PRAISE FOR THE BOOK

"Powerful, provocative, challenging. Anyone interested in contemporary critical theory and radical social change will benefit from reading this book. Kudos to all the contributors!"

—**Jason Del Gandio**, Temple University

"If you want to exist as a liberated soul on the edge of life-worlds, where animals, minerals, clouds, elements, and people all coexist as sacred, read this book. Its intersections take us to another dimension. It's a force to be reckoned with, wielding a transdisciplinary disruptive energy that gets to the heart of true liberation for all."

—**Lea Lani Kinikini**, chief diversity officer, Salt Lake Community College

"Anthony J. Nocella II's and Amber E. George's latest anthology with a diverse group of critical theory scholars around the world provide a liberating pathway forward for abilities liberation, animal liberation, earth liberation, and every other form of liberation possible. This is accomplished through employing Nocella's and George's life-affirming methodology of lifting up the voices, ideas, and methodologies of grassroots scholar-teacher-activists on the peripheries, on our own terms toward win-win recommendations. I especially appreciate Nocella's and George's full-hearted rejection of stigma, repression, othering, and cancel culture which has been devastating to abilities liberation. An exciting, life-affirming, and liberating anthology!"

—**Daniel Salomon**, author of *Autistic Pride* and graduate student in urban studies at Portland State University

"*Critical Animal Studies and Social Justice* makes an impressive contribution to the literature. The content is excellent: Nocella and George deserve great credit for successfully bringing together the ideas and lived experiences of some of the most important global scholar-activists writing at this time."

—**Richard J. White**, reader in economic geography, Sheffield Hallam University

"A must-read book for working toward ending speciesism and for social justice for all. This scholarly text is a radical critique of oppression and domination of the ecological world. This profound total liberation book is one of the most important books within the animal rights movement, edited by Anthony J. Nocella II and Amber E. George."

—**Alisha Page**, director, Save the Kids

"This is a total liberation book that defends radical activism and intersectional voices. Grounded in abolition pedagogy this text fights for freedom and justice. A beautiful and powerful read for anyone interested in ending oppression."

—***Transformative Justice Journal***

"A justice text for all. This environmental studies book brilliantly focuses on human rights, animal rights, and environmental rights."

—***Peace Studies Journal***

Critical Animal Studies and Social Justice

Critical Animal Studies and Theory

Series Editors: Anthony J. Nocella II and Scott C. Hurley

This series addresses human relations with other animals in the context of socio-political relations and economic systems of power. It sees liberation not as a single-issue phenomenon, but rather as inseparably related to human rights, peace and justice, and environmental issues and movements. Rather than emphasizing abstract theory, the series links theory with practice and emphasizes the immense importance of animal advocacy for a humane, democratic, peaceful, and sustainable world. Taking an interdisciplinary approach to questions of social change, moral progress, and ecological sustainability, the *Critical Animal Studies and Theory* series connects with disciplines such as feminism, globalization, economics, science, history, education, critical race theory, environmental studies, media studies, ecopedagogy, art, literature, disability, gender, political science, sociology, religion, anthropology, philosophy, and cultural studies. In keeping with the principles of Critical Animals Studies, the series encourages progressive and committed scholarship and views exploitation of nonhuman animals, such as animal research and studies, as interrelated with other oppressions such as class, gender, and racism. Against apolitical scholarship, the series encourages engaged critical praxis, promotes liberation of all animals and challenges all systems of domination.

Titles in Series

Critical Animal Studies and Social Justice: Critical Theory, Dismantling Speciesism, and Total Liberation edited by Anthony J. Nocella II and Amber E. George

Gender and Sexuality in Critical Animal Studies edited by Amber E. George

Screening the Nonhuman: Representations of Animal Others in the Media edited by Amber E. George and J.L. Schatz

Superheroes and Critical Animal Studies: The Heroic Beasts of Total Liberation edited by J.L. Schatz and Sean Parson.

Critical Animal Studies and Social Justice

Critical Theory, Dismantling Speciesism, and Total Liberation

Edited by

Anthony J. Nocella II and Amber E. George
Forewords by Tyler Lang
and Jordan Halliday

LEXINGTON BOOKS
Lanham • Boulder • New York • London

Published by Lexington Books

An imprint of The Rowman & Littlefield Publishing Group, Inc.

4501 Forbes Boulevard, Suite 200, Lanham, Maryland 20706

www.rowman.com

86-90 Paul Street, London EC2A 4NE

British Library Cataloguing in Publication Information Available

Library of Congress Cataloging-in-Publication Data

Names: Nocella, Anthony J., editor. | George, Amber E., editor. | Halliday, Jordan, 1987- writer of foreword. | Lang, Tyler, writer of foreword.
Title: Critical animal studies and social justice : critical theory, dismantling speciesism, and total liberation / edited by Anthony J. Nocella II and Amber E. George ; foreword by Jordan Halliday and Tyler Lang.
Description: Lanham : Lexington Books, [2021] | Series: Critical animal studies and theory | Includes bibliographical references and index.
Identifiers: LCCN 2021031389 (print) | LCCN 2021031390 (ebook) | ISBN 9781793635228 (cloth) | ISBN 9781793635235 (ebook)
Subjects: LCSH: Animal rights. | Animal welfare. | Animal welfare in literature. | Speciesism.
Classification: LCC HV4708 .C699 2021 (print) | LCC HV4708 (ebook) | DDC 179/.3--dc23
LC record available at https://lccn.loc.gov/2021031389
LC ebook record available at https://lccn.loc.gov/2021031390

This book is dedicated to all those important and loved people that were murdered at the hands of police such as George Floyd, Tamir Rice, Breonna Taylor, Atatiana Jefferson, Aura Rosser, Stephon Clark, Botham Jean, Philandro Castille, Alton Sterling, Michael Brown, Freddie Gray, Michelle Cusseaux, Tanisha Fonville, Eric Garner, Akai Gurley, Gabriella Nevarez, Tanisha Anderson, and Terrance Franklin to just name a few.

Contents

Acknowledgments

We would like to thank everyone at Lexington books especially Sarah and Courtney. We would also like to thank the Institute for Critical Animal Studies, Save the Kids, Utah Reintegration Project, Wisdom Behind the Walls, Poetry Behind the Walls, Arissa Media Group, Salt Lake Community College's JEDI4ST and Department of Criminal Justice, Utah Student Criminology Association at Salt Lake Community College, Academy for Peace Education, Institute for Hip Hop Activism, International Hip Hop Activism Association, Lowrider Studies Journal, Punk Studies Journal, Journal of Hip Hop Studies, Peace Studies Journal, Journal for Critical Animal Studies, Transformative Justice Journal, Green Theory and Praxis Journal, Critical Animal Studies and Theory book series with Lexington Books, and Scott Hurley. We would like to thank all the contributors of the book Tyler Lang, Jordan Halliday Samantha Orsulak, Will Boisseau, Nathan Poirier, Michael Allen and Erica Von Essen, Jessica Holmes, Paislee House, Amanda R. Williams, Ellyse Winter, Tatjana Marjanovic, and Swatilekha Maity. We would like to thank all those that wrote reviews as well Dr. Lea Lani Kinikini, Dr. Richard White, Jim Mason, Alisha Page, Peace Studies Journal, Transformative Justice, Dr. S. Marek Muller, Nathan Poirier, Dr. Jason Del Gandio, and Daniel Salomon. We would also like to thank our friends and family around the world that support us in our activism and scholarship.

Foreword

Tyler Lang

Animal and earth liberation has been a part of my entire adult life. As my interests and views on the world adapt I still seem to return to the overwhelming burden of knowledge that comes with understanding the devastating effects factory farming has on the environment and how it fuels global warming. I can never unlearn how male chicks are callously plucked from a conveyor belt, tossed, and ground alive, because the do not produce capital for the egg industry. I can never forget my first time walking onto a fur farm and seeing thousands of animals hopelessly crammed into wire cages waiting for pelting season, where they would be turned into fur coats for nothing more than vanity and status.

On the night of August 13, 2013 my friend Kevin Olliff and I entered a mink farm in Morris, Illinois. Like all fur farms, the facility was nothing short of barbaric. We had already scouted the farm the night before planning where we could park our vehicle without being on a surveillance camera, searched the facility for security systems, and took note of the tools we would need to dismantle the perimeter fence. We started removing 1 foot tall by 6 foot wide sections of the fence surrounding the farm so the animals would have a way to escape, then we moved on to the sheds where the mink were stored 2–4 animals per cage. I distinctly remember walking into one of the sheds and feeling the floor's elevation rise due to the layers of feces from generations of mink defecating. This explained the nauseating stench that permeated the farm.

Once we were inside of the shed we moved as quickly and quietly as we could. This farm in particular was anxiety inducing because the fur farmers were in their home sleeping only a couple hundred feet away and mink are fairly noisy creatures once disturbed. Shortly after we began opening the cages I paused for a moment and looked around because at first the mink were not leaving their prisons, but rather curiously poking their heads out of the opening. As the mink became braver, they climbed on top of the cage and then finally jumped from the top of the cage to the floor. I remember this moment like it was yesterday. These mink had been crammed into wire cages their whole lives and we had just witnessed what was likely their first time feeling grass beneath their feet. Once one mink leapt from their cage, the rest joined in. Within the hour we emptied every cage in the farm. The mink were running around, both fighting and playing with their brothers and sisters. Before leaving, we spray painted "liberation is love" on the side of the barn.

This action was simple and to the point; we put a fur farm out of business in a single night. Actions like these threaten the foundation of the capitalist machine, because it reveals its weakness; that ultimately ordinary people have the power to stop the exploitation of beings for profit. Direct action has the power to liberate the oppressed and exploited, which are integral pieces to a prospering capitalist economy. Thus, it is no surprise that crimes motivated by liberating animals are labeled as acts of terrorism by the United States federal government.

Something I've learned over the last 17 years of activism is that playing nicely often does not get you anywhere. I've spent years working on campaigns, getting arrested for petty crimes, and having multibillion dollar companies like Beckman Coulter and BlackRock sue us for protesting outside their corporate offices and executives' homes. These corporations would spend hundreds of thousands of dollars hiring private investigators to harass us and record our every move at protests. Even though no crimes were committed, the courts would still grant injunctions against us to prevent us from speaking out for animals.

A pattern I've observed throughout the years is that every time we won—closed a fur farm, forced a corporation to move away from animal testing, etc.– it was because we kept pushing when corporations and the state demanded our obedience. It's when the capitalist structure lost control and the movement kept pushing that I've seen the most success. When Beckman Coulter sued us in 2012, it was the ongoing militant actions by the larger movement that forced them to no longer supply animal testing labs. Having their board of directors homes vandalized and protested in the middle of the night was ultimately the consistency that pushed these companies over the edge.

Critical animal studies is important for activists to understand that we are not only fighting against fur farms and animal labs, but rather a entire system of exploitation. The same exploitative system that allows laboratories to cut into living primates for research also allows migrant families to be separated at the border and thrown in cages so that the American economy can operate uninterrupted. It's not a coincidence that in 2020 the environmental movement is targeting BlackRock for investing in fossil fuels when the animal liberation movement was targeting them in 2012 for investing in animal testing.

Critical Animal Studies and Social Justice: Critical Theory, Dismantling Speciesism, and Total Liberation is a book that will expand your comprehension of the systematic oppression nonhuman animals face in a world dominated by corporate interests and hierarchy. It will provide you with the tools to be a more effective activist to take on the growing challenges that we face as a movement. *Critical Animal Studies and Social Justice: Critical Theory, Dismantling Speciesism, and Total Liberation* will draw the parallel between the exploitation of humans, animals and the natural world. These struggles are intertwined with one another and if we are going to achieve total liberation we need to understand what we are up against.

Foreword

Jordan Halliday

As an academic, total liberation activist, grand jury resister, former movement prisoner, and long-time vegan; the principles guiding the work and research of Critical Animal Studies are values that I feel are extremely important to activists within many movements, but especially within the animal rights movement. This interdisciplinary book edited by Anthony J. Nocella II and Amber E. George consisting of largely new voices including voices from students, most of which have never been published before, is fittingly titled, *Critical Animal Studies and Social Justice: Critical Theory, Dismantling Speciesism, and Total Liberation*. *Critical Animal Studies and Social Justice* accurately reflects many of the values that those within the animal rights movement should be familiar with as activists. This book also encourages those both familiar and unfamiliar to the goal of total liberation through scholarship and activism.

As I write this in the late summer of 2020, in a year that feels equally both long and fast-paced in a weird quantum reality with daily news headlines that would dominate the news during a regular year happening so fast we are quick to forget. A new deadly contagious virus and global pandemic that is believed to have stemmed from a case of exotic "wet market" animal consumption continues to infect the world and take lives at an exponential rate.

Within the United States we are already past 200,000 reported COVID-19 deaths as a result of the novel coronavirus (SARS-CoV-2) and those numbers continue to rise exponentially as of this writing. Keeping in mind that there is speculation that some of the case numbers are being altered and may actually be higher than reported. We are also seeing the rich get richer during the pandemic, in many cases billionaires are adding billions more to their wealth just in the early months of the pandemic alone, risking workers' health, life, and safety to sell nonessential items.

During the pandemic's earlier stages, many workers across the world were either laid-off or asked to work from home, causing a rise in late bill payments and evictions without any plan or aid from the government. Many corporations that were able to offer remote work as an option were against the idea of allowing workers to self-manage from home without someone keeping watch on them. While the evidence has largely seen workers, who are able to effectively do their work remotely without a need to commute to an office.

Initially some areas were allowing only essential workers to work outside of home. Although, the definition of essential was never really defined and we are seeing a large number of primarily Indigenous, Black, Brown, and Latinx migrant workers in various occupations from produce, field, and slaughterhouse workers to housekeeping, construction, and other hard-labor work being defined as "essential." Many of these migrant workers are also working in conditions that do not allow for proper social distancing and/or are being asked to work without being supplied proper personal protective equipment. We have already seen cases of death and mega spreading linked to COVID-positive animal agriculture workers. There are also reliable rumors of these workers passing the virus onto nonhuman animals such as mink on fur farms. There are also concerns that animals might become reservoirs for the virus and possibly even pass mutated variations of the virus back to humans.

In the United States, we have a capitalist government that puts more value on property and commodities over its people; with only 5 percent of the world population, the United States is continuing to rank #1 in both total cases and total deaths from the virus. All this while simultaneously claiming the virus is a hoax or exaggerated and demanding business as usual. This has caused many workers to consider a general strike to address their demands that are not being met by corporations.

In this book you will read about utilizing different types of empathy and building bridges by working intrasectionally with other movements and participating in demonstrations that focus on multiple contexts of exploitation in the pursuit of total liberation. This is timely as civil unrest continues to rise globally as protesters take to the streets advocating for the lives of all Black, Indigenous, and other people of color. We are seeing a growing call for accountability and demands to defund the police as more cases of systemic racism within the criminal justice system are brought to light. These emerging uprisings are not isolated incidents and are taking place across the globe.

There has been an increase in political repression and authoritarianism worldwide; only in part due to the civil unrest. In the United States, we are seeing increased use of chemical agents and "less lethal" weapons banned by the United Nations being utilized by the military and militarized police against its citizens. Protesters in Belarus, Hong Kong, Russia, Colombia, and other countries are being arrested, injured, tortured, killed, and "disappeared."

While talks of fascism and anti-fascism are now commonplace in mainstream news, there still appears to be a complete misunderstanding of the what fascism, anti-fascism, or even what socialism, communism, and anarchism are within the United States, with the rise and support of right-wing authoritarianism and the potential for an autocratic leadership. We are seeing anti-fascists, protesters, social justice movements, and activist organizations erroneously being labeled terrorists, arsonists, rioters, and looters. We are seeing activists getting excessive charges, including potential life sentences for alleged property damage.

In the following chapters you will learn how the definition of intersectionality is being misused and has been diluted within certain movements, especially within the animal rights movement. You'll also read about white fragility, as well as the threats of white supremacy that continue to exist. Unfortunately there has also been an increase of armed violence from self-appointed mostly white civilian militias, setting up checkpoints, and in some cases murdering protesters with guns or vehicles. This is happening as President Trump also dismantles various government/defense departments and installing "active" leadership positions to avoid needing confirmation. He also continues to incite his base in what appears to be one of the slowest preparations for an attempt at a coup d'etat, should he not win the election.

While I am not one to rely on or idolize judges or politicians, we also lost a fierce advocate for feminism, human rights, gender equality, and bodily autonomy with the passing of Justice Ruth Bader Ginsburg. While the right scrambles to implement a new justice just weeks before the 2020 presidential election. We are already seeing attempts to influence and interfere in that election, both national and foreign. The United States government, along with President Trump, and the current administration appear to be openly dismantling the United States Postal Service in order to suppress mail-in voting from opposing states and geographically more liberal locations; which is likely to increase the odds of more votes towards Trump from conservative voters who more often vote in-person. Should Trump still not get the needed votes they might also try to claim election tampering or mail-in voter fraud; additional steps to allow them to further their goals towards right-wing authoritarianism in the United States.

The United States Immigration and Customs Enforcement (ICE) continues to separate families seeking asylum at the border, taking young children away from their families and guardians. Keeping them in isolation at detention camps, often without basic hygienic options or a place to sleep. Whistleblowers continue to come forward with stories of abuse, cover-ups, death, mistreatment, ethical and human rights violations. Recently a nurse has come forward expressing concerns for covering up cases of COVID-19 as well as unwanted forced hysterectomies of detainees, quickly reminding us of the history of eugenics and forced sterilization in the United States.

As we fight for environmental justice, wildfires are spreading all across the world; polluting the air, water, and our lungs. Pollution also continues to exist worldwide, while certain areas, typically those of low-income or Black and Brown communities continue to feel the extra burden of living with factories and facilities that fill the air, soil, and water with contaminants. These industrial polluters aren't always billowing with smokestacks either. We are seeing a large number of factory farms, concentrated animal feeding operations, fur farms, and slaughterhouses disproportionately located in Black and Brown neighborhoods and impoverished communities. This is why I refer to these environmental inequities as environmental racism.

Hurricanes and hurricane level winds continue to uproot communities. For the first time in over 50 years we currently have 5 simultaneously active hurricanes; in fact, this hurricane season is so active that we have even run out of names for them. With Tropical Storm Wilfred taking the 21st name spot for 2020 just recently.

Locally, on the occupied land of the Eastern Shoshone, Goshute, and Núu-agha-tʉvʉ-pʉ̱ (Ute) tribes known as Salt Lake City, Utah; we have experienced unprecedented earthquakes and winds that have continued to damage towns and communities. We are also witnessing the birth of one of the biggest armed and mostly white civilian militias in the country attending Black Lives Matter and Anti-Police Brutality demonstrations in order to harass and intimidate activists and protesters.

Fortunately, we are seeing emerging new voices from a younger generation who are not willing to wait around and are demanding critical change and taking steps towards direct action now. These young new activists also appear to be taking a more progressive and anti-capitalist/anticonsumerist approach to combat global climate change. We are also seeing more demands for more basic socialist ideas such as Universal Health Care and The Green New Deal in the United States.

I fear that the world may not ever return to what we considered "normal" and that history will mark our recent timelines as pre-pandemic, present-day pandemic era, and hopefully post pandemic times. That's why it is important as activists to understand and recognize that oppression can take many ugly and violent forms and as activists we can and should advocate against all forms of violence-based ideologies concurrently, as many forms of oppression are intersected and components of global systems of domination. The best way to build a strong movement is through collaboration with other activists and movements. Critical Animal Studies and the knowledge gained from studying this book help fill in much of that gap and overlap for activists by furthering the goal of total liberation and continued activism.

Introduction

From Fascism to Total Liberation: Getting to Know the Justice, Equity, Diversity, and Inclusion (JEDI) Framework

Anthony J. Nocella II and Amber E. George

DEFINING THE PROBLEM

History has taught us a lot about fascism, authoritarianism, totalitarianism, dictatorship, elitism, domination, oppression, supremacy, and social privilege. This conversation about liberation will begin by defining all of these terms concerning oppression. Fascism is a state that is wanting absolute power. Authoritarianism is when the state enforces strict obedience and discipline. Totalitarianism is when the state has complete social control of those in society. Dictatorship is a type of leadership where one or a few people have ultimate power. Dictatorship + Authoritarianism + Totalitarianism = fascism, therefore, dictatorship is the person/people in control, authoritarianism is how dictators rule, totalitarianism is the state of society, and when put together, fascism thrives.

SYSTEMS

The sociopolitical concepts noted above are similar to the most common types of violence—brutality and torture, which are two terms often misused and used interchangeably. These two terms are similar in that they use violence; brutality is the unjustified use of violence, while torture is the justified use of violence. This is all predicated on having a system of oppression already in place. Oppression originates when there is supremacy + domination = privilege. Supremacy is the idea that something/someone is more valuable than something/someone else. Domination is the abuse of power. Oppression limits the freedom of many individuals based on a common characteristic such as politics, identity, belief, or behavior. Repression is the targeting of a small segment of society that is oppressed. Suppression is reinforcing limited freedoms of an oppression segment. Exploitation is the abuse of power monetarily. Within cultural exploitation, there are two commodification types that make money off other cultural items, while appropriating and generating cultural capital from items from another culture. On the other hand, assimilation is when those oppressed are forced to adapt to the dominant culture. Unlike colonialism, imperialism is the global dominant culture that manipulates another culture to become similar to and dependent on the dominant culture.

OTHERING

The first step in oppressing a group of people is othering them, through stigmatizing them. Label theory has two types of labeling (1) identity, a positive label, which is where the individual labels themselves, and (2) stigma, a negative label, which is where an external group labels the individual. Under the umbrella of label theory, three terms are often misused and used interchangeably. The first is a generalization, which is a broad description based on a fact, a stereotype is a general fixed description, and judgment is a neutral description based on one's limited experience and knowledge. Prejudice is a stereotype and harm, and discrimination is prejudice on an institutional level. With all of that said, it provides the reader with a good lexicon of social justice education.

ROLES FOR SOCIAL TRANSFORMATION

In this realm of promoting peace and justice, there are five roles in creating social transformation (1) peace activists, (2) peacemaker, (3) peacekeeper, (4) peacebuilder, and (5) peace educator. All of these roles are different, but dependent on one another to foster peace and justice.

THEORY FOR SOCIAL TRANSFORMATION

Social transformation is a change in all aspects of society, including the people, institutions, systems, industries, and communities, rather than the narrow scope of social change movements that focuses on one or two aspects of society. What we want to strive for is the mutual liberation of those oppressed and those that are co-conspirators. Liberation is self-directed, while empowerment and being an ally recenters those in power and privilege through neoliberal acts. Social transformation is for revolution, not reform. Thus, if one works in the system, they strive to dismantle it, rather than make the system better. Of course, all of this is easier said than done, as we live in systems we cannot escape. Unfortunately, those of us who are activists and organizers in capitalist developed countries are hypocrites. The only way to initiate change is by exploiting trees to make paper for books or destroying habitats and communities to create phones for which we communicate. For this reason, social transformation and transformative justice are against canceling culture because it promotes shaming and segregation. We must provide space for healing, accountability, responsibility, reconciliation, redemption, and education.

STRATEGY FOR SOCIAL TRANSFORMATION

Equity, Diversity, and Inclusion (EDI) is a theory-to-practice critical pedagogy grounded movement on how first to confront, second resist, and finally dismantle oppression in higher education. Many institutions have offices, departments, and programs dedicated to diversity, equity, and inclusion initiatives. Some degree programs in social justice education, social justice, and justice studies, rarely do all four principles join together. Thus, the Justice, Equity, Diversity, and Inclusion (JEDI) framework for liberation requires that all of society must change (i.e., people, organizations, systems, institutions, states, and industries). For social transformation to be possible, the JEDI four principles must work together in an interdependent relationship. First, one must acknowledge diversity; to claim that you "do not see race or gender" is a problem. Next, we must behave inclusively (i.e., welcoming of diversity in all places). Thirdly, we must address the inequity within the diversity, so all are given what they need to reach their goals. Finally, justice must be served with regard to those lived experiences of oppression that go unaddressed. Once all four of these principles are achieved, which could very well take a lifetime, only then is social transformation possible. Liberation is not a state of being, but a process, and that process we argue is JEDI.

DEFINING CRITICAL ANIMAL STUDIES

Critical animal studies has encountered its fair share of elitist pseudo-activist academics, who post on social media about activism, publish about activism, and teach about activism but are not involved in activism. They are what Hip Hop would refer to as "fronting" and "fake ass." We need to challenge these actions, but not the people. Just as Hip Hop encourages us to "love their haters" and "not give the fronters any airtime," we too in CAS should do the same. We might also ask those scholars who co-opt CAS studies to become more involved with activism. One might ask them to share in public forums how they engage in activist struggles. Furthermore, those who seem intent on co-opting CAS in their scholarship, we must also hold them accountable for promoting anarchism and call them in when this analysis is absent in their work. We need to have real conversations about the fears that some CAS scholars have about not adopting anarchist studies because they worry about offending others or losing their jobs. Finally, we must help those who co-opt CAS to adopt the vision of total liberation in their personal and professional lives. This requires doing activism, becoming vegan, praising organizations such as the Animal Liberation Front, critiquing capitalism, and supporting other underground radical organizations that do direct action. ICAS defines itself as,

> The Institute for Critical Animal Studies (ICAS), rooted in animal liberation and anarchism, is an international intersectional transformative holistic theory-to-action activist led based scholarly think-tank to unapologetically examine, explain, be in solidarity with, and be part of radical and revolutionary actions, theories, groups and movements for total liberation and to dismantle all systems of domination and oppression, in hopes for a just, equitable, inclusive, and peaceful world. (ICAS, 2021)

Institute for Critical Animal Studies (ICAS), the founding organization of CAS defines CAS as,

> Critical animal studies is rooted in animal liberation and anarchism, is an intersectional transformative holistic theory-to-action activist led based movement and field of study to unapologetically examine, explain, be in solidarity with, and be part of radical and revolutionary actions, theories, groups and movements for total liberation and to dismantle all systems of domination and oppression, in hopes for a just, equitable, inclusive, and peaceful world. (ICAS, 2016)

ICAS, first titled as the Center for Animal Liberation Affairs (CALA) was founded in 2001 by Anthony J. Nocella II and Steve Best. The field of critical animal studies was founded in 2005/2006 by Anthony J. Nocella II, Steve

Best, Richard Kahn, and John Sorenson was the first movement in the scholarly world to unite people to fight not only for animal liberation, but for total liberation through an anarchist and intersectional lens. In 2007, Best, Nocella, Kahn, Carol Gigliotti, and Lisa Kemmerer, developed "The Ten Principles of Critical Animal Studies," which follow here:

1. Pursues interdisciplinary collaborative writing and research in a rich and comprehensive manner that includes perspectives typically ignored by animal studies such as political economy.
2. Rejects pseudo-objective academic analysis by explicitly clarifying its normative values and political commitments, such that there are no positivist illusions whatsoever that theory is disinterested or writing and research is nonpolitical. To support experiential understanding and subjectivity.
3. Eschews narrow academic viewpoints and the debilitating theory-for-theory's sake position in order to link theory to practice, analysis to politics, and the academy to the community.
4. Advances a holistic understanding of the commonality of oppressions, such that speciesism, sexism, racism, ableism, statism, classism, militarism, and other hierarchical ideologies and institutions are viewed as parts of a larger, interlocking, global system of domination.
5. Rejects apolitical, conservative, and liberal positions in order to advance an anti-capitalist, and, more generally, a radical anti-hierarchical politics. This orientation seeks to dismantle all structures of exploitation, domination, oppression, torture, killing, and power [by humans to each other and other animals] in favor of decentralizing and democratizing society at all levels and on a global basis.
6. Rejects reformist, single-issue, nation-based, legislative, strictly animal interest politics in favor of alliance politics and solidarity with other struggles against oppression and hierarchy.
7. Champions a politics of total liberation which grasps the need for, and the inseparability of, human, nonhuman animal, and Earth liberation and freedom for all in one comprehensive, though diverse, struggle.
8. Deconstructs and reconstructs the socially constructed binary oppositions between human and nonhuman animals, a move basic to mainstream animal studies, but also looks to illuminate related dichotomies between culture and nature, civilization and wilderness, and other dominator hierarchies to emphasize the historical limits placed upon humanity, nonhuman animals, cultural/political norms, and the liberation of nature as part of a transformative project that seeks to transcend these limits towards greater freedom, peace, and ecological harmony.

9. Openly supports and examines controversial radical politics and strategies used in all kinds of social justice movements, such as those that involve economic sabotage from boycotts to direct action toward the goal of peace.
10. Creates openings for constructive critical dialogue on issues relevant to critical animal studies across a wide-range of academic groups; citizens and grassroots activists; the staffs of policy and social service organizations; and people in private, public, and non-profit sectors. Through—and only through—new paradigms of ecopedagogy, bridge-building with other social movements, and a solidarity-based alliance politics, it is possible to build the new forms of consciousness, knowledge, and social institutions that are necessary to dissolve the hierarchical society that has enslaved this planet for the last ten thousand years. (pp. 4–5)

To keep this movement going, we must be willing to take risks and give up our own freedoms and privileges to support others to live. We must get out behind our desks and into the streets. Critical animal studies and total liberation has no place for respectability politics and collegiality. Social change does not care about being polite, but collaborating in a liberatory, inclusive, equitable, just, and radical manner for total liberation. People that examine different tactics are scholars and effective activists to promote total liberation. Furthermore, the tactic of "cancelling culture" within social justice movements is toxic, abusive, and punitive. Instead we must embrace the flaws in culture with the aims of transforming them to support JEDI initiatives. The 4As of transformative justice must be a beginning point for those that hurt others—(1) Apologize, (2) Acknowledge, (3) Accountability, and (4) Alter. For total liberation to be possible, we must focus on being free, not wild. The concept of "wild" is a social construction that unfairly creates a binary of "us" versus "them." We cannot define ourselves and others using oppressive othering terms. Total liberation unites social justice causes together and is used today in several social justice movements. Total liberation has a number of theoretical values and principles, they include:

1. Being involved in fighting all forms of oppression and domination.
2. Being a scholar, activist, and organizer.
3. Being intersectional and not for oppression Olympics, collegiality, divisive politics, or respectability politics.
4. Being opposed to opportunism, privilege, supremacy, careerism, and reform.
5. Being opposed to systems and theories of oppression and domination such as capitalism and neoliberalism.
6. Opposed to socially constructed binaries.

7. For anarchism, communalism, and direct democracy.
8. Against punishment, shaming, and cancel culture.
9. For transformative justice, healing justice, and community circles.
10. For education not academia or schooling.

Total liberation is what Anthony J. Nocella II and Steve Best co-founded within the Earth and animal liberation movement in 2001 and still growing with collectives, books, articles, conferences, and organizations. These ideas keep growing and developing for one purpose—to destroy oppression and domination.

SELECTED BIBLIOGRAPHY

Adewale, O. & Harper, A. B. (2021). *Brotha vegan: Black men speak on food, identity, health, and society*. Lantern Books.

Albert, M. & Chomsky, N. (2014). *Realizing hope: Life beyond capitalism*. Zed Books.

Anonymous (2019). *Total liberation.* Active Distribution

Arcari, P. (2020). COVID-19 shows why we need to "cease and desist" from commodifying animals. *Medium, Age of Awareness*. https://medium.com/age-of-awareness/covid-19-shows-why-we-need-to-cease-and-desist-from-commodifying-animals-c042e6eb5be5

Best, S. (2014). *The politics of total liberation: Revolution for the 21st century.* Palgrave.

Brueck, J. F. (2017). *Veganism in an oppressive world: A vegans-of-color community project*. Sanctuary Publishers.

Brueck, J. F. (2019). *Veganism of color: Decentering whiteness in human and nonhuman Liberation.* Sanctuary Publishers.

Campbell, C. (2020). "They Are Overwhelmed." China's animal shelters can't cope with the number of pets abandoned due to COVID-19. *Time*. https://time.com/5793363/china-coronavirus-covid19-abandoned-pets-wuhan/

Canning, D., & Reinsborough, P. (2017). *Re-imagining change: How to use story-based strategy to win campaigns, build movements, and change the world.* PM Press.

Clark, J. P. (2019). *Between earth and empire: From the necrocene to the beloved community*. PM Press.

Cohen, N. (2020). Surely the link between abusing animals and the world's health is now clear. *The Guardian*. https://www.theguardian.com/commentisfree/2020/apr/11/surely-the-link-between-abusing-animals-and-the-worlds-health-is-now-clear.

Colling, S. (2020). *Animal resistance in the global capitalist era*. University of Michigan Press.

Corkery, M., Yaffe-Bellany, D., & Swanson, A. (2020, April 29). Powerful meat industry holds more sway after Trump's order. *The New York Times*. https://www.

nytimes.com/2020/04/29/business/coronavirus-trump-meat-plants.html?action=click&module=RelatedLinks&pgtype=Article

Crenshaw, K. (1989). Demarginalizing the intersection of race and sex: A Black feminist critique of antidiscrimination doctrine. *University of Chicago Legal Forum*, 139–168.

de Sadeleer, N., & Godfroid, J. (2020). The Story behind COVID-19: Animal diseases at the crossroads of wildlife, livestock and human health. *European Journal of Risk Regulation*, 11(2), 210–227.

Cudworth, E., White, R.J., & Boisseau, W. (2020). Introduction: For a critically post-humanist sociology in precarious times, *International Journal of Sociology and Social Policy*. Earlycite.

Direct Action Everywhere (2020, July 29). Breaking: Gruesome footage shows pigs roasted alive at Iowa's leading pork supplier amid coronavirus crisis. https://www.directactioneverywhere.com/theliberationist/2020-5-28-breaking-gruesome-footage-shows-pigs-roasted-alive-at-iowas-leading-pork-supplier-amid-coronavirus-crisis

Douglass, F. (1857). *Two speeches by Frederick Douglass: One of West India Emancipation, delivered at Canandaigua, Aug, 4th and the other one the Dred Scott Decision, delivered in New York, on the occasion of the anniversary of the American Abolition Society, May, 1857*. C.P. Dewey Printer.

Dutkiewicz, J., Taylor, A., & Vettese, T. (2020). The Covid-19 pandemic shows we must transform the global food system *The Guardian*. https://www.theguardian.com/commentisfree/2020/apr/16/coronavirus-covid-19-pandemic-food-animals

Dyal J. W. et al. (2020, April). COVID-19 among workers in meat and poultry processing facilities—19 States. *Morbidity and Mortality Weekly Report*, 69(18), 557–561. https://www.cdc.gov/mmwr/volumes/69/wr/mm6918e3.htm

Estes, N. (2019). *Our history is the future: Standing Rock versus the Dakota Access Pipeline, and the long tradition of indigenous resistance*. Verso.

Estes, N., & Dhillon, J. (2019). *Standing with Standing Rock: Voices from the #NoDAPL movement*. University of Minnesota Press.

European Centre for Disease Prevention and Control (2020, September 10). *COVID-19 situation update worldwide*. https://www.ecdc.europa.eu/en/geographical-distribution-2019-ncov-cases.

Gilio-Whitaker, D. (2020). *As long as grass grows: The indigenous fight for environmental justice, from colonization to Standing Rock*. Beacon Press.

Garcés, L. (2020). COVID-19 exposes animal agriculture's vulnerability. *Agriculture and Human Values,* 1–2. https://doi.org/10.1007/s10460-020-10099-5

Gunderman, H., & White, R. J. (2020). Critical posthumanism for all: A call to reject insect speciesism. *International Journal of Sociology and Social Policy*. https://doi.org/10.1108/IJSSP-09-2019-0196

Harper, B. A. (2010). *Sistah vegan: Black female vegans speak on food, identity, health, and society.* Lantern Books.

Hartley-Parkinson, R. (2020). German zoo faces feeding animals to one another as it runs out of cash. *Metro.* https://metro.co.uk/2020/04/15/german-zoo-faces-feeding-animals-one-another-runs-cash-12558117/.

Hogervorst, J. (2020, June 16). Animal testing and Covid-19. *The Ecologist: The Journal for the Post-Industrial Age*. https://theecologist.org/2020/jun/16/animal-testing-and-covid-19

Kendi, I. X. (2019). *How to be an anti-racist.* One World.

Kevany, S. (2020a). Millions of US farm animals to be culled by suffocation, drowning and shooting. *The Guardian* Tuesday 19 May. https://www.theguardian.com/environment/2020/may/19/millions-of-us-farm-animals-to-be-culled-by-suffocation-drowning-and-shooting-coronavirus

Kevany, S. (2020b). A million mink culled in Netherlands and Spain amid Covid-19 fur farming havoc. *The Guardian*. https://www.theguardian.com/world/2020/jul/17/spain-to-cull-nearly-100000-mink-in-coronavirus-outbreak

Ko, A., & Ko, S. (2017). *Aphro-ism: Essays on pop culture, feminism, and black veganism from two sisters*. New York, NY: Lantern Books.

Middleton, J., Reintjes, R., & Lopes, H. (2020). Meat plants—a new front line in the covid-19 pandemic. *BMJ*, 370 doi: https://doi.org/10.1136/bmj.m2716

Nibert, D. (2017). *Animal oppression and capitalism*. Praeger.

Nocella, A. J. II, & George, A. E. (2019). *Intersectionality of critical animal studies: A historical collection*. Peter Lang Publishing.

Nocella, A.J., II Sorenson, J., Socha & Matsuoka, A. (2014a). Introduction: The Emergence of Critical Animal Studies. In. A.J. Nocella, J. Sorenson & A. Matsuoka (Eds.). (2014). *Defining critical animal studies: An intersectional social justice approach for liberation*. Peter Lang.

Nocella, A.J. II, Sorenson, J., Socha, K., & Matsuoka, A. (2014b). *Defining critical animal studies: An intersectional social justice approach for liberation.* Peter Lang.

Nocella, A.J. II, White, R.J., $ Cudworth, E. (2015). *Anarchism and animal liberation: Essays on complementary aspects of total liberation.* McFarland Press.

Nocella, A. J. II, Shannon, D., & Asimakopoulos, J. (2012). *The accumulation of freedom: Writings on anarchist economics*. AK Press.

Moulds, J. (2020). 5 ways the coronavirus is affecting animals around the world. *World Economic Forum.* https://www.weforum.org/agenda/2020/04/coronavirus-animals-wildlife-biodiversity-tiger-boar-pandas-zoos/.

Pellow, D. N. (2014). *Total liberation: The power and promise of animal rights and the radical Earth movement*. University of Minnesota Press.

Polansek, T., & Huffstutter, P.J. (2020, April 27). Piglets aborted, chickens gassed as pandemic slams meat sector. *Reuters Business News.* https://www.reuters.com/article/us-health-coronavirus-livestock-insight/piglets-aborted-chickens-gassed-as-pandemic-slams-meat-sector-idUSKCN2292YS?fbclid=IwAR0TNHZMxERvxbh_G_FoP-mDjjDX01DAOOYt0GnLU7GaXgLJTQ1YgQRSi0

ProVeg e.V. (2020). *Food & pandemics report: Part 1 - making the connection: Animal-based food systems and pandemics.* Report. Berlin.

Reuben, A. (2020). Coronavirus: Why have there been so many outbreaks in meat processing plants? *BBC News.* https://www.bbc.co.uk/news/53137613

Reuters (2020, June 6). Dutch farms ordered to cull 10,000 mink over coronavirus risk. *The Guardian* https://www.theguardian.com/world/2020/jun/06/dutch-mink-farms-ordered-to-cull-10000-animals-over-coronavirus-risk

Salim, M., & González, T. M. (2020). Coronavirus: Chronicle of an announced zoonosis. *Journal MVZ Cordoba,* 25(2). 1–3. https://doi.org/10.21897/rmvz.2048

Socha, K. (2012). *Women, destruction, and the avant-garde: A paradigm for animal liberation.* Brill Rodopi.

Sohrabi, C., Alsafi, Z., O'Neill, N., Khan, M., Kerwan, A., Al-Jabir, A., Iosifidis, C. & Agha, R. (2020). World Health Organization declares global emergency: A review of the 2019 novel coronavirus (COVID-19). *International Journal of Surgery*, 76, 71–76.

Swanson, A., & Yaffe-Bellany, D. (2020, April 29). Trump declares meat supply "critical," aiming to reopen plants. *New York Times*. https://www.nytimes.com/2020/04/28/business/economy/coronavirus-trump-meat-food-supply.html?auth=login-email&login=email

Velavan, T. P., & Meyer, C. G. (2020). The COVID-19 epidemic. *Tropical medicine & international health: TM & IH, 25*(3), 278–280. https://doi.org/10.1111/tmi.13383

Wharton, J. (2020). Pets rounded up and slaughtered to stop spread of coronavirus. *Metro*. https://metro.co.uk/2020/02/21/pets-rounded-slaughtered-stop-spread-coronavirus-12277644/?ito=cbshare

Wadiwel, D. J. (2015). *The war against animals*. Brill Rodoph.

West, C. (2020). *The garden of vegan*. Pimpernell Press Limited.

White, R. J. (2015). Critical animal geographies and anarchist praxis: shifting perspectives from the animal "question" to the animal "condition." In K. Gillespie and R-C. Collard (Ed.). *Critical animal geographies: Power, space and violence in a multispecies world.* Routledge.

White, R. J. (2017). Rising to the challenge of capitalism and the commodification of animals: post-capitalism, anarchist economies and vegan praxis. In D. Nibert (Ed.). *Animal oppression and capitalism.* Praeger.

White, R. J., & Springer, S. (2018). Making space for anarchist geographies in critical animal studies. In Sorenson, J. & Matuoka, A. (Eds). *Critical animal studies: Towards trans-species social justice*. Rowman and Littlefield International.

Chapter One

Toward the Footsteps of Nimrod

Positive Animal Representation in Saki's Short Fiction

Samantha Orsulak

INTRODUCTION

Saki is perhaps one of the most enigmatic writers of British literature, which is perhaps why he is so little studied. Despite his publication dates falling within the first two decades of the twentieth century, he is often hailed as "an embodiment of the Edwardian era," as most of his works offer rich satire on Edwardian, as well as late Victorian, themes of hunting, hypocrisy, and the classification of animals (Langguth, 1981, p. 226). He was born Hector Hugh Munro in 1870, and he chose his pen name, Saki, from Edward Fitzgerald's 1859 translation of Omar Khayyam's *Rubaiyat*. Some critics interpret the reference from the poem to be about Saki's multiple natures of kindness and cruelty, which are often reflected in his dark, witty short stories and distinctive animal characters (Langguth, 1981, p. 62). The interactions among animal and human characters in Saki's stories challenge the reader's beliefs about humans' relationships with animals, especially concerning hunting and anthropocentric attitudes.

This chapter analyzes the various literary representations of animals in Saki's short fiction. Historian Rob Boddice states that authors often portray "animal minds . . . as mirrors of human minds," creating essentially "humans with fur"—animal characters so anthropomorphized they are more of a literary device than actual characters (Boddice, 2008, p. 303; Shapiro & Copeland, 2005, p. 344). While this is true of some authors, Saki gives his fictional animals more developed characterizations. Rather than using animals as simple, one-dimensional mirrors to reflect humans' flaws, Saki creates his animal characters to be as complex as—and often superior to—his human ones. Saki gives animals minds of their own and he regularly pits them against the minds of humans in battles of the wits. It is worthwhile to study Saki's animal minds, as they offer insight into what responsible animal representation can be.

While Saki is never formulaic, his stories often contain a pattern in which human characters' beliefs or behaviors concerning animals are suddenly challenged, punished, or upended. Animal characters perform many versatile roles in Saki's stories; they are often the harbingers of justice, sometimes the victims of cruelty, and occasionally the perpetrators of the crimes. By giving his animal characters a full range of experiences and roles, Saki provides them power and freedom in his stories—something desperately missing in fictional representations of animals.

RESPONSIBLE LITERARY REPRESENTATIONS OF ANIMALS

It is generally acknowledged that representation within media influences one's perception of oneself and others: "Media, in short, are central to what ultimately come to represent our social realities" (Brooks & Hébert, 2006, p. 297). Therefore, it is crucial for animals to receive accurate and empowering representation in media. However, it is not that simple. There are several issues to contend with for giving better representation to animals in fiction.

Firstly, literature must break away from traditions in which animals act only as literary devices. Critic Joseph Salemi attributes Saki's main use of animals to the "old satiric tradition of contrasting human perversion with animal decency" (1989, p. 425). Many of the animal characters in Saki's stories are polite and understanding, while the humans they interact with are rude and superficial. Yet this satirical tradition is not the whole answer to why animals are so pervasive in Saki's fiction, or at times even violent and indecent. When Saki's animal characters do not contrast "human perversion" with their upstanding decency, they are beasts, "red in tooth and claw, indifferent and ruthless, which Saki offers as preferable to the human world of greed, hypocrisy, the intentional infliction of pain and death for anything other than survival, and simple unkindness" (Byrne, 2007, p. 163). Saki provides complicated representations of flaws and virtues in his animals, offering readers a window into what both separates and connects humans and animals. In fact, it is this very virtue of creating dynamic animal characters that makes Saki a worthwhile subject within critical animal studies. The complex animals in Saki's works demonstrate for the rest of literature, as well as the wider world, the potential of representing animals as well-developed, autonomous characters.

Secondly, what does a truly represented animal, free of all possible anthropomorphic influences, really look like? One of the largest problems—and potentially strongest solutions—to animal representations in literature is the vagueness of who an animal really is: "The metaphorical animal's ways of inhabiting literature without somehow being represented therein present tremendous opportunities for recovering and interrogating the material and representational problems specific to animality" (McHugh, 2011, p. 6). While no one can truly create an accurate, unbiased representation of animals, Saki helps negotiate a way toward a more responsible, empowering representation with his animal characters who demonstrate individuality and animality (as we can best understand it).

Thirdly, one must consider that power is inherent in every relationship. Humans' relationship with animals is deeply flawed. Humans overpower animals in acts such as recreational hunting and domestication of species. The very criteria of domestication demand a strict power over a species: Margo DeMello (2012) writes, "Animals are considered to be domesticated when they are kept for a distinct purpose, humans control their breeding, their survival depends on humans, and they develop genetic traits that are not found in the wild" (p. 84). This total domination of other species is inhumane; animals are stripped of their independence and forced to rely on humans for survival. To change the extreme power dynamic within the human-animal relationship, representations of animals in media must change.

We must consider that "all representation is fundamentally and inextricably inscribed in relations of power. Power relations are encoded in media representations, and media representations in turn produce and reproduce power relations by constructing knowledge, values, conceptions and beliefs" (Orgad, 2014). Animal representations in media are problematic because not only are they inherently positioned within a power dynamic with their domesticators and hunters, but also because they are most often defined and characterized through binary opposition. In her 2014 book *Media Representation and the Global Imagination*, Shani Orgad writes that binary oppositions are words or ideas "defined in relation to [their] opposite"; animals are most often defined as a binary opposite to humans.

Furthermore, "Binary oppositions are intimately involved in the production and reproduction of power relations, with one pole signifying the dominant one against which the other pole is defined" (Orgad, 2014). While binary opposition in this context usually refers to concepts such as race and gender—for example, people of color are defined by their separation and distinction from white people—it also applies directly to how humans and animals are defined and represented within media. Animals are very often set as distinct, inferior characters to humans, or they are used as a comparison point to humans' depravity or immorality. If media truly constructs one's reality and creates meaning within culture and society, then it is crucial to portray animals in a positive, empowering light.

Saki is a worthwhile author to study because his representations of animals in his literature are empowering to animals and subversive to the oppressive narrative that his contemporaries tell. He sets his stories in the Edwardian era, a time of lavish hunting parties and celebrated blood sport, compounding on the Victorian era's fixation on humans' distinction from (and assumed superiority to) all other animals. Rather than use his literature to celebrate humans' supposed superiority over animals, Saki satirizes it and often subverts it, offering biting criticism and witty mockery of this anthropocentric idea in his stories in which animals reveal the inferior qualities of humans. His animal characters possess characteristics nontraditional to the binary opposition of animal-human, and they do not give into the power relation of typical representation to which Orgad refers. While Saki's representations of women and minorities are not always empowering, his animal characters are consistently empowered and should be studied for their positive representations within literature.

Some may argue that Saki uses animal characters as a literary device for his critiques of human behavior, which strips the animals of their power and agency as independent characters. However, this argument stems from superficial analysis. While his animal characters are often the ones to highlight human characters' flawed thinking or behavior, they are fully developed characters who display complex emotions and motivations and act independently of human characters within the stories. Additionally, Saki's choice to make the animal characters the ones to point out human characters' flaws flips the power dynamic of the traditional human-animal binary opposition relationship. The animal character is not defined by their distance from humanness, but by their own traits; furthermore, the animal is sometimes the one to physically, mentally, or socially take away the power from the human, not only breaking away from the binary opposition, but completely subverting it as well. Regardless of whether they are useful for criticizing iniquities in humans' views of animals, Saki's animal characters are complex beings with their own characterizations and roles independent from humans.

The story "Sredni Vashtar" (Saki, 1991) follows a young boy Conradin who is under the care of his rather cruel guardian Mrs. de Ropp. Her strict child-rearing policies do not allow for playtime or pets, so Conradin must hide his pet, a ferret, in a shed in their backyard. He begins to worship the animal as a sort of imaginary god and attributes any fortunate events (such as pain or discomfort de Ropp experiences) to the powers of this ferret god,

Sredni Vashtar. When de Ropp is particularly hurtful to Conradin (for example, selling the family hen that he dotes on and loves dearly), Conradin begins to pray for Sredni Vashtar to "do one thing for me," wishing for Vashtar to kill, or at least punish, Mrs. de Ropp (Saki, 1991, p. 138). Soon after, de Ropp deduces that Conradin's frequent visits to the backyard shed means there must be something forbidden in it, so she marches to the shed to remove it.

Conradin watches from the house as de Ropp enters the shed, visualizing what will happen when de Ropp discovers his secret ferret: "He knew that the Woman would come out presently with that pursed smile he loathed so well on her face, and that in an hour or two the gardener would carry away his wonderful god, a god no longer, but a simple brown ferret in a hutch" (p. 139). De Ropp has the most power in the story, as she is both guardian over the child Conradin and a human over the animal Sredni Vashtar. As a seeming binary opposition, Sredni Vashtar is the weaker character juxtaposed to the powerful human de Ropp: when de Ropp enters the shed, Vashtar is a "wonderful god"; when de Ropp leaves the shed, he is "a god no longer, but a simple brown ferret," restricted and powerless in a cage. Conradin's assumption that de Ropp will maintain her position of power within the animal-human relationship represents the societal expectation that animals are and should be subjugated by humans.

However, this is not what actually plays out. Saki not only subverts Conradin and the reader's expectation of de Ropp overpowering Sredni Vashtar by keeping him in the cage and removing him from the property, he also subverts the power dynamic and transfers de Ropp's power to Vashtar. Conradin waits for de Ropp to leave the shed having possessed Vashtar, but instead "out through that doorway came a long, low, yellow-and-brown beast, with eyes a-blink at the waning daylight, and dark wet stains around the fur of jaws and throat" (Saki, 1991, p. 140). The animal overpowers the human. Sredni Vashtar frees both himself and Conradin from de Ropp: the moment he realizes that Vashtar has killed his imperious guardian, "Conradin drop[s] on his knees" in gratitude and makes himself toast with as much butter as he likes—a symbol of his freedom from the tyrannical, bread-and-butter-withholding Mrs. de Ropp (p. 140). Sredni Vashtar acts as a symbolic equalizer, stripping Mrs. de Ropp of her unequal power and giving some of it to Conradin and himself. A ferret overpowering a human directly challenges the Victorian and Edwardian belief that humans are superior to animals.

Through Conradin's worship, Sredni Vashtar becomes the hero of the story and saves him from the oppressive guardianship of de Ropp (although whether she is truly oppressive or merely excessively strict is subjective). By portraying the ferret in a sympathetic light, Saki suggests that Vashtar's killing de Ropp is acceptable and that humans are not so superior to animals that they cannot be affected by them. Furthermore, the idea of Conradin's hero slaying who he views as his oppressor creates a sense of deserved justice, as she had abused her power as guardian, and it suggests the idea that the human gets what she deserves at the hands of the animal—a provocative idea in a culture so celebratory of blood sports.

DOMESTICITY V. WILDNESS IN LITERARY ANIMAL REPRESENTATIONS

Just as men and women were relegated to separate spheres of the public and private within Victorian and Edwardian society, animals were relegated to separate spheres. Animals were categorized as either peaceful, domestic creatures to be kept as pets (mostly dogs, cats, and birds), or as violent, wild beasts (Danahay, 2017). Danahay argues that both women and pets (particularly dogs, cats, and birds) were seen as domestic because they "were securely located within the protective boundaries of the domestic sphere" (2017). He points out that there are war horses, but "there is, by contrast, no such thing as a 'war cow'"; even though dogs and cats have "teeth and claws and [can] scratch and bite," they are relegated to the private sphere as peaceful companions (Danahay, 2017). This restriction placed on animals (as well as humans) reflects in media representations, creating problematic, one-dimensional characters who do not reflect real animals accurately.

Saki criticizes this restrictive categorization by creating animal characters who blur the lines between domestic and wild. His characters range from a murderous pet ferret to a polite ox to a cat who passive-aggressively ruins a dinner party. By challenging his readers' perceptions and expectations of animals both domestic and wild, Saki pushes them to reevaluate the way in which humans categorize, and thereby diminish, animals.

The most blatant way in which Saki subverts this trend of categorizing animals is his placement of "wild" animals in domestic spaces and vice versa. His "The Stalled Ox" (Saki, 1991) is a story about a large, threatening-looking ox who has wandered into a woman's delicate garden and later her house—two spaces representative of the private sphere. The woman seeks out her neighbor's help, but both of them see the ox as dangerous and are afraid to engage with it. The ox, "a huge mottled brute" with "large blood-shot eyes," looks like it has the potential for violence, and the human characters expect it to "[lower] its head" and "[stamp] its feet," clearly placing the ox in the "wild" category of animals (Saki, 1991, p. 346, 347).

Yet, Saki subverts expectations and the ox behaves in a polite, peaceful way. When the ox understands it is not welcome, it immediately leaves the garden (entering the house instead). In fact, the ox's considerate complaisance is quite comical: "The ox seemed to realise at once that it was to go;

it gave a hurried final pluck at the [flower]bed where the chrysanthemums had been, and strode swiftly up the garden" (p. 347). The ox's politeness is contrasted with the woman's "raging retort[s]" and furious stomping in anger at the ox eating her flowers (p. 348). Saki not only moves the ox from the violent, wild category to the peaceful, domestic one, he also moves the woman from the peaceful domestic sphere to the violent public one, further seen in her angrily marching into town to call the police. Saki's consistent subversion of categories for animals and women help in the fight to give them more accurate representation in literature. By going outside the traditional spheres, Saki pushes his readers to reconsider the complexity of women and animals; they should not be dismissed as submissive things to be kept at home, but rather be recognized as powerful beings fully capable of moving within all spheres.

Interestingly, many of Saki's animal characters who cross the boundaries between wild and domestic are accompanied by women who also leave the domestic sphere. For example, in "Esmé" (1991), a head-strong, independent Englishwoman titled the Baroness befriends a wandering pet hyena, Esmé, when the Baroness and her hunting companion get lost during a hunting party. Throughout the story, Esmé weaves between the human-imposed animal spheres of wild and domestic. Esmé behaves as a friendly domesticated animal, greeting the Baroness and her friend with "demonstrations of friendliness," coming when called, and trotting "cheerfully" alongside the women's horses like a faithful pet; yet, when a young child comes along, he eats it quite ferociously (p. 102, 103). The Baroness also blurs boundaries, demonstrating leadership and financial skills through her taking charge when they get lost and initiating a financial transaction—two characteristics typical of the public sphere.

Additionally, she is quite aggressive and arguably anti-domestic, seen in her response to Esmé's eating the young child: when her friend wonders if "the poor little thing suffered much," the Baroness responds in the affirmative, adding, "It may have been crying from sheer temper. Children sometimes do" (p. 104). This lack of maternal concern for the child and dismissal of its pain as an annoying habit of childhood reveals the Baroness's absence from the domestic sphere. Creating characters that do not fit in simple boxes allows Saki to assert humans' and animals' individuality and complexity, giving them better agency and stronger representation within literature.

Saki further challenges the separation of the domestic and wild spheres through the concept of showing—or not showing—shame. Daniella Cadiz Bedini (2014) argues that experiencing shame of one's body demonstrates one's humanity, as nonhuman animals are not ashamed and therefore do not cover up their bodies like humans do (p. 28). She explains that shame and covering one's body extends to controlling one's bodily urges and functions. This choice to control one's body by denying or restricting its physical urges "is seen as an element of separation from the 'animal kingdom' (which becomes characterized as lacking in shame, so having no need to cover up the body and its processes)" (Bedini, 2014, p. 28). Essentially, if an animal, human or nonhuman, displays shame or attempts to control their body, they are demonstrating a sense of humanity and civility.

Saki criticizes this concept through "Esmé." In the story, Esmé carries the young child in his mouth for a portion of their journey, unbeknownst to the Baroness and her hunting partner. When the women discover this, they shout at Esmé to drop the child. In response, he quickly "bound[s] aside into some thick bushes, where [they] [can]not follow" (Saki, 1991, p. 104). Interestingly, the Baroness notes, "When the beast joined us again, after an absence of a few minutes, there was an air of patient understanding about him, as though he knew that he had done something of which we disapproved, but which he felt to be thoroughly justifiable" (p. 104). While the Baroness may perhaps be anthropomorphizing Esmé at this moment, it is significant that she comments on his personal lack of shame as well as his acknowledgment of the women's attempts to shame him. Esmé (through the eyes of the Baroness) recognizes that the women think his act of eating the child is shameful, yet he feels "thoroughly justifi[ed]" in it, with no shame at all.

While some readers may view Esmé's behavior as a way in which Saki is proving that Esmé is a violent, wild animal incapable of peace or shame, careful analysis of the Baroness's observation suggests that Esmé's choice to not feel shame means the opposite. Esmé carries the child for a considerable amount of time. It is only after the women shout at him that he decides to eat it. This suggests that he is capable of controlling his bodily urges, as he delays eating the child. Also, he chooses to ignore the women's orders for him to not eat the child, yet he recognizes that the women view the act as shameful. This demonstrates that Esmé makes the conscious decision to not feel ashamed: he "patient[ly] understand[s]" the women's view of the act as shameful and respectfully disagrees. Therefore, Esmé is capable of shame, yet he chooses not to feel it. Saki does not create a one-dimensional "wild" beast, but rather a sophisticated animal character who displays complex thought and challenges the reader to consider whether shame and attempting to control one's body is really what sets humans above animals.

HUNTING

"Mrs. Packletide's Tiger"

Saki includes various hunting scenes and elements into some of his stories, often subverting or challenging hunting culture and the beliefs that hunters hold about animals. In 1911, Saki wrote his short story "Mrs. Packletide's Tiger" (1991), satirizing the popular genre of the hunting narrative and criticizing the immorality of killing animals. Saki subverts the typical hunting narrative's celebration of violent domination over others by replacing the motives, characters, and events of the hunting narrative to mock its belief in humans' superiority to animals. Instead of following the traditional plot of a rugged hunter single-handedly conquering a powerful predator to quench his masculine thirst for blood, Saki's satire follows the not-so-heroic feat of an overweight, middle-aged woman who pays for a hunting safari to one-up her neighbor. While this story is one of his more comical satires, Saki's criticism is not any less serious or severe.

In her influential 1987 book *The Animal Estate*, Harriet Ritvo dedicates a chapter to the history and culture surrounding big-game hunting at the end of the nineteenth century, offering critical insight into the beliefs and behaviors that Saki satirizes. Her explanations provide critical historical context for better understanding Saki's denunciation of hunting. According to Ritvo, "The first books dealing specifically with the chase of exotic big game appeared early in the nineteenth century," and evolved throughout several decades, maintaining the popularity of the genre as hunting remained a major factor in British life (1987, p. 256). Ritvo writes that as the British Empire continued to expand its colonies in Asia and Africa, British hunters could travel to more exotic places more easily. Hunting-narrative authors then rationalized their desire to travel across continents to access more big-game animals by portraying the hunter-protagonists within the narratives as the saviors of the native populations; hunters who killed tigers and big-game animals "saved" the people who lived nearby from the supposedly ferocious beasts. Even though the now-colonized people had lived beside these animals for countless generations prior to British intrusion, hunting narratives often depicted "beleaguered natives [beseeching] valiant sportsmen to rid them of such scourges" (Ritvo, 1987, p. 276). That the Asian and African people truly did see the British hunters as "valiant sportsmen" is highly doubtful; the fact that the British hunters saw themselves and their sport as noble and beneficial to others is informative of hunting culture in the late nineteenth century and an aspect that Saki heavily criticizes in his fiction. While there are clear racial implications to unpack with this idea of a white, Western savior, this chapter focuses on the characterizations and representations of fictional animals.

In his story, Saki mocks hunters' rationales for killing animals through Mrs. Packletide's motivations. He begins his story by declaring that Mrs. Packletide intends to kill a tiger, but her motives are not the usual ones: "Not that the lust to kill had suddenly descended on her, or that she felt that she would leave India safer and more wholesome than she had found it, with one fraction less of wild beast per million of inhabitants" (Saki, 1991, p. 115). By declaring what Packletide's motivations are not, Saki identifies two major themes within the hunting narrative genre and sets them up for criticism.

The first reason authors during the Victorian and Edwardian eras used a hunting trope was to satiate violent, instinctual desire to kill and prove themselves as distinguished, dominant men. This also served the dual purpose of altruistically protecting people in the colonies from being preyed upon by animals. Ritvo writes that many viewed hunting as "the chance of violent domination"; "this enjoyment derived ultimately from the satisfaction of a lust for blood" (1987, 270). In his book on hunting history, Boddice writes, "Nineteenth-century attitudes toward hunting relied upon the notion that it was *natural* for men to hunt" and was seen as "an exemplar of manly virtue," offering hunters a way to demonstrate their own manliness (2008, p. 261). In fact, some considered hunting—especially of big game like tigers—to be the only "'real sport' [to] release [their] blood-lust, which contributed . . . to their innate sense of masculine identity" (McKenzie, 2009, p. 76). Saki's humor comes out in his placing an out-of-shape, aging woman from suburbia in the role of the masculine hunter, lusting for blood and "violent domination."

The other main appeal for hunting—the desire to "save" Asian and African populations from predatory animals—frequently appears in hunting narratives of Saki's time, as authors qualified their adventures as "equally beneficial to the rulers and the ruled" (Ritvo, 1987, p. 276). This seemingly charitable incentive is ironically named as the other motive Packletide does not have: that "she would leave India safer and more wholesome" by removing "one fraction less of wild beast" from the land (Saki, 1991, p. 115). Saki's condemning voice shines through the humor as he cuts down this popular line of reasoning by arguing her one hunting trip would scarcely affect the ratio of "wild beast per million of inhabitants." By measuring one's improvement of an entire country by "beast per million," Saki points out the absurdity of hunters' rationalizations for their expeditions. Saki's inclusion of the main rationales for hunting in his introduction of Packletide's story sets the foundation for his criticism and subversion of the nineteenth-century hunting narrative.

Saki's humorous satire of hunting narratives continues with his explanation of Packletide's actual intention for wanting to hunt a tiger. The narrator reveals that her motivation is that her neighbor "Loona Bimberton had recently been carried eleven miles in an aeroplane by an Algerian aviator, and talked of nothing else; only a personally procured tiger-skin and a heavy harvest of Press photographs could successfully counter that sort of thing" (Saki, 1991, p. 115). Saki disputes the belief in hunting as a noble sport by comparing hunters' motives with Packletide's, implying that they are equally petty. He also ironically associates her with great figures of hunting; the narrator claims that she is following in "the footsteps of Nimrod," the legendary hunter in the Bible's Book of Genesis, and Packletide dresses as Diana, the

Roman goddess of hunting, at a costume party after her hunt (p. 115). These god-like comparisons serve to push the biting humor in Saki's criticism of hunters' skewed views of themselves as dominant figures within the animal kingdom. Furthermore, Saki mocks hunters who think they are playing God and saving villages and towns from animals. This belief is quintessentially anthropocentric, as humans are not invulnerable to other animals. By satirizing this and other anthropocentric beliefs within big-game hunting culture, Saki works to de-glorify big-game hunting.

Saki also criticizes hunting with his reversal of several key characteristics of the hunting narrative. One such change is his portrayal of the Asian and African people who would assist in tracking the animal for the British hunter. Ritvo explains that in their hunting narratives, British hunters would provide contradictory views of the paid assistants who helped them in their hunting excursions. The writers would openly admit that without the aid of trackers, their hunts would be unsuccessful, yet they often complained that the local assistants who helped them "presented an endless series of obstacles to efficient management" of a hunting expedition or stretched the truth and claimed they hunted on their own (Ritvo, 1987, p. 261). Saki criticizes this trend by presenting the assistants in his hunting narrative as exaggeratedly efficient managers of Packletide's hunt.

When Packletide offers one thousand rupees for the experience of shooting a tiger, an Indian village comes together to manage the entire experience: "The prospect of earning the thousand rupees had stimulated the sporting and commercial instinct of the villagers"; mothers would silence their babies to allow the "venerable herd-robber" enough sleep, and "the cheaper kinds of goats [are] left about with elaborate carelessness to keep him satisfied with his present quarters" (Saki, 1991, p. 116). The village takes absurdly extreme measures to ensure that Packletide can hunt her tiger, giving the reader an over-the-top satirical jab at British hunters who complain of inefficient assistants or take credit for the hunt themselves. The villagers' extreme measures to ensure the tiger is ready to be hunted points out British hunters' hypocrisy in needing local assistants and trackers to help them find their game and yet viewing them as hindrances to their hunts.

Saki even includes the village's encouragement of the tiger by baiting it with their children—the very people hunters supposedly were saving by hunting tigers: children are "posted" outside "to head the tiger back in the unlikely event of his attempting to roam away to fresh hunting-grounds" (Saki, 1991, p. 116). This elaborate criticism of hunters works two-fold, as it illustrates how hunters were not as independent or Nimrodian as they claimed to be in their hunting narratives, and it mocks the idea that they were saving the villages from these fearsome beasts. The direct contrast of baiting the tiger with their children and the notion that a hunter "would leave India safer and more wholesome" is yet another clever criticism Saki offers in his story.

Saki continues his satirical hunting narrative with his description of Packletide's shooting the tiger. Ritvo writes that in hunting narratives, the author would often describe the moments of the kill as if he were in complete isolation, willfully ignoring the entire troupe of paid assistants, trackers, and fellow huntsmen nearby. It was important that the hunter was seen as locked in a "tête-à-tête with his prey," as "the ultimate challenge posed by a dangerous and enraged quarry" was faced alone by the hunter and "required the raw force and the delight in violence that hunting narratives were structured to emphasize and celebrate" (Ritvo, 1987, p. 263). Yet this fierce, one-on-one battle to the death is exactly what Packletide does not experience. She sits in a "comfortable and conveniently placed" platform that she has paid the villagers to build, with her paid companion Ms. Mebbin next to her, and the "village headman, who [is] in ambush in a neighboring tree" (Saki, 1991, p. 117). What's more, the moment the tiger collapses, "a crowd of excited natives [swarm] on to the scene," evidently very nearby (p. 117). Packletide is anything but isolated in her hunt. Again, Saki points out the absurdity of hunting narrative authors' claims of their superiority as hunters, as she not only needs the village to manage the entire experience for her, but also they surround the hunting area, "swarm[ing]" it as soon as she has pulled the trigger.

In fact, a major element of the story's humor is that Packletide's one act of authentic hunting—shooting her rifle at the "beast of prey" accidentally hits the tethered goat meant as bait, and the tiger "succumb[s] to heart failure, caused by the sudden report of the rifle, accelerated by senile decay" (Saki, 1991, p. 117). Mebbin's blunt way of describing the great hunt—"How [Packletide] shot the goat and frightened the tiger to death"—reinforces Saki's criticism of hunters' portrayals of their adventures in their narratives as one-on-one battles with fierce beasts, when in reality they often leave the work to their paid assistants and pull the trigger (p. 118). The pitiful death of the tiger works on two levels. Firstly, the tiger's old age garners sympathy and calls into question the necessity of hunting by more empathetic readers. Secondly, the tiger's frailty and death from heart failure instead of the gun derogate hunters who think they are conquering the world's fiercest beasts when in reality they are killing a living being with physical limitations with a gun from afar. The combination of an overweight suburban woman and an elderly, weakened tiger add extra weight to Saki's criticism of hunters' perceptions of themselves as mighty masters of nature conquering ferocious jungle monsters.

Packletide's shooting the goat also allows Saki to comment on the inhumanity of using animals as live bait. Killing the goat in the same manner as big game challenges hunters' categorization of animals and acceptable treatment of them: in many hunters' eyes, tigers are wild and aggressive, meant to be shot with large guns and conquered; goats are domesticated and peaceful, associated with the private sphere and the home and therefore should be treated with gentleness. For both Edwardian and modern-day readers, the animals' deaths are unacceptable. For the modern reader, the animals' deaths are wrong and immoral for the very fact that they are killed. However, for the Edwardian reader, it is wrong for Packletide to not "properly" have killed the tiger with the gun and for killing the goat, a helpless animal of the home, with a violent, aggressive weapon. Portraying the animal characters' deaths as offensive and needless contributes to Saki's condemnation of big-game hunting as absurd and unjustifiable.

One of the reasons that Saki's satire is so effective is that he targets the beliefs behind unethical behaviors rather than just the actions. For example, he pokes fun at hunting narrative authors' self-image as Herculean sportsmen and the supreme predators of the animal kingdom instead of outright criticizing hunting. Saki's story in which a petty, average woman spooks a tiger to death and parades herself as Diana provides an over-the-top, comedic satire of hunting and its use by men to prove their masculinity *ad absurdum*. Saki's narrative proves repeatedly the true absurdity of killing others to support one's self-image or reputation in society. To take away a life for something as insignificant as a few moments of confidence is something that absolutely needs to be stopped universally and immediately. Saki's use of satire and humor to convey his criticism is a risky tool in that it can be misconstrued as making light of a serious topic; however, by emphasizing the absurdity of what he criticizes through over-the-top satire, Saki is clear in his denunciation of harming animals. Studying Saki's fiction offers a better understanding of past and present sentiments toward animals and humans' relationships with them, aiding in the ultimate goal of maintaining peaceful, beneficial coexistence among all animals.

"Laura"

"Laura" is another humorous story in which Saki challenges humans' supposed superiority to, and placement within, the animal kingdom. Here, Laura is a witty, facetious woman who takes out "petty vindictive revenges" on her friend Amanda's fussy, fidgety husband, Egbert (Saki, 1991, p. 242). Laura tells Amanda of her belief in reincarnation and that she plans to reincarnate as an otter; shortly after, Laura dies, and the story continues as Egbert is plagued by a very pernicious otter.

"Laura" provides a hunting scene which Saki uses to poke fun at hunters and their irrational, anthropocentric perceptions of the animals they hunt. Often, hunters justify their sport by viewing animals as equally intelligent or clever as the hunter and therefore more difficult and worthy to kill: "Hunting apologists consistently . . . took a line of argument that tacitly acknowledged the cleverness of the fox, stating that hunting was truly sporting *because* of the fair psychological battle between predator and prey" (Boddice, 2008, p. 289). This illogical view of animals acts as a double-edged sword: if the animal is not as intelligent as the hunter, the hunter is no longer the strong, masculine dominator of nature and becomes an emasculated exterminator of the weak; if the animal is too intelligent, the hunter must admit he has been outwitted by a "lower" animal and cannot as easily claim superiority at the top of the animal kingdom. Saki plays on this illogical line of thinking in hunting culture by writing a story in which a hunter is clearly surpassed in intelligence by an otter.

Egbert has several psychological battles with the otter (assumedly Laura reincarnated) and loses all of them. The otter initiates the first battle by dragging Egbert's four prized Sussex chickens into his new, expensive garden and eating them, destroying the delicate flowers in the process. With a heavy dose of situational irony, Egbert claims, "it almost seems as if the brute that did the deed had special knowledge how to be as devastating as possible in a short space of time," and responds by "strengthening [his] poultry yard defenses" (Saki, 1991, p. 243, 244). He admits that it is such an even match of wits that he cannot consider hunting it as anything but "a case of necessity" and immediately plans an official otter hunt (p. 244). Egbert's desperation reveals his perception of the otter as psychologically comparable, if not superior, to himself. The otter soon outwits Egbert again, killing the rest of his chickens and destroying his strawberry plants. While Egbert plans his offensive attack by calling in the otter hounds "at the earliest possible moment," the otter steals and eats a salmon on his rug (p. 244). So far, the otter has managed to one-up Egbert seemingly every time he leaves the house. She has managed to enter his poultry yard, his garden, and his house, penetrating his defenses and destroying what his wife claims he is most devoted to: "his poultry and his garden" (p. 242).

This otter uses the same methods to exasperate Egbert that hunters use to find and kill otters. According to H.A. Bryden (1904), otter hunting "is conducted entirely upon foot" by people wading through streams and rivers with long poles attempting to force otters out of their dens (p. 250). Upon discovery of an otter, participants in the hunt call for their pack of otter hounds, "and the otter usually meets his end . . . by the teeth of the hounds" (p. 253). In Saki's story, the otter reverses the roles, psychologically acting as the predator by persistently attacking and invading Egbert's home. By never explicitly stating whether Laura is the otter, Saki asserts the possibility that animals can outwit humans and the belief that animals should be considered intelligent beings and treated accordingly.

According to an article from Cambridge University Press on otter hunting in the 1900s, hunting otters was different from hunting other animals: "[One] aspect of otter hunting that attracted critical attention was the type of people involved and the behavior it induced. Men, women and children could all actively participate together in this sport" (Allen et al., 2016, pp. 88–89). While big-game hunting was treated as a demonstration of one's manly strength, otter hunting was a family activity, as seen in a 1908 pamphlet's description of an otter hunt as "a middle-aged woman, hurrying along, mile after mile, through wet grass and muddy pools" tracking her prey (qtd. in Allen et al., p. 89). With otter hunting being a sport commonly associated with children, it is humorous to consider that Egbert, an adult, finds it too challenging.

When the otter has "massacred" the rest of his speckled Sussex and torn through his strawberry plants, Egbert demands the death of the otter. When Amanda claims that it is "hardly sporting to hunt an animal when it has so little chance of taking refuge anywhere," Egbert replies, "I'm not thinking about sport. I want to have the animal killed as soon as possible" (Saki, 1991, p. 244). Egbert's desperate desire to get rid of the otter rather than any excitement to hunt it shows him to be unequal in the hunt: as Boddice explains, people viewed hunting as fair sport because the "psychological battle between predator and prey" is evenly matched (2008, p. 289). Therefore, Egbert's claim that he is "not thinking about sport" when he demands that the otter be killed immediately acts as an admission that the otter is psychologically superior. Saki plays out this disparity in wits in Egbert and the otter's battles, satirizing hunting culture's illogical and inhumane justification of hunting small animals like foxes and otters.

Saki confronts the cultural belief of humans' superiority in the animal kingdom and therefore our right to hunt other animals by providing a hunted animal character who can be considered partially human. Amanda's reactions to Laura's and Egbert's interactions reveal the cultural ideas Saki challenges. When Laura shares her desire to reincarnate as an otter, Amanda is horrified: "How dreadful to be hunted and harried and finally worried to death!" (Saki, 1991, p. 242). It is only after she imagines Laura, a human, as an otter that Amanda can sympathize with animals. However, it does not last long, as several days later she announces, "I've asked quite a lot of people down for golf and fishing" (p. 243). Her foray into sympathizing with animals ends with her plans to harm some (fishing), implying that the cause of this momentary compassion for them is Laura's humanness. Amanda's perception of Laura as both a human and an otter blurs the lines between the species, creating a literal anthropomorphism, and allows the empathy she feels for humans to temporarily transfer to animals. Amanda's conditional sympathy highlights the problem—and solution—of humans' limited compassion; if people can view animals not as a strict "other," but as fellow living beings (like the way Saki creates his animal and human characters), then their sympathy can reach all animals, human and nonhuman.

Saki uses Amanda's reactions to Egbert's efforts to kill the otter to further criticize humans' lack of compassion for nonhuman animals. Because she truly believes Egbert has hunted and killed her friend Laura, Amanda has an "attack of nervous prostration" (Saki, 1991, p. 245). Amanda's emotional commiseration for the otter is undeniably due to the fact that she believes it is a human reincarnated as the otter; when she changes her mind and believes that it was merely an "adventurous otter in search of a variation of diet" and not her friend in an animal body, she has a complete "recovery of health and mental balance," no longer caring that her husband has killed the animal (p. 245). Amanda's changes in emotional response to the otter's death presses readers to reevaluate their beliefs about hunting and people's limited ability to sympathize with animals. "Laura" mocks hunters' justifications for killing small-game animals as well as society's lack of compassion for animals, just as "Mrs. Packletide's Tiger" ridicules big-game hunters for their anthropocentric egotism. Saki's stories such as "Mrs. Packletide's Tiger" and "Laura" work to criticize the immorality of hunting and highlight humans' abusive relationship with animals.

CONCLUSION

The animal characters in Saki's stories challenge traditions and ideas such as hunting and human superiority to animals. In several stories, animals challenge the cultural value of a life: in "Laura," Amanda can only sympathize with a hunted animal if she believes it is human, meaning that she values human lives much higher than animal lives; in a story titled "The Penance," children practice an eye-for-an-eye system of justice by promising to kill a man's child because he killed their cat, shocking the man and begging the question, why is it acceptable for one life to end but not the other?

Susan McHugh writes, "Animality gains intellectual appeal for some literary critics as a repressed deconstructive element, a marker of difference internalized in human species being. This implies that animal subjectivity remains significant only as an essentially negative force against which the human is asserted" (2009, p. 489). This (needless) desire for the presence of humanness within animal studies is reflected in Saki critic Joseph Salemi's argument that "animals play so large a role in Saki's fiction [because] they represent what human beings . . . really are beneath the surface . . . in Saki's view, the playful conflict between man and beast represents the more serious and unremitting conflict between what we are and what we strive to seem"

(1989, p. 426). Critics like Salemi that McHugh refers to in the quote above cannot seem to produce worthwhile literary criticism without relying on projecting humanness onto animality—they reinforce the binary opposition in which the animal must be defined by its relation to the human, further ingraining humans' power over animals. It is this very notion that humanness is a foundational or mandatory part of animal studies that makes studying Saki's animal characters within an animal studies lens crucial.

Saki has been interrogating the representation of animals and animality since the beginning of the twentieth century. His animal characters demonstrate individuality and animality and often demand that readers rethink their views and treatment of animals. Animal characters such as Saki's prove "useful for interrogating key elements of identity and society, inspiring as well as confronting the limitations of knowledge" (McHugh, 2011, p. 211). Saki's animal characters push the boundaries of literature and confront reader expectations. They kill and are killed, politely leave gardens and tear up flower beds, and provide complex personalities that represent dynamic living beings with thoughts, emotions, and meaningful lives. A.J. Langguth finishes his landmark biography of Saki stating, "If genius is doing a thing perfectly, he was a genius. If genius is doing all things perfectly, he was not. Does it matter? He makes us laugh" (1981, p. 280). Saki does much more than make us laugh. He makes us think and rethink.

SELECTED BIBLIOGRAPHY

Allen, D Watkins, David Matless. (2008). "An incredibly vile sport": Campaigns against otter hunting in Britain, 1900–39. (2016). *Rural History,* 271, 79–101.

Bedini, D. C. (2014). Behaving like animals: Shame and the human-animal border in "The unbearable lightness of being and disgrace. " *Journal for Critical Animal Studies*, 12(4).

Boddice, R. (2008). *A history of attitudes and behaviours toward animals in eighteenth-and nineteenth-century Britain: Anthropocentrism and the emergence of animals*. Edwin Mellen Press.

Brooks, D. E., & Hébert, L. P. (2006). Gender, race, and media representation. In *Gender and communication in mediated contexts* (pp. 297–318).

Bryden, H. A. (1904). *Nature and sport in Britain*. G. Richards.

Byrne, S. (2007). *The unbearable Saki: The work of H.H. Munro.* Oxford U Press.

Danahay, M. A. (2017). Nature red in hoof and paw: Domestic animals and violence in Victorian art. *Victorian Animal Dreams*, 97–119.

DeMello, M. (2012). *Animals and society: An introduction to human-animal studies.* Columbia University Press.

Langguth, A. J. (1981). *Saki: Life of Hector Hugh Munro*. Hamish Hamilton.

McHugh, Susan. (2009). Literary animal agents. *English Faculty Publications*, University of New England, 487–495.

———. (2011). *Animal stories: Narrating across species lines*. Minneapolis: University of Minnesota Press.

Mckenzie, Callum. (2000). The British big-game hunting tradition, masculinity and fraternalism with particular reference to the "The Shikar Club," *The Sports Historian*, 20(1), 70–96.

Orgad, S. (2014). *Media representation and the global imagination*. John Wiley & Sons.

Ritvo, Harriet. (1987). *The animal estate: The English and other creatures in the Victorian Age*. Harvard University Press.

Saki. (1991). *The Complete Saki*. Penguin Classics.

Salemi, Joseph. (1989). An asp lurking in an apple-charlotte: Animal violence in Saki's "The Chronicles of Clovis." *Studies in Short Fiction*, 36(4), 423–430.

Shapiro, Kenneth and Marion Copeland. (2005). Toward a critical theory of animal issues in fiction. *Society & Animals*, 13(4), 343–346.

Chapter Two

Making No Appeal to the State

Ending Animal Abuse through Total Liberation and Direct Action

Will Boisseau

INTRODUCTION

This chapter takes a radical animal studies approach, influenced by anarchist theory and practice, to argue that concepts of solidarity and total liberation can better serve nonhuman animals than arguments that focus on animal "rights" or "welfare." I further argue that the anarchist concepts of total liberation and direct action offer non-state ways of agitating for an end to animal oppression.

The chapter considers critiques of rights and welfare from anarchist, feminist, and radical animal activist perspectives. For instance, the Feminists for Animal Rights (1990) group argued that the terminology of rights "represents an ordering of the world that is inherently hierarchical, dualistic and competitive" (p. 1). Other animal activists have similarly noted the hierarchical nature of rights which provides animals with honorary protections who are perceived to have the most human-like qualities.

The next section of the chapter explores how animal activists aim to end animal abuse through non-state solutions using the concept of total liberation and direct action. This part of the chapter is particularly influenced by anarchist theory. Anarchist activists seek non-state solutions. The inspiration for this chapter stems from interviews I have conducted with over fifty animal activists in the U.K. and North America. One interviewee told me that they believed that "law and capitalism are intimately connected, that law's basic norm is the protection of private property, that the entire system of laws and courts are built on/to serve this basic notion [of property]." A radical feminist approach supports the anarchist belief that legislative solutions will not amend oppressive social relations and legal changes may further legitimize the liberal state and the animal oppression it upholds.

RIGHTS AND WELFARE

In this section, terms such as animal welfare, rights, and liberation are defined and critiqued. Animal welfare is the belief that animals should be treated humanely whilst avoiding unnecessary suffering. A belief in animal welfare means that animals can still be consumed as food, hunted, or used in experiments but should not be done with gratuitous or unnecessary violence. On the other hand, an animal rights position states that animals should not be used instrumentally as a means to human ends under any circumstance. Finally, an animal liberation approach accepts the premise of animal rights, but focuses on the domestication of animals and has adopted tactics including direct action and the liberation of animals.

Even with these definitions, such terms are still often contested. Tom Regan (2004) explains that words such as "humane" and "welfare" "can either conceal or reveal the truth," "depending on who is using them" (p. 203). In everyday language, anyone concerned with improving some aspect of animal use is grouped together using one term, thus "someone who advocates that pigs have larger stalls, so as to improve the quality of their short lives, is described as a believer in an animal right" (Donaldson & Kymlicka, 2011, p. 19).

A focus on animal welfare has been heavily criticized by proponents of animal *rights*, such as Gary Francione (1996), who argued that the "most ardent defenders of institutionalised animal exploitation themselves endorse animal welfare" (p. 1). Moreover, Francione (1996) believes that welfare groups will never challenge the property status of animals or seek fundamental change because "these groups, which are far more like bourgeois charities than revolutionary organisations, are not likely to have a go at the institution of private property" (p. 187).

An animal *rights* position, which gained prominence since the 1970s with Regan, Peter Singer, and Francione, states that animals should not be used instrumentally as a means to human ends under any circumstances. Steven Best and Anthony Nocella (2004) set out the difference between a rights and a welfare approach. An animal rights position aims to abolish animal suffering "demanding not bigger cages and 'humane treatment,' but rather empty cages and total liberation"; animal rights philosophy insists that "animals are subjects of their own life and no one's to own"; and finally animal rights theory "puts human and nonhuman animals on an equal moral plane and rejects all exploitative use of animals, whether human beings benefit or not" (pp. 26–27).

Steven Best (2014) explains that whilst liberationists "often rely on rights-based assumptions while upholding abolitionists" goals' they also aim to "free animals from captivity and to attack exploiters through various means" including diverse forms of direct action and economic sabotage (p. 82). Therefore, liberationists might focus on the property status and confinement of animals whereas rights advocates would focus on the pain experienced by animals. Whilst animal rights and liberation are often used synonymously, both are often regarded as incompatible with animal welfare. As Corey Lee Wrenn (2011) argues, "welfareism . . . only serves to make nonhuman animal exploitation more efficient and is thus counterproductive" (p. 21). For Wrenn, "there is little hope of reconciling these two approaches" (Ibid).

Many activists argue that animal welfare helps in the smooth running and continued exploitation of animals. Moreover, welfare improvements work only to appease the public and steal the thunder of those seeking systemic transformations. The distinction is both a theoretical and a tactical split. It is maintained because of many animal activists' reluctance to make compromises on behalf of other animals. This is partly due to the feeling that such compromises will not work. Other activists perceive such compromises as a speciesist betrayal that the animals in factory farms, and other places of abuse, would not themselves agree to if they were able to formulate their own political demands. The ALF (c. 1998) position is that:

We don't talk to those people who kill animals . . . You can't compromise with us as long as the victims all die on one side. We're not open to discussion, because we can't take you seriously in a discussion when you drown in the blood of animals (*Animal Liberation through Direct Action*).

Clearly there is a large difference between rights/liberation and welfare approaches.

Activists believe that a liberation approach is compatible with revolutionary anti-statism because:

> The crumbs from the political tables of compromise will not achieve liberation of our mother earth and her animals, they will only result in false faith in a political and corporate structure that cannot survive without animal and earth abuse. (Western Wildlife Unit)

Other campaign groups may use the term animal rights whilst theoretically distancing themselves from the concept of rights. For instance, Feminists for Animal Rights (1990) believed that "rights are inherently paternalistic" because "even so-called inalienable rights have to derive from somewhere"; and rather than challenge all hierarchy and power structures, the concept of rights instead simply made recipients of such rights "honorary straight white men" (p. 12). Anarchists have also critiqued the concepts of both rights and liberation. For instance, Watkinson and O'Driscoll (2014) believe that rights rely on enforcement from a state and Brian Dominick (1995) has come to believe that liberation is "a particularly human concept" and "beyond the capabilities of any [nonhuman] animal" (p. 16). From an anarchist perspective both rights and welfare rely on state enforcement. On the other hand, liberation involves activists taking direct action to free animals from places of abuse.

ANIMAL OPPRESSION

The belief that animals are subjected to an intersecting form of oppression is important to anarchist understandings of animal liberation. This belief developed from Peter Singer's concept of speciesism. Still, radical animal scholars do not regard speciesism as a mere prejudice equivalent to other forms of bigotry. Rather, it is a system of oppression that must be understood as benefiting humans due to their hierarchical position above other animals, although in different ways and to different degrees. David Nibert (2002) explains the three elements of mutually reinforcing mechanisms of oppression: firstly, economic exploitation of "the Other." Secondly, iniquitous social power which is politically reflected and reproduced by the state. And finally, an ideology that is emergent from and produces economic relations. This helps explain speciesism as a belief system that legitimizes and fosters exploitation and oppression. These mutually reinforcing mechanisms also relate to patriarchy, white supremacy, and other forms of oppression. Nibert follows the approach of Iris Marion Young (1990) who describes oppression as the overarching concept in which systematic institutional processes prevent people from developing their potential through exploitation, marginalization, powerlessness, and violence which are subsections of oppression (p. 38). Erika Cudworth (2005) perceives domination as the overarching concept which includes oppression, exploitation and marginalization. Oppression limits life chances and inhibits individuals and groups to flourish; exploitation amounts to the use of someone (or something) as a resource for the ends of the user; and marginalization is the conceptualizing or making of someone as relatively insignificant. In this way speciesism is part of a complex web interfacing in a network of oppression. Val Plumwood (1993) argues that different forms of oppression—such as those involving gender, nature, race, colonialism, and class—exist in a web of relations (p. 2). This web means that different forms of intersecting oppressions are unique and autonomous, yet at the same time rely on a unified model of operation with a common structure and ideology. Such intersecting frameworks of oppression may include hierarchical thinking, value-dualisms, "power-over" concepts of power, concepts of privilege, and the logic of domination (Cudworth, 2005). Whilst different forms of oppression might be based on common structures and ideologies, the lived experience of such oppression is, of course, experienced in multiple different ways. Animals caught in the animal-industrial complex do not simply have limited life chances but are bred into existence in ways which best serve the industries that exploit them. Their very existence is based on their use as a resource, they are not simply made to seem relatively insignificant but tortured, turned into living commodities, and killed for consumption.

The fact that radical animal activists believe that animals experience oppression makes their aims less compatible with welfare and rights approaches. Firstly, ending oppression requires systemic changes, whereas welfare and rights only offer piecemeal solutions. Secondly, the state is always key to upholding oppressive systems and therefore animal activists would not seek to legitimize the state by asking it to weaken an oppressive system it upholds. Anarchist animal advocates would argue that it is misguided to prioritize state legislation as a means of ending animal abuse. A radical feminist approach supports the anarchist belief that legislative solutions will not amend oppressive social relations. For instance, Catharine MacKinnon (1989) argues that feminists will only make minor gains through laws in "male supremacist societies" (p. 238). CAS scholars can apply the same framework to animal activists in anthropocentric societies. MacKinnon argues that, in the liberal state, laws appear "neutral, abstract, elevated, [and] pervasive" and as such institutionalized power of a dominant group over an oppressed group is made to "seem a feature of life, not a one-sided construct imposed by force for the advantage of a dominant group" (p. 238). For MacKinnon, the fact that law is interpreted as legitimate makes the social dominance that law upholds become invisible:

> Liberal legalism is thus a medium for making male dominance both invisible and legitimate by adapting the male point of view in law at the same time as it enforces that view on society. (p. 237)

Similarly, anarchist animal activists would argue that legal changes in anthropocentric societies will not challenge the speciesist standpoint that liberal legalism legitimizes; these anarchists do not regard the state as a neutral tool, instead they believe that the state is inherently opposed to animal rights ends, and as such campaigning for legal changes may further legitimize the liberal state and the animal oppression it upholds. Moreover, anarchist animal activists may point to the continued exploitation and oppression of human groups at the hands of states, and suggest that it is unlikely that states that have been prepared to treat humans instrumentally will be willing to change the status of animals.

OPPOSITION TO THE STATE

Opposition to the state (alongside opposition to capitalism and other forms of socially constructed hierarchy) is a key anarchist position adopted by radical animal activists. Anarchists view the state as a complex array of social and political institutions which uphold internalized power relations and also has interests of its own; moreover, the state is a "psychological phenomenon" which creates a certain "way of thinking about the world and understanding social organization" (Cudworth, 2007, pp. 142–146). Anarchist opposition to the state does not imply that self-identified anarchists would reduce their ideology to "any single position"; and anarchists do recognize "the possibility of thinking about resistance within the body of the state" (Kinna, 2005, pp. 54–55). Anarchist activists will be wary of appealing to the state as the "arbiter of justice," when it is the same state which enforces many of the injustices they oppose (Croatoan).

The anti-state position of anarchism has led to a strong connection between anarchism and animal liberation because many, though by no means all, animal liberation activists are hostile to state structures. David Nibert (2002) argues that the oppression of animals is fundamentally linked to the "capitalist state" because "the physical, political, economic, ideological, and diversionary powers of the state support and build such entangled oppressions while giving such atrocities legal and social respectability" (p. 185). Indeed, Nibert and Bob Torres (2007) believe that the ideological framework within which oppression operates needs a state to facilitate and enforce the dominant group's exploitation of oppressed groups (p. 8).

One does not have to be anti-statist to believe that "governments are in league with the dairy and meat industries," in terms of subsidies and preferential treatment to seemingly powerful farmers' unions (Spencer, 2002, p. 332). Those involved in the animal liberation movement tend to agree that these industries are "sanctioned, protected, and funded by the state" (Mann, 2007, p. 596).

Radical animal activists have adopted a tactical repertoire which does not rely on appeals to state reform because they are opposed to the state and believe that animal oppression is upheld by the state. In the next section, the concepts of total liberation and direct action are explored.

TOTAL LIBERATION

The concept of total liberation is used to promote a movement that simultaneously campaigns for human, animal, and Earth liberation and "in order to advance an anti-capitalist and, more generally anti-hierarchical politics" that seeks to "dismantle all structures of exploitation, domination, oppression, torture, killing, and power in favour of decentralising and democratizing society" (Best et al., p. 5).

As used by the animal and Earth liberation movements, the concept of total liberation was adapted from previous struggles. Most notably, Frantz Fanon used the term total liberation to call for "colonized and working-class people to free their minds from, and fight back against, colonial enslavement" (Colling et al., p. 56). However, the use of total liberation to describe the connections between human, animal, and Earth liberation was developed by Steven Best (2014) to argue that "human liberation is incomplete—as it would still be rooted in domination and oppression—if it does not include these other facets" (p. 52). David Pellow and Hollie Nyseth Brehm (2015) believe that the concept of total liberation has emerged as a dominant social movement frame due to the combination of radical environmental and animal rights activists with "the politics of social justice" (p. 193). According to Pellow and Nyseth Brehm, anarchism is a central component of the total liberation frame, along with anti-capitalism, support for direct action, and "an ethic of justice and anti-oppression for people, nonhumans and the ecosystems" (ibid).

Anarchists believe that the state is key to enforcing these intersecting systems of oppression that total liberation seeks to dismantle. It is only through direct action that animal activists can seek to undermine the animal-industrial complex.

DIRECT ACTION

In this final section, the importance of direct action for animal activists who want to campaign for animal liberation without appealing to the state and whilst recognizing the importance of total liberation is expanded.

Direct action, which is an "action without intermediaries, whereby an individual or a group uses their own power and resources to change reality in a desired direction" and which demands "taking social change into one's own hands, by intervening directly in a situation rather than appealing to an external agent (typically a government) for its rectification," has traditionally been associated with anarchism, and anarchists "take great pride" in this connection (Gordon, 2008, p. 17; Franks, 2006, p. 115).

Direct action for animals is associated with the formation of the ALF in 1976, although the Hunt Saboteurs Association (HAS) developed such tactics during the 1960s. By 1972 members of the HSA "decided more militant action was needed," and so a small group of activists formed the Band of Mercy, who engaged in property damage in defense of animals (ALF, undated, pp. 3–4). The Band of Mercy, named after a nineteenth-century RSPCA youth group, began their campaign by "destroying guns and sabotaging hunter's vehicles by breaking windows and slashing tyres" (ibid). The group, including Ronnie Lee, expanded their attention to other areas of animal abuse, and received national attention by "burning seal hunting boats as well as pharmaceutical laboratories" (interview with Ronnie Lee, 2013). Lee and fellow activist Cliff Goodman were "eventually . . . arrested and ended up [receiving] three-year sentences of which we only did a year." As Lee explains:

> It was when I came out from that jail sentence that the Animal Liberation Front was formed because there were a lot of people who heard about [us], who then wanted to get involved in it from hunt sabs and different groups. I think we were concerned that the name Band of Mercy sounded like some sort of religious group, it didn't say anything about animals, it didn't say anything about what we were about which was animal liberation, so we decided to change the name to the Animal Liberation Front. (interview with Ronnie Lee, 2013)

Lee believes that the ALF always had a connection to anarchism "in the sense that both believed in direct action, I was very much a believer in direct action in those days to protect animals . . . I think that was where the common ground was" (Interview with Ronnie Lee, 2013). Direct action here is more than just a tactic, it is a "process whereby activists develop decentralized and egalitarian politics based on cells, affinity groups, and consensus decision-making models" (Nocella, 2011, p. 16). Direct action is not only a key part of a movement's action repertoire, but can help bolster a group's collective identity. Participants in direct action may feel a "visceral empowerment" whereby activists "immediately feel in control of a situation that was previously defined by others" (Schnurer, 2004, p. 112). Moreover, direct action is not regarded as an appendage to political lobbying; instead it is the strategy that will bring about animal liberation by itself. One activist argued that "I obviously do hope that Government will intervene but whether it does or not is immaterial as the ALF will achieve what I want—all animal abuse ended" (ALF, 1983, p. 3). Ronnie Lee agreed that:

> We do not need the RSPCA to put pressure on the Government to end animal abuse because with sufficient action and efficient organisation we can end animal abuse *with our own hands* without reference to any governments . . . true animal and human liberation will not come by means of negotiations with governments but only through their abolition. (ALF, 1984, p. 4)

CONCLUSION

Direct action has been used by radical animal activists for a number of reasons: it relies on a liberation approach, it aims to end the oppression of animals, it does not rely on appeals to the state, and it is compatible with total liberation. Although the chapter has considered direct action in the form of ALF activism—rescuing animals from places of abuse and causing economic damage to animal abusers—there are numerous forms of direct action that one can take. Groups like the Anarchist Teapot and Food Not Bombs provide this solidarity and direct action by distributing vegan food at protest sites, environmental or peace camps, on picket lines, and at benefit gigs. Other forms of animal activism have tied in with feminist initiatives that provide safe spaces for victims of domestic abuse and their companion animals. Animal activists have also combined their promotion of veganism with other initiatives focused on local communities growing their own food such as the Transition Network.

The use of direct action allows groups to build trust and solidarity in small groups that typically use a consensus decision making, and a non-hierarchical, framework. When individuals and groups build confidence and trust it is then possible to move on more ambitious projects. The important thing about direct action is that it doesn't rely on appeals to a higher power, but it is about individuals coming together and achieving positive social change through their own solidarity and collective action. As one activist told me, the reason they are attracted to radical animal activism is because: It was very clearly a direct action grassroots movement, it was like: we're not asking the government to stop testing on animals, we're not asking the government nothing, we're closing this company down ourselves. And so the grassroots movement was very vibrant and alive and kicking.

SELECTED BIBLIOGRAPHY

ALF. (1983, April). *ALF supporters' group newsletter*, 4.

ALF. (1984, October). *ALF supporters' group newsletter*, 13.

ALF. (c.1988). *Animal liberation through direct action.*

Best, S., & Nocella II, A. J. (2004). Introduction: Behind the mask: Uncovering the animal Liberation Front. In Best, S., & Nocella II, A. J. (Eds.). *Terrorists or freedom fighters?: Reflections on the liberation of animals*. Lantern Books.

Best, S., Nocella II, A. J., Kahn, R., Gigliotti, C., &. Kemmerer, L. (2007). Introducing critical animal studies. *Animal Liberation Philosophy and Policy Journal*, 5(1), 4–5.

Best, S. (2014). *The politics of total liberation: Revolution for the 21st century*. Palgrave Macmillan.

Colling, S. Parson, S., & Arrigoni, A. (2014). Until all are free: Total liberation through revolutionary decolonization, groundless solidarity, and a relationship framework. In Nocella II, A. J. Sorenson, J. Socha, K. Matsuoka, A (Eds.), *Defining critical animal studies: An intersectional approach for liberation*. Peter Lang.

Croatoan. (2012). *Who is Oakland: Anti-oppression activism, the politics of safety, and state co-optation*. https://escalatingidentity.wordpress.com/2012/04/30/who-is-oakland-anti-oppression-politics-decolonization-and-the-state/

Cudworth, E. (2005). *Developing ecofeminist theory: The complexity of difference*. Palgrave Macmillan.

Cudworth, E. (2007). Anarchism: The politics of anti-statism. In Cudworth, E. Hall, T. McGovern, J. (Eds.), *The modern state: Theories and ideologies*. Edinburgh University Press.

Dominick, B. A. (1995.) *Animal liberation and social revolution: A vegan perspective on anarchism and an anarchist perspective on veganism*. Critical Mess Media.

Donladson, S. Kymlicka, W. (2011). *Zoopolis: A political theory of animal rights*. Oxford University Press.

Feminists for Animal Rights. (1990). *Feminists for animal rights newsletter*. 3–4.

Francione, G. L. (1996). *Rain without thunder: The ideology of the animal rights movement*. Temple University Press.

Franks, B. (2006). *Rebel alliances: The means and ends of contemporary British Anarchism*. AK Press and Dark Star.

Gordon, U. (2008). *Anarchy alive! Anti-authoritarian politics from practice to theory*. Pluto Press.

Kinna, R. (2005). *Anarchism: A beginner's guide*. Oneworld.

MacKinnon, C. A. (1989). *Towards a feminist theory of the state*. Harvard University Press.

Mann, K. (2007). *From dusk 'til dawn: an insider's view of the growth of the animal liberation movement*. Puppy Pincher Press.

Nibert, D. A. (2002). *Animal rights/human rights: Entanglements of oppression and liberation*. Rowman & Littlefield.

Nocella II, A. J. (2011). A dis-ability perspective on the stigmatization of dissent: Critical pedagogy, critical criminology, and critical animal studies. *Social Science – Dissertations*, 178.

Pellow, D. N., & Brehm, H. N. (2015). From the new ecological paradigm to total liberation: The emergence of a social movement frame, *The Sociological Quarterly*, 56, 185–212.

Plumwood, V. (1993). *Feminism and the mastery of nature*. Routledge.

Regan, T. (2004). *Empty cages: Facing the challenge of animal rights*. Rowman and Littlefield.

Schnurer, M. (2004). At the gates of hell: The ALF and the legacy of Holocaust resistance. In Best, S., & Nocella II, A. J. (Eds.), *Terrorists or freedom fighters?: Reflections on the liberation of animals*. Lantern Books.

Spencer, C. (2002). *Vegetarianism: A history*. Grub Street.

Torres, B. (2007). *Making a killing: The political economy of animal rights*. AK Press.

Watkinson, K., & O'Driscoll, D. (2014). *From animals to anarchism: Open letter #3*. Dysophia.

Webb, R. (c. 1999). ALF Press Office News, *Arkangel*, 21.

Western Wildlife Unit, *Memories of Freedom*.

Wrenn, C. L. (2011). Resisting the Globalization of Speciesism: Vegan Abolitionism as a Site for Consumer-Based Social Change, *Journal for Critical Animal Studies*, Vol. 9, No. 3. pp. 9–27.

Young, I. M. (1990). *Justice and the Politics of Difference*. Princeton University Press.

Chapter Three

The Lamb with Ear Tag #8710

Suffering as "Good Welfare" in Animal Science

Nathan Poirier

INTRODUCTION

February 12, 2019, was the first time I held an animal whose sole purpose for being created was to be killed for meat (and some wool along the way). During a tour of a sheep farming facility, a lamb had been taken out of her pen for animal science students to hold and take pictures with. As the lamb with ear tag #8710 was passed to me by another student to hold, I was struck by how warm her body felt, even through my winter coat and sweater. I held this lamb for about 10 minutes, during which time she silently leaned against my chest. This experience is one that should encourage connection to an animal by affectionate touch and photographs.

Yet, this was not the intended, nor the likely result. The lamb with ear tag #8710's existence is completely controlled to extract as much profit from her as possible over her artificially shortened life. Starting before she was born, her birth, death, and every stage in between is planned out by the farmers and researchers at this facility. Additionally, the photo opportunity itself felt uncomfortably close to "white savior" pictures frequently taken and posted on social media by white travelers and volunteers to places where people live in poverty (Gharib, 2017; Bandyopadhyay, 2019). As this chapter will outline, the discipline of animal science and likely the students involved in these pictures, see themselves as heroes to farmed animals. Indeed, browse the website for any animal science department and the rhetoric of caring for and protecting "farmed" animals will be prevalent.

In this chapter, I present an extended analysis of observations obtained during the Spring 2019 semester in which I joined an undergraduate introductory animal science class on tours, called "labs," of the teaching and research facilities of farmed animals at Michigan State University (MSU), the premier land-grant university in the United States. This chapter is an expansion of a previous journal article completed to satisfy requirements for my doctoral program (Poirier, 2021). This limited the ability of this previous article to be as oriented toward critical animal studies (CAS) as it should be. With only slight overlap of primary findings, this chapter compliments and goes well beyond the previous paper by critiquing the role of animal scientists within the animal industrial complex. Readers are encouraged to view the previous publication for further details on various aspects of this study. The present chapter shows how the concept of animal welfare is socially constructed within this pedagogical field setting and argues that, as animal scientists construct the term, animal welfare can justify and even promote animal suffering, if inadvertently. This is because the concept of animal welfare is constructed to balance production efficiency, profit, animal science research, and garnering positive public perception of animal agriculture. A particular intersection of the animal industrial complex and the education industrial complex (Repka, 2019a; Nelson, 2011; Noske, 1997; Twine, 2012) is investigated through the social construction of animal welfare in the context of formal animal science undergraduate education.

Although the course is offered through the Animal Science department, it also often enrolls veterinary science, zoology, and other undergraduate majors. This diversity in student enrollment reflects the (inter)connections of the animal industrial complex (Pedersen, 2019; Noske, 1997). I attended labs for the horse, sheep, "beef" cattle, "dairy" cattle, poultry, and pig facilities, although this chapter will focus on cows, pigs, and chickens as this is where suffering was most prevalent. Being a participant observer is pertinent to learning about the construction of animal welfare because welfare is an applied concept involving human-nonhuman interactions that produce visual information. Further, formal education is a social institution, and "Since institutions exist as external reality, the individual cannot understand them by introspection. [W]e must 'go out' and learn about them" (Berger & Luckmann, 1966, p. 78).

Since I advocate for abolishing animal agriculture, I felt as if I should experience intensive farming facilities for myself. It is one thing to read about agribusiness but is an entirely different experience to witness it live in operation. Scholars and activists can, of course, work to liberate farmed animals without visiting farms. But direct observation can analyze and expose myths employed by the animal industrial complex to sustain itself (Dinker & Pedersen, 2019). Witnessing animal farming helps to anchor knowledge claims and enhance analyses that inform activism. Visiting farms allows one to survey the premises, learn entry and exit points, observe the type of housing and confinement structures, note surveillance equipment, and learn how the farm is staffed. These are all informative components in planning successful and effective direct actions (Anonymous, 2004).

As such, the aim of the chapter is to expose contradictions and the inherently problematic nature of animal welfare. This is done with the intent to further promote a society structured to provide as much freedom as possible for animals (human and nonhuman) and the environment (Nocella et al., 2014; Nocella et al., 2019a). Further, this chapter adapts and extends the notion of anarchism to include human domination over nonhumans as an unacceptable and unjustifiable form of authority (McLaughlin, 2016; Nocella et al., 2015). In line with anarchism, this chapter, and critical animal studies more generally, encourages strong skepticism towards rhetoric that justifies the exploitation, captivity, and/or oppression of an *other* and, correspondingly, encourages radical activism as a means by which to dismantle such situations.

SOME BACKGROUND ON ANIMAL SCIENCE

The definitions and meaning of concepts of animal welfare in animal science are socially constructed and shift over time and place through ongoing social interaction (Berger & Luckmann, 1966; Fisher, 2019). Each cultural group confers its own definitions of their surroundings which creates meaning through a unique combination of values, beliefs, and experiences. The social paradigm of anthropocentrism, the belief that animals exist to serve generalized human needs and desires is particularly salient to animal science. Animal science is a narrow scientific field that is primarily production-oriented and unabashedly operates on a hierarchical and anthropocentric human-animal binary. Paul Waldau notes that while animal science relies heavily on technical science, many broader issues such as animal sentience, intelligence, and cognition are deliberately downplayed as of "at best of secondary interest" (Waldau, 2013, p. 69). Such considerations are problematic and inconvenient for maximally efficient and profitable animal exploitation. Animal scientists thus dismiss many situations in which animals suffer in favor of scientific studies that increase the sustainability and profitability of agribusiness. Those concerned with animal welfare take the murder of animals as a given—they only question how they are killed, not that they are killed (Duxbury, 2019).

The history of animal science departments in academia has colonialism and statism at its core foundation. The Morrill Acts of 1862 and 1890 created "land-grant universities" specifically to promote animal agriculture, the education of farmers, promote technology use in agribusiness, and encourage (white) U.S. citizens to settle in and "develop" the west (Neo & Emel, 2017, p. 49). Dozens of national and regional animal science associations and departments were institutionalized to achieve this goal. These organizations have political ties at the state level through the Department of Agriculture and by donations to political campaigns. Such an alliance of corporate and state interests has progressed to labeling those who threaten the hegemony of agribusiness as terrorists (Best & Nocella, 2004). Power is exercised through strict security measures built into state and federal law premised on harsh consequences for transgressors, a web of surveillance techniques, and seclusion of facilities and farm/slaughterhouse labor from public view.

Since animal science departments often act as a pipeline for students to be funneled into the animal agriculture industry, they have a stake in promoting agribusiness (Pedersen, 2019, p. 21). Thus, how an animal science curriculum defines and promotes animal welfare directly contributes to the mutually reinforcing nature of the animal and educational complexes. In this vein, Pedersen (2019) analyzes how students in secondary and higher education learn about relationships with animals through various modes of scientific education. She ethnographically examines a range of students, those in secondary school, college, professional (e.g., veterinary), and graduate school, but focuses on secondary and veterinary students. Ellis and Irvine (2010) interview children in 4-H programs (an organization often with direct connections to animal science departments) about how they manage their emotions as they sell animals for slaughter who they have raised and gotten to know over a year. Their study takes place within the context of informal education at animal auctions. Repka (2019) explores how the animal and education industrial complexes are interrelated within formal secondary education classrooms. The present analysis complements and extends these previous works by focusing on formal education about farmed animals "in the field," specifically within animal science at the introductory undergraduate level.

JUSTIFICATION OF HARMFUL PRACTICES

From my observations throughout lab visits, two major discourses emerged regarding animal welfare: control and comfort (Poirier, 2021). The term "control" emphasizes how animals are confined and used for human interests. "Comfort" denotes discourse used by lab guides to emphasize the benefits that result from human control (for broader discussion of mechanisms that serve to (re)assure people that animal exploitation is ethical and beneficial, see Joy (2009); Arcari (2020); Aaltola (2016)). Comfort rhetoric serves as a *redemption narrative*, a narrative serving to reduce cognitive dissonance over being involved in what might be seen as harmful practices (Ellis & Irvine, 2010). Together, control and comfort function in ways that allow animal suffering in the name of welfare. Overall, welfare rhetoric revolved around the food products that could be obtained from animals. Welfare was discussed as important insofar as it contributed toward improving the quality, efficiency, the perceived respectability, and ultimately the profitability of animal food products. It is telling how observations of the animal science labs revealed that control over animals was almost always presented first, followed by comfort rhetoric. This highlights the central role of control. That students may view intensive animal control objectionable is anticipated and steps are taken to redirect emotions and deflect critique.

One such instance occurred in what is known as a "squeeze shoot." A squeeze shoot is a technological apparatus meant to restrain and compress a cow's body to calm them when handled (Grandin, 1992). Echoing Granding, the lab guide reassured students that cows are more relaxed in the shoot by likening its effect to a hug (Field notes, February 26). The use and rhetoric of the squeeze shoot conveyed the notion that animal welfare was attended to during what could be perceived as a stressful procedure (e.g., being restrained and given shots) even though most cows were hesitant to enter the shoot, tried to back out, and were often startled by having the doors suddenly clamp around their necks. During observations, one cow began to pass out after struggling to get free when the shoot doors closed around their neck. The cow slowly sank down to the floor. After a student questioned what was happening, the lab guide informed students that this sometimes occurs when cows resist being confined in the squeeze shoot. Turning their head causes the doors to compress their windpipe which can lead to loss of consciousness. The students are told that this is fairly routine as cows do not like to be huddled together and forced one-by-one into a large mechanical object. It seems uncontroversial to say that choking oneself out causes suffering. Yet, such an instance was stated as fairly common and as a side effect of "good" welfare.

From the day they are born, the university's dairy calves are housed separately from their mothers and other adult cows. Although the cow-calf bond is known to be particularly strong, any emotional pain felt by either mother or calf was summarily waved aside by explaining that when calves are separated from their mothers, they cry for three days and "then they're good" (Field notes, March 12). Such rhetoric suggests that cow-calf suffering is inherent to these processes through the separation of mother from infant (for a slightly extended ecofeminist analysis of cow-calf separation, see Gaard, 2017, pp 62–66). It also masks suffering by conveying that the calfs' situation is one in which each individual's welfare is in mind. Human mothers who have cared for, lived with, and raised their children can only imagine the anguish of being forcefully separated, while this experience has been all too real for many migrant families (Perlo, 2019).

A further instance of routine suffering occurred when students witnessed the following demonstration of disbudding on a calf:

> The calf is first given short-and long-term pain medication orally about 5 minutes before beginning. Then the calf's snout is placed in a metal muzzle secured to a fence, holding the calf in place. The dehorning tool burned off a silver-dollar sized portion of the bud. After applying the heat once, the lab guide encouraged students to look at the visible ring of the calf's now exposed skull. The lab guide put heat to the calf's bud several more times to finish disbudding. With each application, the calf jerked forcefully and tried to pull away from the heat and muzzle. Before this procedure, as the lab guide entered the calf's fenced-in hutch, the calf bounded out and licked the lab guide's hand. After disbudding the first bud, the calf was released from the muzzle and immediately cowered in the back of her hutch. (Field notes, March 19)

Clearly, the calf suffered. Yet, after each application of the heat, the lab guide assured the students that the calf felt little to no pain and that this procedure was done for everyone's own good. In this way, what is explained as a welfare measure also entails suffering. Every calf is forced through this painful procedure, which still had to be repeated for the other bud on this particular calf.

At the poultry facility, laying hens are kept in cage-free and "enriched colony" housing systems. The difference is that cage-free systems have a backside that is open from floor to ceiling (but still fenced) where the chickens are free to stretch their wings. Chickens at the bottom of the pecking order are at constant risk of being pecked by over 100 other birds. Thus, these birds have more freedom than battery cages but must survive indoors, moving around on wire mesh under crowded and cramped conditions. Furthermore, they have no opportunity to nest, roost, or mate freely as they are artificially inseminated. Beyond animals used for food, the poultry facility had just completed a two-year toxicity test on Japanese quail. While the type of test was not mentioned, this shows that animal scientists are willing to subject animals to torture in the name of "good" welfare.

The conditions for the pigs on the MSU farm are just as grim. Gestating pigs are kept in single metal stalls not much larger than the pig herself, called gestation crates. One of the lab guides mentioned that gestation crates are preferred over group housing for the pigs' protection. In single crates, each pig is tended to individually which suggests that the manager can make sure each pig's needs are met. Crates also protect sows from each other as group housing can lead to competition for food and water which in turn can lead to violence among sows, stress, and death. The stalls are also believed to not inhibit a pig's natural behaviors. Pigs are admitted to be social and intelligent animals and since the crates consist of metal bars, pigs can still socialize with neighboring pigs through the space between bars. While animal scientists would argue otherwise, this does not allow pigs to adequately express their natural behaviors. It is informative to think about how many have struggled in maintaining social relationships during COVID-19 "social distancing" protocols and use this to imagine what it must be like for highly intelligent and social animals such as pigs to not be able to interact with others, in an effort to empathize with confined nonhuman animals. Pigs were also observed to be constantly bumping up against the walls of their stalls in efforts to move or turn around. These pigs undoubtedly suffer.

THE CORRUPTION AND PERVERSION OF WELFARE

As part of animal welfare science, captivity, abuse, and killing animals for consumption are normalized as welfare became essentially synonymous with human control over animal lives, bodies, and environments (Poirier, 2021). Simultaneously, these practices are made to seem natural, necessary, mutually beneficial, and legitimated by rhetoric that anticipates student (and perhaps by extension, public citizen) concern over treatment of these animals. Such control is further legitimated as animal welfare science is proclaimed to be authoritative, built on human-animal interactions that have evolved over thousands of years (Fisher, 2019).

Tours of farming facilities also revealed that "good" animal welfare is constructed anthropocentrically such that *certain humans* perceive that animals' needs are met. Animal scientists or animal experimenters conduct experiments to determine what they consider to be satisfactory conditions for captive animals. As mentioned earlier, these departments often receive funding from vested parties—agribusiness, animal testing, etc. As such, it is a select group of humans with connections to and a stake in upholding human supremacy and the animal industrial complex that largely determine welfare standards. Welfare is constructed around human-imposed captivity of farmed animals for exploitation. The animals themselves are never asked what they would want. Although this notion might sound ridiculous to some, the point is that humans assume they can and do know what is best for nonhuman animals. But many needs are not met or met only nominally.

For instance, while pigs were readily admitted as requiring social interactions with each other, being able to see, hear, and touch snouts through bars on gestation crates is considered sufficient or "good welfare." But the pigs cannot move beyond standing up or laying down, they cannot physically interact with each other. They may not even be able to effectively communicate with other pigs besides their immediate neighbors. They are not able to play, root, or teach their young how to be pigs. They are also not able to choose to be (fully) solitary if and when it is desired. The individual attention given to the pigs is what the lab guides declare best for the pigs. This facility was currently conducting an experiment for group-housed sows as opposed to gestation crates. It was explicitly admitted that employees of this facility do not believe group housing is best for the sows because the pigs cannot handle increased freedom, apparently they will inevitably harm each other. So it is only the few employees who decide what is best for the hundreds of pigs at this facility who are endowed with their authority not from the pigs themselves, but from their research institution which recognizes their socially constructed credentials.

Direct observations of the situations of agricultural animals at MSU's teaching of animal welfare in animal science labs indicate that these animals suffer throughout their lives, yet are repeatedly said to be optimally cared for. As examples in this chapter show, suffering is inherent to capitalist and speciesist production that is couched in "welfare" terms. My observations show that MSU is not trying to minimize awareness of farmed animal suffering, but in many instances are actively calling suffering "good" welfare: Cows cause themselves to pass out in squeeze shoots from fear and panic; calves are separated from their mothers while both cry for each other; calves endure heat sources applied to their skull; fowl are tested for chemical toxicity; and pigs are kept in cages barely larger than their bodies for nearly their entire life. All of these are considered necessary for efficient and cheaper animal production. In each instance, suffering results. And, all of these instances of animal suffering are said to promote "good" welfare. Perplexingly, the concept of "good" welfare appears to be premised on the guarantee of continued suffering.

These observations parallel two arguments made by Wadiwel (2015) who argues that (1) human superiority over other animals is founded on human sovereignty and (2) that violence is constructed as its opposite—care. Likewise, I find that farmed animal welfare is founded on complete human control over animals. MSU's educational professionals constantly justify this control through comfort rhetoric—in both straightforward and insidious forms—to reassure future animal scientists and the general public that animal agriculture is moral because they care deeply about farmed animals. University-educated animal scientists who espouse the holistic benefits of farmed animal treatment co-opt notions of prestige and objectivity generally attributed to higher educational institutions to lend an added degree of authority to their ideologically and economically driven constructions of welfare (Nelson, 2011). Animal science students who become animal scientists perpetuate the same rhetoric, thus sustaining and further entrenching animal exploitation within cultures. Indeed, this is the point of socialization, to teach novices the ways of a discipline so that they can carry it into the future (Poirier, 2021; Pedersen, 2019).

Repka (2019a) uses three types of curriculum to study the animal industrial complex within secondary education in the U.S. The explicit (or formal) curriculum, consisting of substantive material from books and assignments, is what educational experts intend students to learn. The implicit, or hidden, curriculum refers to lessons students learn indirectly through the structure of educational institutions. For instance, being served animal products for school lunch implicitly teaches students that animals exist for human consumption. Lastly, the null curriculum is the avoidance or omission (intentional or otherwise) of certain disciplines or topics from the explicit curriculum. All three types were prevalent in the animal science labs I observed.

The explicit curriculum consists of being told voluminous amounts of information about the economic and reproductive aspects of farmed animals' lives. For each animal species, students were given a breakdown of life-cycle stages, design of confinement structures, how long animals live on farms, how much animals are "worth," how often they reproduce, what and how much feed is received, anatomy, animal behavior, and welfare. This comprised the bulk of information given at each lab. The hidden curriculum, as argued in this chapter, consists of informally teaching students that animal suffering either doesn't exist or is part of "good" welfare. The null curriculum is the omission of why animals are kept on farms in the first place or other ethical considerations. For example, lab guides never mentioned animal sanctuaries or vegetarianism, gender issues with artificial insemination and manipulation of reproductive systems, or the massive environmental destruction due to animal farming. These omissions construct such issues as unimportant and inhibit critical thinking that forestalls the ability for dissenting thoughts to enter students' minds (Repka, 2019).

These types of academic programs normalize animal suffering within agribusiness because they omit alternative discourses and critiques of the animal industrial complex. They also create students who are lulled into passive acceptors or even active supporters of the industry. In terms of pedagogy and activism, direct observation helps to expose mechanisms by which animal-use industries "exploit our emotions in order to exploit the animals" (Dinker & Pedersen, 2019, p. 50) so that such discourses and practices can be resisted. However, the control-comfort mechanism accomplishes emotion management that can stifle resistance (Ellis & Irvine, 2010). The exceeding amount of control that goes into animal science operations reflects the fact that the *perceived* ordinariness of animal agriculture and animal product consumption is rendered normal only through massive coordinated efforts by the animal industrial complex, anchored in this case by animal scientists who control every facet of farmed animals' lives and deaths.

If control over others can be constructed as "care," then many exploitative and violent situations can be made to seem beneficial. This extends to human groups as well. American slavery was frequently justified by "paternalism" which suggested that Blacks could not take care of themselves so whites had to control them. In this way, slavery was presented as a form of care (Spiegel, 1996). Likewise, colonialism is frequently justified under the banner of benevolence as in the U.S. genocide of Native Americans through Manifest Destiny rhetoric and the Doctrine of Discovery; Indigenous peoples were portrayed as uncivilized and in need of white salvation (Miller, 2008). Similarly, in president Mckinley's Benevolent Assimilation Proclamation concerning the Philippine-American War, in which the U.S. framed colonization of the Philippines as a benevolent acquisition under the Treaty of Paris, McKinley stated: "the mission of the U.S. is one of BENEVOLENT ASSIMILATION. . . . In the fulfillment of this high mission, supporting the temperate administration of affairs for the greatest good of the governed, there must be sedulously maintained the strong arm of authority . . ." (quoted in Stanescu, 2012). In these cases and others, "care" is constructed as control over others who are exploited with impunity and without guilt for the benefit of a more dominant group. Also, each of these instances—slavery, Native American genocide, and "Benevolent Assimilation"—is linked to war and exploitation of nonhuman animals and the environment highlighting the interconnections between all types of illegitimate authority and the need for total liberation (Nocella et al., 2013; McLaughlin, 2016).

CONCLUSION

This study focused on the problems of animal welfare as taught by animal scientists. A shortcoming of this chapter is that it does not discuss alternative discourses and pedagogies, potential for student resistance, or other ways to help animals. However, there are many sources that offer suggestions along these lines from a critical animal studies approach (Pedersen, 2019, ch. 8; Nocella II et al., 2019b; Anonymous, 2004; Martusewicz et al., 2020; Repka, 2019b).

To be clear, this chapter does not assert that welfare measures cannot *reduce* suffering in certain situations. They can. Nor does it argue that animal scientists actively want farmed animals to suffer. Rather, animal welfare science inherently maintains suffering at some level because it is constrained by human supremacy, professional prestige, profit and industry promotion (Waldau, 2013, pp. 68–72). Animal scientists operate under a construction of welfare where what animals receive, how much and when, are largely dictated by efficiency, profit, and to a lesser extent, public concerns (when they threaten profit). Emotion management is at play in animal science pedagogy through comfort rhetoric which teaches students that sentimentality for animals is misplaced (Ellis & Irvine, 2010). As the variety of examples in this chapter illustrate, "The development of such a diversity of mechanisms for forestalling and overriding sympathetic opposition to harming animals shows that human resistance is always a potential threat to the continuation of the animal exploitation industries" (Luke, 1995, pp. 311–312). Therefore, animal suffering is rhetorically transformed into animal welfare. These constraints are why CAS believes the industry cannot be reformed and should be dismantled using radical direct actions where necessary.

What helps to make welfare rhetoric persuasive is its degree of truth. However, it is a reductionist version of truth that is exploited along with the animals. The animals *are* given food, water, protection from predators and disease, and these *are* elements of care. But they are not the entirety of care. CAS recognizes that animal welfare is simply one component of care—and one that is premised on human domination and violation, at that. Animal welfare science reflects a construction of animals as passive objects and property who can be exploited, albeit with a capacity to suffer. Simultaneously, animal welfare is constructed as a means by which to refine animal exploitation and suffering but not to end them (Duxbury, 2019, p. 30). This way, suffering and care exist simultaneously without any apparent contradiction as their meanings become conflated. This is how students can emotionally connect with the lamb with ear tag #8710, allow her to suffer, and send her to slaughter.

SELECTED BIBLIOGRAPHY

Aatola, E. (2016). The problem of akrasia: Moral cultivation and socio-political resistance. In P. Cavalieri (Ed.), *Philosophy and the politics of animal liberation* (pp. 117–148). Palgrave.

Anonymous. (2004). Letters from the underground: Parts I and II. In S. Best, & A. J. Nocella II (Eds.), *Terrorists or freedom fighters? Reflections on animal liberation* (pp. 354–361). Lantern Books.

Arcari, P. (2020). *Making sense of "food" animals: A critical exploration of the persistence of "meat."* Palgrave.

Bandyopadhay, R. (2019). Volunteer tourism and "the white man's burden": globalization of suffering, white savior complex, religion and modernity. *Journal of Sustainable Tourism, 27*(3), 327–343.

Berger, P.L., & Luckmann, T. (1966). *The social construction of reality: A treatise in the sociology of knowledge.* Penguin Books.

Best, S., & Nocella II, A. J. (2004). *Terrorists or freedom fighters? Reflections on animal liberation.* Lantern Books.

Dinker, K. G., & Pedersen, H. (2019). "Critical animal pedagogy: Explorations toward reflective practice." In A. J. Nocella II, C. Drew, A. E. George, S. Ketenci, J. Lupinacci, I. Purdy, & J. L. Schatz (Eds.), *Education for total liberation: Critical animal pedagogy and teaching against speciesism.* Peter Lang.

Duxbury, C. (2019). Property, pain, and pastoral power: The advent of animal welfare in the review of the 1876 Cruelty to Animals Act, 1947–1965. *Journal for Critical Animal Studies, 16*(2), 3–33.

Fisher, M. (2019). *Animal welfare science, husbandry and ethics: The evolving story of our relationship with farm animals.* 5M Publishing.

Gaard, G. (2017). *Critical ecofeminism*. Lexington Books.

Gharib, M. (2017). Volunteering abroad? Read this before you post that selfie. *NPR.* https://www.npr.org/sections/goatsandsoda/2017/11/26/565694874/volunteering-abroad-read-this-before-you-post-that-selfie.

Grandin, T. (1992). Calming Effects of Deep Touch Pressure in Patients with Autistic Disorder, College Students, and Animals. https://www.grandin.com/inc/squeeze.html.

Joy, M. (2009). *Why we love dogs, eat pigs, and wear cows: An introduction to carnism*. Conari Press.

Luke, B. (1995). Taming ourselves or going feral? Toward a nonpatriarchal metaethic of animal liberation. In C. J. Adams & J. Donovan (Eds.), Animals & women: Feminist theoretical explorations (pp. 290–319). Duke University Press.

Martusewicz, R., Edmunson, J., & Lupinacci, J. (Eds.). (2020). *Ecojustice education: Toward diverse, democratic, and sustainable, communities* (3rd Ed.). Routledge.

McLaughlin, P. (2016). *Anarchism and authority: A philosophical introduction to classical anarchism*. Routledge.

Miller, R. J. (2008). *Native America, discovered and conquered: Thomas Jefferson, Lewis and Clark, and manifest destiny.* Praeger.

Nelson, C. (2011). Higher education's industrial model. In S. Best, R. Kahn, A. J. Nocella II, & P. McLaren (Eds.), *The global industrial complex: Systems of domination and oppression* (pp. 155–168). Lexington Books.

Neo, H., & Emel, J. (2017). *Geographies of meat: Politics, economy and culture.* Routledge.

Nocella II, A. J., Salter, C., & Bentley, J. K. C. (Eds.). (2013). *Animals and war: confronting the military-animal industrial complex*. Lexington Books.

Nocella II, A. J., Sorenson, J., Socha, K., & Matsuoka, A. (Eds.). (2014). *Defining critical animal studies: An intersectional social justice approach for liberation.* Peter Lang.

Nocella II, A. J., White, R. J., & Cudworth, E. (Eds.). (2015). *Anarchism and animal liberation: essays on complementary elements of total liberation*. McFarland.

Nocella II, A. J., & George, A. E. (Eds.). (2019a). Intersectionality of critical animal studies: A Historical Collection. Peter Lang.

Nocella II, A. J., Drew, C., George, A. E., Ketenci, S., Lupinacci, J., Purdy, I., & Schatz, JL (Eds.). (2019b). *Education for total liberation: Critical animal pedagogy and teaching against speciesism*. Peter Lang.

Noske, B. (1997). *Beyond boundaries: Humans and animals.* Black Rose Books.

Pedersen, H. (2019). *Schizoanalysis and animal science education*. Bloomsbury Publishing.

Perlo, K. W. (2019). Defending PETA's dairy/migrant families advert: Mother-love as an ethical model. *Journal for Critical Animal Studies, 16*(3), 3–27.

Poirier, N. (2021, forthcoming). Learning to exploit: The socialization of animal science undergraduates. *Sociological Inquiry, 91*.

Repka, M. (2019a). Intersecting oppressions: The animal industrial complex and the educational industrial complex. In A. J. Nocella II, C. Drew, A. E. George, S. Ketenci, J. Lupinacci, I. Purdy, & JL. Schatz (Eds.), *Education for total liberation: Critical animal pedagogy and teaching against speciesism* (pp. 99–120). Peter Lang.

Repka, M. (2019b). Radical environmentalism and teacher: A pedagogy of activism. In A. J. Nocella II, S. Parson, A. E. George, & S. Eccles (Eds.), *A historical scholarly collection of writings on the earth liberation front* (pp. 253–268). Peter Lang.

Spiegel, M. (1996). *The dreaded comparison: Human and animal slavery.* Mirror Books.

Stanescu, V. (2012). Man's best friend: Why human rights needs animal rights. *Journal for Critical Animal Studies, 10*(2), 69–100.

Twine, R. (2012). Revealing the "animal-industrial complex"—A concept & method for critical animal studies? *Journal for Critical Animal Studies, 10*(1), 12–39.

Wadiwel, D. J. (2015). *The war against animals.* Brill.

Waldau, P. (2013). *Animal studies: An introduction.* Oxford University Press.

Chapter Four

On the *Dharma* of Critical Animal Studies

Animal Spirituality and Total Liberation

Michael Allen and Erica Von Essen

INTRODUCTION

Are religious or spiritual insights accessible *only* to humans or are they also accessible to nonhuman animals? The Indian religious traditions of Hinduism, Jainism, and Buddhism are ambivalent concerning the question of whether nonhuman animals (henceforth animals) are capable of spiritual insight (Jaini, 1991). On the one hand, these Indian traditions see capability for moral and spiritual insight as the *differentia specifica* (Parel, 2006; 2008) of human animals (henceforth humans). Gandhi philosophically embraces this conception of such capabilities as unique to humanity in his modern reinterpretation of the classical Indian doctrine of the purusharthas, or goals of life. According to him, only humans as opposed to animals are capable of spiritual liberation. On the other hand, Hinduism, Jainism, and Buddhism often present animals not philosophically but rather mythologically as capable of moral and spiritual insights equal to human lay devotees in fables.

Can critical animal studies (CAS) learn anything from these myths and fables? Do animal spirituality stories inform and support any of its distinctive political goals? One central goal of CAS is to embrace "a politics of total liberation" (Best et al., 2007). This politics is "total" insofar as it "grasps the need for, and the inseparability of, human, nonhuman animal, and Earth liberation and freedom for all-in-one comprehensive, though diverse, struggle"

(Best et al., 2007). Indeed, it refers to "the process of *understanding* human, animal and earth liberation movements in relation to one another and *building bridges* around interrelated issues such as democracy and ecology, sustainability and veganism, and social justice and animal rights" (Best 2014, p. xii; our italics). This inevitably raises a question about whose "understanding" of interrelationships, and whose agency in "building bridges" around such issues, is at stake in the politics of total liberation. Is the understanding and agency requisite for such a politics exclusively human or might animals also contribute to the *total* liberation of all species?

CRITICAL ANIMAL STUDIES AND ANIMAL SPIRITUALITY

CAS aligns itself with neuroscience and cognitive ethology (Best, 2014). Neuroscience demonstrates the structural similarities of animal and human brains, while cognitive ethology attributes minds to animals based on close empirical observation (Bekoff, 2001; 2010). In these respects, neuroscience and ethology have "repercussions for our *spirituality*" (Yarri, 2006, p. 26). Our appreciating or "minding" animals enables us to "envision a unified, peaceable kingdom . . . based on respect, compassion, forgiveness and love" (Bekoff 2001, p. 647). Minding animals helps us humans grow spiritually, achieving a kind of liberation otherwise unobtainable for us. Nevertheless, CAS is strangely silent on the question of animals minding us. Why should we not also say that their minding us helps them grow spiritually? In other words, why should we not say humans and animals reciprocally facilitate one another's spiritual growth, establishing an egalitarianism of the spirit?

Perhaps the most obvious answer to this question is that the capabilities for spiritual growth are unique to humans. Indeed, the rudimentary forms of social morality of which animals are capable prove insufficient for animals to *envision the same unified, peaceable kingdom*. That is, animal minds cannot grasp the spiritual unity of all planetary life. This chapter, however, challenges any such assumption that only humans are capable of spiritual growth and *spiritual liberation*.

It first discusses neuroscience and ethology and its bearings on spirituality in animals. It then considers the animal spirituality traditions of Hinduism, Buddhism, and Jainism. It next turns from these animal spirituality traditions to a critical engagement with Gandhi concerning moksha as the differentia specifica of humanity and his political reinterpretation of classical Indian doctrine of the *purusharthas*, or goals of life. *Arguing against Gandhi*, it denies that only humans as opposed to animals are capable of spiritual liberation. Moreover, it contends that animals are potential contributors to total interspecies liberation. In this respect, we do not mean to suggest that Gandhi himself was an incipient total liberationist. On the contrary, despite his sympathy for the suffering of animals, Gandhi explicitly repudiated their capacities for spiritual and political liberation. Indeed, he is unclear to what extent he genuinely attributed these capacities to all humanity, as evidenced from recent studies concerning his reinforcement of racist stereotypes concerning Black South Africans (Desai & Vahed, 2015).

The purpose of this chapter is quite different. It shows that recent work in neuroscience and ethology supports the view that animals are capable of spiritual liberation and capable of contributing to a total vision of interspecies emancipatory life-goals. Hence, rejecting Gandhi on spiritual liberation as the differentia specifica of humanity, and extending the political interpretation of the purusharthas across species lines, it argues for the equal capabilities of humans and animals minding each other in a total interspecies liberations struggle.

A broad definition of spirituality includes "non-material, intangible, and introspective experiences of the sort humans have" (Bekoff, 2009). This broad definition of spirituality—as an experience of the intangible—raises the following questions:

> Do animals marvel at their surroundings, have a sense of awe when they see a rainbow, find themselves by a waterfall, or ponder their environs? Do they ask where does lightning come from? Do they go into a "zone" when they play with others, forgetting about everything else save for the joy of playing? What are they feeling when they perform funeral rituals? (Bekoff, 2009)

Further,

> [do] animals experience the joy of simply being alive? And if so, how would they express it so that we would know they do? (Bekoff, 2009)

That said, however, answers remain speculative to the extent humans cannot literally enter the minds of animals. Nevertheless, this merely extends the philosophical problem of "other minds" from humans to animals: how can one know that any other beings—animal or human—possess minds capable of introspection on such feelings and experiences? Nevertheless, rejecting Cartesian solipsism, some neuroscientists and cognitive ethologists attribute the existence of minds to animals based on structural similarities between animal and human brains and ethological observations of how animals behave in their various natural and social environments (Bekoff, 2010; Best, 2014).

According to neuroscience, the limbic system of our brains evolved before the cerebral cortex, governing higher cognitive functions. Indeed, resting beneath the cortex and governing most emotional responses, the limbic brain is the pre-human product—and even pre-hominid—evolution. Consequently, most other animals on the planet share this fundamental brain structure. In this respect, some researchers contend the limbic brain is not only the source of such pre-cortal responses to imminent danger as "flight or fight," but also paradigmatically religious, or mystical, experiences of awe or wonderment. For example, Goodall (2005) considers the phenomenon of an adult male chimpanzee dancing at a waterfall as a precursor to religious ritual. Viz.:

> As he gets closer, and the roar of the falling water gets louder, his pace quickens, his hair becomes fully erect, and upon reaching the stream he may perform a magnificent display close to the foot of the falls. Standing upright, he sways rhythmically from foot to foot, stamping in the shallow, rushing water, picking up and hurling great rocks. Sometimes he climbs up the slender vines that hang down from the trees high above and swings out into the spray of the falling water. This "waterfall dance" may last ten or fifteen minutes.

She asks:

> [i]s it not possible that these performances are stimulated by feelings akin to wonder and awe? After a waterfall display, the performer may sit on a rock, his eyes following the falling water. What is it, this water?

Indeed,

> [i]f the chimpanzee could share his feelings and questions with others, might these wild elemental displays become ritualized into some form of animistic religion? Would they worship the falls, the deluge from the sky, the thunder and lightning—the gods of the elements? So all-powerful; so incomprehensible.

Hence, neurological similarities of brain function between animals and humans partly motivate Goodall's question. One might object that attributions of religious feelings outstrip the findings of neuroscience. Nevertheless, research supports similarities in how animals and humans process emotions. For example, traumatized animals often respond to the same medications and therapies that work for traumatized humans (Vlahos, 2008). If animals experience raw emotions of distress and disturbance similarly to humans, then they might also experience raw and primitive emotions like awe and wonderment similarly.

However, ethological observation also motivates Goodall's question from the perspective of critical anthropomorphism (Griffin, 2001; Bekoff, 2010).

Wary of falsely attributing human thoughts and feelings to animals, this perspective avoids the "opposite mistake" of discounting "what is right before our eyes" (Bekoff, 2010, p. 54). Animals experience many of the same emotions as us—love, fear, aggression, anger, joy, grief. This is right before our eyes as "lay observers already know"; something to which researchers are only now "catching up" (Bekoff, 2010, p. 77). Critical anthropomorphism thus invites us to ask us whether what is before our eyes in the case of Goodall's chimpanzee is a display of feeling we would not hesitate to call spiritual in the case of humans. It also asks us whether similar spiritual feelings are evident in displays of grief over lost companions (Bekoff, 2010; Smith, 2012) or displays of altruism.

In this latter respect, Bender (2014, p. 51) relates a story "so outlandish that few people would believe it had it not been filmed" by a documentary crew. A female leopard kills a female baboon but desists from feeding on its carcass when she discovers an infant baboon still clinging to its mother's dead body. Indeed, ignoring her "kill" instinct, the leopard proceeded to nurse the ailing infant baboon through the rest of the day and the night until it eventually died of exposure the next morning. According to Bender, we may properly describe this baboon as an extraordinary "animal *bodhisattva*" or "saint," going beyond the material and tangible "to help a creature in trouble without stopping to ask "What's in it for me?" or "What's in it for my species?" (Bender, 2014, p. 52).

Indeed, Bender's description of animals as *bodhisattvas* or saints gains support from the Indian animal spirituality tradition in Hinduism, Buddhism, and Jainism. Consistent with the Western Abrahamic religions (Kymlicka & Donaldson, 2014; Allen & von Essen, 2018), the Indian spirituality tradition sometimes endorses human superiority over animals (Jaini, 1991; Parel, 2006; 2008). For example, according to the *Hiopadesa*,

> Men are the same as animals
> As far as food, sleep, fear, and sex are concerned.
> They are distinguished only because of *dharma*:
> A man who lacks *dharma* is the same as the animals. (Jaini, 1991, p. 270)

Dharma thus comprises exclusively human capabilities to fulfill moral and spiritual duties (Jaina, 1991). Nevertheless, the Indian tradition also powerfully contradicts this view of the moral and spiritual superiority of humans over animals in numerous myths and fables. For example, in the Hindu story, *Gaja moksha*, a crocodile catches an elephant and drags it down into a lake. However, the elephant recalls and recites a hymn it learned in a previous physical incarnation. Lord Vishnu appears, kills the crocodile and saves the elephant. At that moment, the elephant loses its animal body and assumes the form of four-armed Vishnu, achieving similitude (*samya*) with the Lord.

However, some caution is in order interpreting this story. On the one hand, it demonstrates an animal's capability to attain spiritual liberation from the earthy coil. This seems to establish equivalency of spiritual capacities across species lines. On the other hand, though, liberation is only possible because of a "hidden human being . . . temporarily enmeshed in animal destiny" (Jaini, 1991, p. 271). The story assumes a "hidden human" necessary to facilitate spiritual transcendence from within the form of an animal. This effectively prohibits universalizing the "claim that animals are capable of progressing towards salvation" (Jaini, 1991, p. 271). Indeed, it is not the animal per se but the hidden human from a past incarnation who achieves salvation and does so only by intervention from a deity.

In many Buddhist animal fables, however, it is the bodhisattva or saint who appears in animal form. Not only does he lead an exemplary life practicing moral discipline as an animal-manifestation, but he also teaches *dharma* to humans. In the *Hasti-Jataka* in the *Jatakamala*, the bodhisattva-elephant provides his own body for the sustenance of lost travelers. Fearful they would be incapable of taking his life, however, he resorts to subterfuge by telling the travelers an animal has fallen from a cliff. Hurrying ahead, the bodhisattva-elephant throws himself from the cliff, killing himself. Later realizing it was the same animal as before, the travelers praise the magnanimity of its charitable self-sacrifice. Indeed, the author of the *Jatakamala* remarks: "Even though born as animals, there is seen the charitable activities of great beings, performed according to their capacities" (Jaini, 1991, p. 274).

However, this story assumes not simply a "hidden human" but a "hidden bodhisattva or saint" as necessary to exemplify and teach the *dharma* to humans. Again, it is not the animal per se but the bodhisattva or saint, manifest within its bodily form, that exemplifies and teaches. Reminiscent of the previous Hindu story, this Buddhist story prohibits "universalizing" any claim to the effect that animals are capable of practicing and teaching the *dharma*, independently of a hidden saint manifest within them.

Nevertheless, the Indian animal spirituality tradition also presents stories of animals who benefit from religious instruction in the dharma from the bodhisattva or saint. A Buddhist story tells of a water buffalo who is successfully instructed by the Buddha to refrain from terrorizing the residents of a village. The Buddha preaches to the buffalo about impermanence, lack of substance, and nirvana. Indeed, he reminds the water buffalo of his previous births in which he had also been a teacher of *dharma*. Overcome with remorse, the buffalo dies, and is reborn in the *Devaloka*. Of course, this story still assumes a "hidden human," if not a "hidden bodhisattva or saint," manifest in the buffalo. Nevertheless, its importance is that it shows such an animal is "capable of insights" (Jaini, 1991, p. 276) possible for any lay practitioner of *dharma*.

Indeed, a Jain story goes a step further by attributing to an animal the capability of undertaking religious vows. When Mahavira's soul is reborn as a lion, two Jain monks recognize that it can benefit from religious discourse. The monks instruct this lion on the value of kindness, admonishing him to refrain from killing. Moved by their instruction, it abstains from food, dies, and is reborn in heaven. This lion is thus "on a par with Jaina laymen . . . adhering to such vows as non-violence and non-possession" (Jaini, 1991, p. 280).

Hence, contrary to Bender (2014), the buffalo and the lion in these stories are not extraordinary animal bodhisattvas or saints, any more than they are "manifestations" of the latter in temporary animal form. Instead, they display moral and spiritual capabilities equivalent to ordinary, lay human practitioners of *dharma* (Jaini, 1991). However, this still establishes a point of great importance for CAS and the project of total liberation: that animals and humans are equal in their capacities for spiritual insight and transcendence. Like humans, they have "spiritual aspirations," which are the "subtle seed of liberation" from the yoke of materialism (Jaini, 1991, p. 281). If not *bodhisattvas* or saints, animals are neither better nor worse than ordinary humans concerning these capabilities.

So far, this chapter has explored in two different ways animals possess spiritual capabilities: (1) by appeal to neuroscience and ethology (2) by appeal to myth and narrative in the Indian animal spirituality tradition. Next, it turns to the Indian doctrine of the *purusharthas* or goals of life. It does so for the following reason. Integral to both classical and modern Indian political theory, the *purusharthas* doctrine present a political vision of intersecting life-goals that are ultimately in the service of spiritual liberation. Animals possessing equal capabilities for spiritual insight or transcendence has obvious implications for the *purusharthas* doctrine. Indeed, it argues that the doctrine provides CAS with a resource for including animals in its vision of total animal/human liberation.

The classical doctrine of the *purusharthas* lays out four aims of life. These are ethics and religion (*dharma)*, wealth and power (*artha*), pleasure *(kama*), and spiritual liberation or transcendence (*moksha*). The first three aims of life all point towards the ultimate-aim of spiritual liberation or *moksha*. Etymologically, *purusha* means "immaterial spirit" while *artha* means "for the sake of." Consequently, *purushartha* means, "that which is done for the sake of the immaterial spirit" (Parel, 2008, p. 46). These goals are perceived as intersectional in the sense that one must not only experience liberation from selfish material desires (first goal), but also material exploitation and abuse (second goal) along with suffering and pain (third goal) before one may ultimately attain spiritual transcendence (fourth goal). Hence, liberation is total because it is a function of combining a comprehensive set of emancipatory life-goals.

However, it is also total in the sense that all who are capable of spiritual liberation can pursue this combination of life-goals to achieve transcendence. Nevertheless, the classical doctrine of the *purusharthas* fails to provide any guarantee that all those capable of transcendence could attain it. In ancient India, the totality of life-goals is embedded politically in a hierarchical caste system maintained by a kingly state seeking imperial aggrandizement and conquest. Consequently, spiritual liberation is detached from politics and worldly affairs instead of synonymous with withdrawal and otherworldliness (Parel 2006, 2008). As for animals, the classical *purusharthas* doctrine is silent concerning their spiritual capabilities, unlike the animal spirituality tradition with its wealth of myths and fables.

In the twentieth century, however, Gandhi reinterpreted the *purusharthas* by appealing to a modern egalitarian standard of political freedom (*swaraj).* He developed this reinterpretation to provide a conceptual framework for the Indian national independence movement against British colonial rule (Parel, 2016). To this extent, he saw the political reinterpretation as flattening long established hierarchies of caste and rejecting all ambitions for imperial domination. Gandhi contended political freedom (*swaraj*), along with economic and social reform, should become the "very means to" (Parel, 2016, p. 15) spiritual liberation (*moksha*) *for everyone* regardless of caste. It is the very means insofar as everyone—untouchable (*Dalit*) and priest (*Brahmin*)—has a "voice" in collaboratively shaping the shared terms of social cooperation. Hence, according to this framework, everyone is empowered to combine the intersectional life-goals of the *purusharthas* and attain the ultimate-goal of transcendence.

As noted earlier, however, Gandhi did not consistently apply the political reinterpretation to all humanity, reinforcing racial hierarchies in South Africa (Desai & Vahed, 2015). Moreover, he fails completely to include animal capabilities for moral and spiritual conduct in his purportedly egalitarian reinterpretation of the *purusharthas*. Instead, contending such capabilities are exclusive to humanity as its *differentia specifica* (Parel, 2016). Gandhi reaffirms the *Hiopadesa*: "[Men] are distinguished only because of *dharma*." Indeed, he appeals to animal life in two distinct ways. On the one hand, he regards them as governed exclusively by the violent law of beasts. Hence, "Man has by painful striving to surmount and survive the animal in him [. . . He] must, therefore, if he is to realize his dignity and his own mission, cease to take part in the destruction and refuse to prey upon his weaker fellow creatures" (Burgat, 2003, p. 230). On the other hand, Gandhi appeals to animals as "poems of pity" (Burgat, 2003, p. 231). To this extent, he contends "Cow-protection to me . . . means protection of all that lives and is helpless and weak in the world" (Burgat, 2003, p. 230).

Both kinds of Gandhian appeal—to animals as violent and amoral and as weak and helpless—thus support a species inegalitarian conception of animals as *incapable* of performing the duties of *dharma*. Indeed, contrary to the fables in the animal spirituality tradition discussed above, they can only ever be on the "receiving end" of moral and spiritual conduct by humans, as the subjects of protection and compassion. In other words, Gandhi denies animals are also on the "giving end" of such conduct. Perhaps they "give" in the sense that they symbolize what humans should not and should be. They should not be violent towards any fellow creatures and rather be compassionate towards the helpless. Beyond this, however, animals do not "give and take" with humans by engaging in morally and spiritually equivalent conduct based on performing duties such as nonviolence and non-possession. Further, they do not engage in give and take with humans based on equal citizenship, contributing to shaping social norms. Consequently, the appropriate goal for human animal interactions is not strict equality of citizenship rights and duties as much as equity, acknowledging humans and animals give and receive differently based on differential capabilities.

This is a point of considerable importance for the present analysis of the *purusharthas* and CAS's vision of total animal/human liberation. As including the goal of *co*-transcendence for animals and humans, the *purusharthas* must be interpreted against Gandhi to permit that animals are capable of political freedom (*swaraj*). Consequently, CAS could synthesize neuroscience and ethology with the animal spirituality traditions; that is, how it could indeed synthesize them in an appropriate *political* vision of the totality of emancipatory life-goals for animals and humans.

Neuroscientific and ethological evidence points to the possibility of total liberation modeled on the goals of the *purusharthas* based on the evidence that animals experience the ultimate-goal of spiritual transcendence. However, this scientific literature focuses primarily on their experiencing transcendence through encounters with nature, such as chimpanzee waterfall dances. This is not a form of transcendence achieved by observing religious duties of *dharma* or political duties of citizenship. As for the animal spirituality tradition, this explicitly presents animals as following religious if not political duties. Nevertheless, it operates at the level of myth and fable rather than scientific evidence. Indeed, myths and fables may be interpreted as attributing to animals' capabilities for observing *dharma* only vicariously. To this extent, the tradition attributes uniquely human abilities to animals to teach moral and religious lessons *to humans*.

Nevertheless, accepting this latter point concerning vicariousness, the animal spirituality tradition still contributes to CAS's political vision. As stated above, total liberation requires a conception of spiritual transcendence attained through the give and take of social interactions *rather than encounters with nature*. By focusing on animals performing the duties of *dharma*, the spirituality tradition reengages some of our deepest intuitions about animals as social members possessing a moral compass that is not entirely dissimilar from our own. Myths and fables encourage relearning childhood affections for animals (Luke, 2007; von Essen & Allen, 2017), drawing on extant sentiments. However, does the scientific literature also lend support to animal/human co-transcendence through social interactions? This chapter contends that it does, at least, to the extent ethological observations show animals possess the basis of social morality in their capacities for empathy towards members of their own and other species.

Many animals can intuitively grasp *fairness* in their interactions with other beings including humans (Bekoff, 2001; Yarri, 2006), even though they may lack the brain structure necessary to grasp higher concepts of duty and obligation. Nevertheless, reengaging buried sentiments and observing the neurological and ethological basis for morality in animals is insufficient to ensure that animals can liberate themselves from exploitation and abuse in human households, industry, and so on. After all, this is the fundamental insight of the *purusharthas*: combining liberations—economic, hedonistic, and so on—is the practical condition for transcendence. Indeed, it is the insight to which Gandhi adds the vital caveat that political liberation is the means to combining diverse emancipatory goals to transcend merely tangible experiences of the social, not just the natural world.

To be sure, Gandhi himself restricts the equal political freedom of citizens to humans, as stressed above. However, this restriction appears arbitrary considering the scope of empathetic give and take between the species. For example, Donaldson and Kymlicka (2011; 2015a) argue domesticated animals may contribute to shaping norms of social cooperation with humans, despite their obvious incapacity to fulfill the traditional duties of citizenship, such as participation in public deliberation or voting (Scruton, 2001). Assuming we pay attention to them (von Essen & Allen, 2017), their interactions with us communicate their sense of fairness regarding our various expectations of them in the workplace and domestic life. Such internatural communication (von Essen & Allen, 2017) may consist of non-linguistic or behavioral expressions of grievance over unfair treatment in distributing rewards and punishments (Brosnan & DeWaal, 2003).

Alternatively, expressions of grievance may consist of direct acts of resistance (Carter & Charles, 2013) to their exploitation for exclusively human ends of profit, gustation, entertainment, or companionship (Russell, 2003).

Animal resistance may include non-cooperation, self-harm, or running away (Wadiwel, 2016; Hribal, 2013). Animals thus exercise viable forms of political agency, non-linguistically communicating their preferences and sense of fairness to humans (Donaldson & Kymlicka, 2011). For their part, humans should view their agency as morally considerable in the same way that they should view the sub-linguistic communications and resistances of humans with severe cognitive disabilities (Wong, 2011). Indeed, every effort is made to accommodate the latter's distinctive modes of non-linguistic communication and represent their grievances and preferences in multiple institutional contexts ranging from clinical consultations to parliamentary deliberations (Eckersley, 1999; Donaldson & Kymlicka, 2011; 2015a).

By parity of reasoning, then, humans should extend the same conception of representing humans with disabilities operating below the level of linguistic participation to animals as equally belonging and contributing to social cooperation. Hence, if they can be represented politically as non-linguistic social participants, then it follows that they can also shape the terms of cooperation through appropriate human proxies. Shaping these terms through such proxies, they collaborate with humans in facilitating their liberation from exploitation and abuse. A collaboration of this sort, in turn, facilitates the moral and spiritual growth of humans to the extent they abandon morally indefensible behaviors and develop an enlarged sense of community and belonging.

Moreover, the political agency and representation of animals combines their life-goals of the *purusharthas* by providing them with a political path beyond exploitation, towards spiritual liberation. In other words, it provides them with a route to transcendence not in the context of interactions with the natural world but rather diverse interactions in a shared, interspecies political community. Thus, animal spirituality may be understood by analogy with Gandhi's notion of nonviolent social experiments with Truth (Gray & Hughes, 2015), expanding one's circle of interactions and interrelationships. Such experiments are nonviolent to the extent they flatten hierarchies, facilitating multiple, intersecting liberations. Of course, appeal to this analogy entails a *consistent* application of his political reinterpretation of the *purusharthas* Gandhi himself never achieved. In other words, it should be rendered consistent by including interactions across all human and animal perspectives in such a community.

According to Gandhi, all humanity and not just its saints become capable of such experiments, given their political liberation from exploitation and oppressive hierarchy (Parel 2006; 2008). Indeed, expanding the circle of inclusive community and belonging (Lal, 2016), such experiments are grounded primarily in experience rather than rationality and higher cognitions (Gray & Hughes, 2015). Animals can engage in social experiments in Truth with humans, expanding the boundaries of interspecies community and belonging. Such experiments are manifest today in many ways. They manifest in the proxy representation of animals in policy deliberations (Eckersley, 1999; von Essen & Allen, 2017), and also, for instance, in the Farmed Animal Sanctuary movement (Donaldson & Kymlicka, 2015b). These sanctuaries treat animals originally raised for slaughter as equal community members with their own personalities and preferences, as well as emphatic capacities for creating new relationships with one another and human supervising or visiting the facility.

Such interspecies experiments in Truth—and equal community belonging—are further manifest in recent efforts to experimentally determine the preferences and aptitudes of animals incorporated into the economy as, say, therapy animals or police K9s (Donaldson & Kymlicka, 2015a). Here, the objective is to match occupations with personalities to give working animals meaningful and fulfilling careers. Consequently, like humans, these animals may also find spiritual purpose in their occupational roles, combining economic functionality with meaning and fulfillment transcending base materiality.

Animals are capable of experimenting with humans in alternative normative structures for social cooperation. Based on their capabilities for empathy and a sense of fairness, animals are capable of such interspecies experimentation, even if they are incapable of higher cognition. This is consistent with Gandhi's political reinterpretation of the *purusharthas* once his anthropocentric view of moral and spiritual growth as the *differentia specifica* of humanity is rejected. Grounded in both fable and science, such experiments in Truth facilitate the *purusharthas*' intersecting emancipatory life-goals, including transcendence. Indeed, they also provide CAS with a template for extending its vision of total animal and human liberation into the spiritual domain.

SUMMARY

In sum, this chapter has brought together several different literatures—mythological, scientific, and political—each of which contributes to extending the goal of spiritual liberation or transcendence to animals as well as humans. If this analysis is correct, then it should supplement CAS' vision of total animal/human liberation. It takes seriously transcendence as an emancipatory goal intimately connected to species egalitarianism and non-hierarchy. This vision of liberation is total in the sense that it intersects and combines the life-goals of freedom from exploitation and abuse with the goal of transcendence. It is also total in that it intersects and combines these emancipatory life-goals from the perspectives of both animals and humans, as equally belonging to the social and political order.

CAS might be interpreted appropriately as a form of *dharma* to the extent its program supports emancipatory experiments in Truth concerning interspecies relations that extend to spiritual liberation or transcendence for animals and humans alike.

SELECTED BIBLIOGRAPHY

Allen, M., & von Essen, E. (2018). Religion, critical animal studies, and the political turn: Nonhuman animal belonging and participation from secular and religious perspectives. *Journal for Critical Animal Studies, 15*(4), 4–25.

Bekoff, M. (2001). The evolution of animal play, emotions, and social morality: On science, theology, spirituality, personhood, and love. *Zygon 36*(4), 616–665.

Bekoff, M. (2009, Nov 9). Do animals have spiritual experiences? Yes they do. *Psychology Today* https://www.psychologytoday.com/us/blog/animal-emotions/200911/do-animals-have-spiritual-experiences-yes-they-do

Bekoff, M. (2010). *The animal manifesto: Six reasons for expanding our compassion footprint*. New World Library.

Bender, L. (2014). *Animal wisdom: Learning from the spiritual lives of animals*. North Atlantic Books.

Best, S. (2014). *The politics of total liberation: Revolution for the 21st Century*. Palgrave Macmillan.

Best, S., Nocella, A. J., I., Kahn, R., Gigliotti, L. M., & Kemmerer, L. (2007). Introducing critical animal studies. *Critical Animal Studies, 1*(5).

Brosnan, S. F., & De Waal, F. B. (2003). Monkeys reject unequal pay. *Nature, 425*(6955), 297–299. doi: 10.1038/nature01963

Carter, B., & Nickie, C. (2013). Animal, agency, and resistance. *Journal for the Theory of Social Behavior 43*(3), 322–340.

Desai, A., & Vahed, G. (2015). *The South African Gandhi: Stretcher bearer of empire*. Standford Univerity Press.

Donaldson, S., & Kymlicka, W. (2011). *Zoopolis: A political theory of animal rights*. Oxford University Press.

Donaldson, S., & Kymlicka, W. (2015a). Farmed animal sanctuaries: The heart of the movement? *Animals and Politics 1*, 50–74.

Donaldson, S., & Kymlicka, W. (2015b). Interspecies politics: A reply to Hinchcliffe and Ladwig. *Journal of Political Philosophy 23*(3) 321–344.

Eckersley, R. (1999). The discourse ethic and the problem of representing nature. *Environmental Politics 8*(2): 24–49.

Goodall, J. (2005). Primate spirituality. In Taylor, B. (Ed.) *Encyclopedia of religion and nature*. Continuum.

Gray, S., & Hughes, T. (2015). Gandhi's devotional political thought. *Philosophy East and West 65*(2) 375–400.

Griffin, D. (2001). *Animal minds: Beyond cognition to consciousness*. University of Chicago Press.

Hribal, J. (2013). *Fear of the animal planet: The hidden history of animal resistence.* CounterPunch.

Jaini, P. (1991). Animals as agents in ahimsa action and spiritual life. *Journal of Dharma, 16*(3), 278–281.

Kymlicka, W., & Donaldson, S. (2014). Animal rights, multiculturalism and the left. *Journal of Social Philosophy* 45(1), 116–135.

Lal, S. (2016). Gandhi's Synthesis of liberal and communitarian values: Its basis and insights. *Journal of East-West Thought 6*(3), 29–43.

Luke, B. (2007). Justice, caring and animal liberation. In J. Donovan & C. J. Adams (Eds.), *The feminist care tradition in animal ethics* (pp. 125–152). Columbia University Press.

Parel, A. J. (2008). Gandhi and the emergence of the modern Indian political canon. *Review of Politics, 70,* 40–63.

Parel, A. J. (2006). *Gandhi's philosophy and the quest for harmony*. Cambridge University Press

Russell, N. (2003). The wild side of animal domestication. *Society & Animals, 10*(3), 285–302.

Smith, K. (2012). *Governing animals: Animal welfare and the liberal state*. Oxford University Press.

Scruton, R. (2001). Animal rights and wrongs. Continuum.

Yarri, D. (2006). Animals a kin: The religious significance of Marc Bekoff's Work. *Zygon, 41*(1), 221–228.

Vlahos, J. (2008). Pill popping pets. *New York Times Magazine*. https://www.nytimes.com/2008/07/13/magazine/13pets-t.html

Von Essen, E., & Allen, M. (2017). Solidarity between human and non-human animals: representing animal voices in policy deliberation. *Environmental Communication,* 11(5), 641–653.

Wadiwel, D. J. (2016). Do fish resist? *Critical Studies Review, 22*(1), 47. doi: 10.5130/csr.v22i1.4363

Wong, S. I. (2010). Duties of justice to citizens with cognitive disabilities. In Kittay, E. F. & Carlson, L. (Eds.), *Cognitive disability and its challenge to moral Philosophy* (pp. 127–146). Wiley-Blackwell.

Chapter Five

Teaching Public Activism in the Humanities

Navigating a Classroom Climate in Crisis

Jessica Holmes

INTRODUCTION

Teachers in critical animal studies and across humanities disciplines increasingly embrace collaboration and intersectional, interdisciplinary dialogue in their classrooms. Amid the worsening global climate crisis and the youth-led strikes occurring across the world, college students repeatedly express a desire for institutional opportunities to *do* more, be more *active* in applying what they learn, and discuss public and personal accountability through scholarship. In animal studies, environmental studies, and human rights classes, students are expected to digest potentially traumatic content and engage in discourses of crisis, yet do not always feel sufficiently empowered as individuals or as an academic community to tackle such problems. Additionally, students are often required to approach these problems without the necessary imaginative and critical thinking skills so arduously taught in humanities programs—skills that would better equip them as social activists. Critical Animal Studies seeks to foreground activism, political engagement, and praxis. The interdisciplinary priorities of Critical Animal Studies are "to link theory to practice, analysis to politics, and the academy to the community" (Best et al., 2007). In this way, Critical Animal Studies models for academically related fields how to use activism to inform and cultivate a radically minded, socially equitable, pro-liberation scholarly practice.

Learning about public activism in the college classroom presents an opportunity for students to understand and engage more deeply in their community. It also encourages them to harness institutional tools and resources to transform hope, resilience, and empowerment into social change. This chapter discusses creating an adaptable interdisciplinary framework for educators within the humanities to teach activism in Critical Animal Studies courses. This framework enables instructors and students to investigate the relationship between scholarship and activism to enrich each other mutually. With the right pedagogical tools, teaching public activism can enliven student learning and empower classroom populations. The goal in developing public-facing resources and models (such as this chapter) is to share pedagogical tools that other educator-activists can adapt to fit diverse scholarly contexts. For instance, CAS's total liberation goals directly align with increasingly espoused pedagogical priorities championed within anti-racist discourse, equitable education, and environmental sustainability. Additionally, directly integrating activist practices into college curricula can address the mental health struggles facing educators and students on higher education campuses while simultaneously producing beneficial outcomes for the larger community. What follows are five key pedagogical goals around which I develop my own courses on (or including) social activism. These goals are not comprehensive; they continue to evolve as local and global contexts evolve, and as the nature of activism progresses—hopefully toward a future of greater and ultimately *total* liberation for all beings and for the Earth they call home.

GOAL #1: GENERATE COLLABORATIVE, STUDENT-DRIVEN DEFINITIONS OF *ACTIVISM*

I begin courses on social activism with a definitional inquiry. An argument for teaching rhetoric, vocabulary, and language is on some level an argument for the importance of humanities training at large; that is to say, language matters. Most of my students are not English majors, but many are scientists (or scientists-in-training). Scientists need not look far for examples in which the failure to use appropriate vocabulary results in deadly, real-world consequences. Politicians and media outlets regularly prove unwilling to employ even such simple, accurate terms such as "crisis" and "emergency" in their portrayal of climate issues. If we cannot identify the problem accurately, how can we hope to solve it?

When asked to define and illustrate the terms *activism* and *activist*, many students (and people) make immediate associations with cliché images of tree-hugging hippies or self-righteous extremists who hold signs, block roads, and break laws. This is relatively unsurprising given mainstream media's long-time depiction of activists in a negative light. A quick synonym search of "activist" on *Thesaurus.com* yields the following top results: *lobbyist, militant, zealot, tree hugger, propagandist, protestor, abolitionist, fanatic*. Alternatively, students who provide positive associations with the term *activist* often name exclusively readily available, aspirational examples of activists—in my experience, namely Martin Luther King, Jr. and occasionally Rosa Parks (tremendous activists indeed, but both are too often cited by students with little knowledge about the specific ideologies, backgrounds, lives and movements behind these individuals). According to such associations, activism seems to be for many college students an identity category that is either undesirable or unachievable.

The *Oxford English Dictionary* defines activism as: "The policy of active participation or engagement in a particular sphere of activity; *spec*. the use of vigorous campaigning to bring about political or social change." When I prompt my students on the first day of class, "raise your hand if you consider yourself an activist," zero to five percent raise their hands. This is despite the fact that a great number of my students volunteer their time and energy for local causes, participate in registered student organizations, and use social media to practice civil engagement. Their hesitancy in adopting the identity of *activist* when prompted strikes me as both illogical and highly relatable. After all, it has been only a few short years since I began calling myself an "activist"—and to be honest, the term still feels uncomfortable when applied to little-old-me. Perhaps my unease with the term implies some unspecified level of engagement to which I'm not sure I measure up. Or perhaps because in my own imagined democracy, to be a community member inherently implicates active engagement in that community, meaning there are no activists, only community citizens; or rather all citizens are activists. I was attending protests, participating in community organizing, engaging in campus leadership and educational outreach in my area, as well as filming, editing, and producing hundreds of advocacy videos for social media—in other words directly partaking in "active participation or engagement" in the realms of environmental and animal rights—and yet I never once dared refer to myself as an "activist." Is it any wonder my eighteen-year-old students don't either?

For this reason, students in my classes first explore the definition of *activism*, and later, after considerable efforts to elicit an inclusive, diverse understanding of activism, they consider the identity category of *activist*. We apply the literary conception of *genre* to various examples of contemporary and historical activism, enabling students to broaden (or narrow) their own definitions of activism through exposure to manifold models. Students learn that while street protests and property destruction are indeed strong examples of activism, they are not the only forms of activism, and are certainly not the only forms of activism available to students. Ultimately, the definition(s) of *activism* carried forward in my classroom are student-driven. Through peer collaboration and reflective, as well as research-based, writing, with sufficient exposure to examples, students become better equipped to revisit and revise preconceived assumptions about *activism.*

Later in the term, we revisit the question of to whom the term *activist* can and should be applied. Students are typically eager to apply the term to others—for instance socially attentive artists, animal sanctuary carers, or educators (some examples offered up by students that fall outside the standard clichés). However, students rarely prove as eager to apply the term to themselves. For example, in a recent environmental humanities course focused on climate crisis, multiple class members reported making radical changes to their lifestyles based on the course content they had studied. Some drastically lowered their plastic use, transitioned to eating a plant-based diet, started biking to school and work, began shopping at thrift stores, and altered their social media practices. They also engaged in community conversations and leadership by sharing materials with friends and family, attending local and campus events, applying for sustainability grant projects, and attending environmentally focused protests.

Many students were going to such admirable lengths to create change and accountability in their own lives and social circles (well beyond the confines of class requirements), and yet during office hours, class discussions and reflective writing assignments, most reported feeling overwhelmed by feelings of guilt, anger, and hopelessness. These feelings, in my experience, rarely translate to a sense of empowerment. Desperation and exhaustion are poor fuels for activism, especially in the long-term. They underscore the need for a broad discussion of self-care, compassion fatigue, and activist burnout within the context of fighting for social and ecological justice, as well as the indispensability of developing a supportive classroom community when teaching public activism. Neither I nor my courses argue that anything and everything vaguely beneficial to a cause should automatically qualify as activism; but the ability to recognize and take pride in engaged acts of consciousness and empathy, as well as the persistent pursuit of justice on an individual and collective level, must be learned and reinforced if any pro-liberation movement is to sustain itself. While many of my students remain reluctant to self-apply the *activist* label (even using broader, more inclusive definitions of *activism*), they are ultimately quite confident in applying it to one another. In this way, an ongoing definitional inquiry has led to the discussion and development of various activist identities among students.

GOAL #2: PRACTICE PERFORMING CRITICAL READINGS OF SPECIFIC PUBLIC ACTIONS ACROSS MULTIPLE MOVEMENTS

In thinking about broad definitions and categories of *activism*, my courses engage grassroots "genres" such as: protest and demonstration, strikes and boycotts, petitioning, corporate pressure campaigns, political campaigns, rallies, social media activism, civil disobedience, underground resistance, pamphleting and dissemination of literature, educational outreach, open rescue, vigils, art and "artivism," mutual aid, and more. Within each genre, students are asked to examine specific examples with keen attention to motivation(s), goal(s), strategies and tactics, relative successes (and how to track the success of actions, as well as the success of broader, movement-based efforts toward justice and liberation). Students are invited to look at examples on a local, national, and global scale, but focus is importantly placed on campus activism. Through their writing, research, and collaborative projects for the respective course, students answer questions like: What groups and organizations are engaging in campus activism? How are these groups funded? What are their values, goals, strategies, and tactics? In groups, students might perform a collaborative "case study" of a particular example of local or campus activism, in which they read about and research the group, analyze connections to and distinctions from other groups (both inside and outside the respective movement), interview key organizers or participants, and either witness or participate in the group's action(s).

My students rightly point out that not everybody can or is willing to hit the streets with a sign and a bullhorn. Based on the inclusive, diverse, student-driven definitions of *activism* generated in the early stages of the course, I encourage students to discover creative expression and action on campus, in addition to more conventional models of activism. These models might include art as activism, teaching or educational activism, or even examples of activist-minded mental health or self-care practice. After performing their collaborative "case study," in the final stages of the course, students are given a chance to explore their own preferred way(s) of getting active. My public activism course typically culminates in an extended exercise (either group or individual), in which students imagine and map out their own (hypothetical or actual) activism project, applying the knowledge they have gained in the course. Examples of creative "actions" carried out for this project include the composition of a vegan cookbook, an eco-conscious online zine, sustainable product development, public service campaigns, poetry writing and multimodal performance art, sidewalk chalk art purposed as educational outreach, a food justice-informed phone app, a film screening and discussion, a sustainability product labeling campaign on campus, and many more.

By exploring a specific area of activism of their choice, students can engage in creative, critical, and collaborative reflection, including reflection upon the question of how an understanding of and participation in public activism might deepen the impact and stakes of academic scholarship and/or how scholarship might enrich public activism. In this way, we can see public activism education working in tandem with the teaching of conventional humanities skills such as critical thinking and analysis in order to simultaneously support academic curricula *and* pro-liberation mobilization and action.

GOAL #3: CREATE AND MAINTAIN SPACE FOR EXPLORING THE AFFECTIVE DIMENSIONS OF CLASSROOM CONTENT AND PUBLIC ACTIVISM

Before studying animal exploitation, ecological devastation, and social inequity, students enter the classroom in a state of crisis. According to the National Alliance on Mental Illness (NAMI) one in four young adults between the ages of 18 and 24 have a diagnosable mental health condition (2019). Over 70 percent of students living with a mental health condition experience a mental health crisis on campus; over a third do not report the crisis. Over 80 percent of college students report feeling overwhelmed by all they had to do in the past year and 45 percent report having felt hopeless. Suicide is the second leading cause of death among college students in the United States (SafeColleges, 2020). Mental health experts are only just beginning to scratch the surface of psychological challenges unique to living in the so-called Anthropocene era; terms such as *eco-grief*, *climate anxiety*, *pre-traumatic stress disorder*, and *solastalgia* have begun to emerge. Scholars such as psychologist Clare Mann have also written about the mental and social struggles of living as a vegan in a non-vegan world; Mann introduces the term *vystopia*, which she defines as the "existential crisis experienced by vegans, arising out of an awareness of the trance-like collusion with a dystopian world" (2018). The existing mental health crisis running rampant on college campuses combined with the potential of the traumatic content contemplated in Critical Animal Studies and related courses to exacerbate existing mental health challenges and/or incite new ones necessitates mental health support inside the classroom (as well as outside). Courses on public activism must create and maintain space(s) in which to explore the affective dimensions of classroom content.

To begin cultivating such a space, I make it a pedagogical priority to openly invite discussions of emotion, affect, and mental health in my courses.

This process includes informal classroom conversations and activities, and the incorporation of mental health clauses into formal documents such as syllabi and/or course descriptions. I also actively integrate mindfulness-based activities into as many class sessions as possible, based on the growing body of research on the benefits of mindfulness practice within an educational context. My aim is always to cultivate a learning environment, not a testing environment. According to NAMI, mental health issues are the top impediment to academic success (2019). Particularly within the context of a course on activism, I find that affective exploration of materials often translates to more positive, practical action as well as higher quality academic work.

Some examples of pedagogical strategies that foster empowerment, resilience, and community-building in the college classroom are student-led resilience training, public engagement opportunities, and occasions for creative expression. In my courses, student-led resilience training is based on a combination of individual student incomes and collaborative research; resulting leadership projects have included student-led class-wide meditations, visualization exercises, collaborative music playlists and service-learning projects. Resilience-training may or may not overlap with public engagement opportunities—my public activism students are required to attend and reflect upon (through writing) at least one public engagement function, such as a public lecture, a protest, a sanctuary visitation or volunteer day, or an art showcase. Finally, as discussed in the previous section, occasions for creative expression are directly scaffolded into writing assignment sequences, meaning students may produce non-traditional "texts," such as paintings, performances, and poems, informed by their study of public activism. It is naïve to think that even the most research-informed, compassionate pedagogy will be able to eliminate the mental health struggles of students; but by combining and connecting the study of activism with the study of affect, public activism educators at the very least eschew a dangerous neglect of student mental health experiences, and in the best case scenario enhance student activism engagement, academic success, and general well-being.

GOAL #4: ILLUMINATE THE INTERSECTIONALITY OF VARIOUS JUSTICE MOVEMENTS AS WELL AS THE STAKES OF CLASSROOM CONTENT

Collective liberation operates under the well-founded assumption of shared goals across movements. Many students enter the college classroom never having seriously considered the connections between seemingly separate topics such as racism and speciesism, feminism and the dairy industry, or fossil fuel companies and genocide. The project of advancing public activism as an area of academic study serves not only to underscore individual causes and movements, but importantly heightens understanding of what is described in Critical Animal Studies as “a larger, interlocking, global system of domination” (Best et al., 2007). One of the benefits of embracing an intersectional approach when teaching public activism is that it makes classroom content highly adaptable to fit a wide array of teaching contexts, topics, and disciplines. And, while courses on animal rights activism or environmental activism certainly hold potential and value in their own right, teaching individual issues within the context of and in relationship to each other, as well as to the broader pattern of systematic oppression, tends to enhance student interest, as well as collaboration within and across the academy.

Activism is usually most effective when it is historically informed. I ask my students to consider, through their writing, which practices and movements throughout history they are drawing on when they attend or participate in an action. How do these movements work together and how do they sometimes come into conflict? And what types of coalitions might be most likely to overturn oppressive structures of power and profit in the future? By applying critically informed, intersectional lenses to a wide array of examples in activism, students are better able to analyze, synthesize, and “read” any given action, as well as to define for themselves precisely what constitutes success, in which contexts, and at what cost.

When presenting examples of oppression, I find it useful to emphasize areas of concrete intersectional overlap—for instance, examining the human and worker rights violations that occur in factory farming systems (not just the plight of animals), or examining the impacts of environmental devastation on racial justice (not just the ecological impact of deforestation, air pollution, and overfishing). The more examples of oppression coursework can connect and the more tightly it can connect them, the clearer the stakes of that work become for students, particularly among diverse campus populations.

The length of the typical academic term presents some challenges when thinking about the sheer amount of intersectional coverage pursued by any given course. However, an intersectional approach to public activism pedagogy by no means equates to a comprehensive approach. Just as typical English courses seek to model for students the process of gathering and synthesizing various materials in order to pursue their own chosen research pathways, an intersectional humanities course in public activism need only model sufficient examples in order to illuminate for students the presence and nature of the “larger, interlocking, global system of domination,” and ideally to animate critically informed projects and actions based on individual student inquiries and interests.

GOAL #5: ENCOURAGE INTERDISCIPLINARY COLLABORATION, COMMUNITY PARTNERSHIPS, AND THE PURSUIT OF PUBLIC GOOD THROUGH STUDENT WORK

Any study of activism, however cursory, is sure to highlight the power of and the natural human inclination toward community-building, teamwork, and solidarity across difference. If academia is to serve the public good, our classrooms must directly reflect and engage these values. We must develop among our students not only the well-crafted skills of critical thinking and active organizing, but an unshakable aptitude for contemplating the personal and public stakes of their work and the social, political, and ethical commitments to which they hold fast. The study of activism constitutes a form of public scholarship, which is to say it advances scholarship as a publicly engaged practice and seeks to further the democratization of knowledge and the liberation of all beings and the Earth.

Facilitating grassroots partnerships beyond the confines of an academic campus or institution requires some legwork on the part of instructors but is integral to the study of public activism. Examples of engaging community networks include field trips, volunteer opportunities, guest speaker series, letter writing, direct public outreach, and service-learning course components. Partnerships such as these provide concrete models upon which students can build in their own work. Many academic institutions also house non-departmental organizations or resources, such as mental health centers, minority and diversity affairs offices, and leadership and public service centers, which may provide additional, accessible opportunities for community-building and the furthering of public good, and which can be linked or integrated directly into curricula.

Fostering interdisciplinarity within Critical Animal Rights or any public activism classroom might include connecting and collaborating with instructors across multiple fields of scholarship (whether on curriculum development, pedagogical philosophies, or community-building strategies), integrating extracurricular engagement outside the respective field as foundational to the coursework, and applying humanities lenses of study to content from or anchored in alternative academic disciplines. Partnerships between the sciences and humanities have been particularly fruitful in my own experience teaching undergraduates at an R1 public institution, and public activism courses (though highly adaptable) fit well within increasingly prominent programs such the Certificate in Public Scholarship, the Interdisciplinary Writing Program and the Department of Comparative History of Ideas (University of Washington). Due to the highly intersectional nature of Critical Animal

Studies and its opposition to widespread mainstream scholarly approaches (such as those based on speciesism, insularity, or the claim of apoliticization), it is in some respect difficult to situate within the academy. However, as educators and advocates, we must continue to build dialogues, relationships, and coalitions across the disciplines in order to more visibly and strongly foreground the nature and consequences of planetary crisis and to carve out pathways toward transformative change.

CONCLUSION

In conclusion, the intersectional and interdisciplinary nature of climate change and the plight of human and nonhuman animals alike demand radical new pedagogical and institutional approaches to education, including the teaching of public activism in college classrooms. The above guidelines aspire to offer a starting point and evolving, adaptable model to instructors seeking to incorporate more public activism pedagogy into their courses. Equipped with the necessary foundation and tools, and in collaboration with their fellow colleagues and community allies, educators will be able to provide students with diverse, resonant frameworks by which to expand student learning of and engagement with climate, social justice, and Critical Animal Studies issues, as well as their own peers and communities at large. Through the study and practice of activism *as* academic scholarship, we seek to generate innovative forms of publicly engaged collaboration, critical thinking, and resilience both inside and outside the college classroom and, through action, to collectively restore the "humanity" within the humanities.

SELECTED BIBLIOGRAPHY

Best, S., Nocella, A. J., Kahn, R., Gigliotti, C., & Kemmerer, L. (2007). Introducing critical animal studies. http://www.criticalanimalstudies.org/

Dictionary.com. (2020) Activist. In *Thesaurus.com*. www.dictionary.com

National Alliance on Mental Illness. (2020). *Mental Health by the Numbers.* www.nami.org

Oxford University Press. (2020) Activism. In *Oxford English Dictionary.* www.oed.com

SafeColleges, Vector Solutions. (2019). *Suicide Second Highest Cause of Death Among College Students.* www.safecolleges.com

Chapter Six

The Preservation of Injustice

Human Supremacy, Domination, and Privilege

Paislee House and Amanda R. Williams

INTRODUCTION

For thousands of years, the prevailing narratives of the human species have been exceptionalism, dominance, and supremacy.[1] These narratives have been pushed not by the evolutionary journey of the human species but instead by Western religious and philosophical thought, colonization, and capitalism (Montford & Taylor, 2020). Similar to other hierarchies, such as that of men over women or white people over people of color, the human supremacy narrative is a social invention, and the resulting privileges of the dominant groups are unearned and unjust. Stripped of the stories of human superiority, stories that originate from human sources instead of from the natural world, our responsibility to other beings becomes a mandate. Overdue is an expansion of our justice movements to include more-than-humans. Human supremacy and the privileges it grants to a single animal species is an injustice that we must work together to eradicate.

The word Privilege comes from the Latin roots *privus* and *lex*. The full Latin word *privilegium* originally meant a "law applying to one person, bill of law in favor of or against an individual." After being shaped by Old French, it was not until the fourteenth century when the Middle English word *privilege* came to be used for an "advantage granted," which is how it is still used today (Online Etymology Dictionary, 2021). Privilege is most commonly used in the context of human-animal social justice. White privilege, male privilege, class privilege, ability privilege, these are well-known frameworks that human animals concerned with equality and justice work to upend. Today, privilege has been generally defined along the following lines: "a special, unearned advantage or entitlement, used to one's own benefit or to the detriment of others; often, the groups that benefit from it are unaware of it" (Black & Stone, 2005, p. 244). Michael Kimmel (2018) likens privilege to "running with the wind at your back. It feels like just plain running, and we rarely if ever get a chance to see how we are sustained, supported, and even propelled by that wind." These definitions are narrowed when applied in different sociological contexts. White privilege, for example, has been defined as, "An advantage, good, or resource that people with ascribed white racial identities receive and/or have greater access to and that people with ascribed nonwhite racial identities are denied and/or have less access to, primarily as a consequence of their ascribed racial identity and not because of what they do or do not do as individuals" (Bunyasi & Smith, 2019, p. 109). Overall, social privilege can be seen as the inverse to social inequality because its focus is on how power structures in society aid privileged people versus how those structures oppress others.

Of course, this topic is nuanced because privilege doesn't exist in a vacuum, and various forms of privilege can interact in a myriad of situations (Kimmel, 2018). In the current American sociopolitical moment, the re-energized fight for racial justice has produced an increasing number of conversations around privilege. "Check your privilege" has become a phrase hurled from all sides. Some argue that the frequency and fluidity with which the term is being applied has caused it to lose its meaning (Sebastian, 2020). Others say that all this talk of privilege causes people to "wallow in guilt" instead of truly challenging structural injustice (Malik, 2020). Some even argue that privilege does not exist, particularly referring to racial privilege (Arora, 2020). However, the consensus among those who study social privilege is that it is a real phenomenon with real consequences.

One common argument against blanketing an entire group of people with a particular privilege, such as white privilege or human-species privilege, is that when someone is living without financial security, they cannot have privilege. Gina Crosley-Corcoran (2014) addresses this sentiment in an article on the topic of white privilege specifically. Crosley-Corcoran experienced a childhood of severe poverty growing up in Illinois without heat or running water. Despite her family's own economic paucity, she writes that "it's impossible to deny that being born with white skin in America affords people certain unearned privileges in life that people of another skin color simpl[y] are not afforded" (Crosley-Corcoran, 2014, p. 1). She goes on to give examples[2] like turning on the television and seeing people of her race represented, being told about our national heritage or "civilization" as something that white people made, and not being singled out based on race by police. Crosley-Corcoran's (2014) piece underscores the latter part of Black and Stone's (2005) definition of privilege, that "often, the groups that benefit from it are unaware of it" (p. 244).

Something that is missing from many common definitions of privilege is that it exists on a spectrum. Some people may not have as much of a particular privilege as others. This chapter places its focus on human-species privilege, which all human animals possess at some level. However, not all human animals are treated the same. In a world dominated by white supremacy and racism, for example, people of color have been and are often still treated as "subhuman" and compared to other animals pejoratively for the sake of discrimination (Jackson, 2020). This social reality for many people of color manifests in a lack of access to many facets of human-species privilege. While the term privilege certainly gets misused and perhaps even has the potential to cause a type of justice paralysis, there is still power in its acknowledgment, opening up the gates to the possibility of change. Privilege is not the be-all-end-all of analyses or the end of a self-improvement checklist. Instead, it is the first stop on a long journey toward dismantling oppressive power structures and working to eliminate its own existence.

The concept of privilege is said to have been born from the writings of American sociologist, historian, and civil rights activist W.E.B. Du Bois (1903), most notably in his book *The Souls of Black Folk*. He wrote about what he called a "double consciousness" that Black people have, a "sense of always looking at one's self through the eyes of others, of measuring one's soul by the tape of a world that looks on in amused contempt and pity" (Du Bois, 1903, p. 2). Du Bois observed that while Black people had to know about white Americans and recognize racial discrimination, white people didn't think much about Black Americans nor the effects of their discrimination (Sullivan, 2006).

It was not until the 1980s that the concept of social privilege really caught fire in the academic space, and Peggy McIntosh—American feminist, anti-racism activist, scholar, and pioneer in the field of inclusive education—has been credited with sparking the flame. McIntosh (1988) published the article, "White Privilege and Male Privilege: A Personal Account of Coming to See Correspondences through Work in Women's Studies." In it, she listed forty-six privileges that she experienced as a white, cisgender, heterosexual woman in the United States. In this article and in her writings overall, she encourages others to reflect on their own unearned advantages as parts of large and overlapping systems of power (McIntosh, 2019). From her article, "White Privilege: Unpacking the Invisible Knapsack," McIntosh (1989) writes:

> Thinking through unacknowledged male privilege as a phenomenon, I realized that, since hierarchies in our society are interlocking, there was most likely a phenomenon of white privilege that was similarly denied and protected. As a white person, I realized I had been taught about racism as something that puts others at a disadvantage, but had been taught not to see one of its corollary aspects, white privilege, which puts me at an advantage. (p. 1)

The formal concept of privilege was studied more intensely in the years following McIntosh's early publications (O'Brien, 2009). However, the concept rarely left the human-animal arena.

In the mainstream, Western academic world, the framework of human-species privilege has not been a popular means of examining human-animal relationships. A variety of factors play into this mainstream exclusion. There is indeed a lack of institutional support for animal-liberation-related causes (Duin, 2012). On top of that, the academic space has been slow to diversify its staff, curriculums, and research (Roberts, 2020). Equally unhelpful has been a historic siloing of academic subjects such as philosophy, law, sociology, political theory, ethology, environmental studies, and animal studies, which creates barriers to the cross-pollination of concepts across academic disciplines (Nocella et al., 2014). The largest factor of all, of course, is the persistent belief in the superiority of human animals and their interests.

Although not part of the dominant discourses of most areas of study, scholarship around species privilege can be found more explicitly in the writings of some individual scholars. In the area of critical disability studies, for example, Daniel Salomon (2010), an autistic scholar and animal advocate, writes about neurotypical privileging and how it connects human-animal and more-than-human animal issues. He says, "neurotypicalism privileges a form of cognitive processing characteristic of peoples who have a neurotypical (non-autistic) brain structure, while at least implicitly finding other forms of cognitive processing to be inferior, such as those natural to autists and nonhuman animals" (Salomon, 2010, p. 47). It stands to reason that the framework of human-species privilege would be compared to that of ability privilege, given that the main ways human supremacists separate themselves from more-than-human animals is based on ability (e.g., intelligence).

Some feminist scholars have also included a species-privilege framework into the area of feminist studies. In "Rethinking Cross-Species Relations: Feminist Interventions," Natalie Corinne Hansen (2010) writes, "As with other categories of difference, species difference is constructed to benefit specific actors: *Homo sapiens*. Left unexamined, assumptions of species privilege justify many levels of inequality, from the dehumanization of 'enemy combatants' to globalized predations on natural resources" (para 2).

Carol J. Adams, a long-time ecofeminist scholar and animal-rights activist, published several books on the relationship between the oppression of women and the oppression of more-than-human animals, including her most famous *The Sexual Politics of Meat*. On the topic of pleasure derived from eating more-than-human animal bodies, Adams (1995) comments, "But there is no pleasure without privilege, the privilege to be a member of the dominant culture that's dominating women, people of color, and animals. We need to get the privilege acknowledged and the social structures that create privilege, and the way the privilege is rewarded through pleasure, a pleasure which actually arises from someone else's harm" (p. 7).

There are some biocentric environmentalists, too, who employ the concept of species privilege in their work. Paul Taylor (1986) wrote *Respect for Nature*, a book that as Bob Bruner (2017) argues is "considered to be the first rigorous, philosophical defense of biocentric ethics" (para 7). Biocentrism is an ethical view that gives inherent value to all living things, and it is only in the human mind that our species is superior, or privileged. Relative to the natural world, Taylor (1981) argues, "we should not consider ourselves privileged beings in relation to other species. This is the fact that the well-being of humans is dependent upon the ecological soundness and health of many plant and animal communities, while their soundness and health does not in the least depend upon human well-being" (p. 7). Taylor's work reinforces the fact that human superiority is entirely invented, and it is sustained by the domination of and violence toward those deemed less than human. The privileges we gain from that domination and violence are not the products of the natural order of things but instead undeserved self-service. Based on the existing scholarship, various generalized definitions of privilege in traditional dictionaries—and informed by the language around human privilege that already exists globally, both in academia and outside academia, where concepts of human-species privilege are more robustly discussed—the authors' definition of human privilege is a system of advantage based on species that affords unearned preferential treatment and benefits to human animals while oppressing more-than-human animals and the more-than-human world.

PRIVILEGE IN CONTEXT

Unlike human privilege, the concepts of human supremacy, anthropocentrism, and speciesism—the systems that produce human privilege—have been explored in depth by writers in both the academic and popular realms. From the philosophies of more-than-human-animal suffering of Eastern religions and Western utilitarians to the philosophies of anti-hierarchy from ecofeminists, biocentrists, anarchists, and Critical Animal Studies (CAS) scholars, human-animal dominance has not gone unquestioned. Some of the most important work today is the work that expands its focus beyond the scope of more-than-human-animal oppression. Humans are animals, which means both human and more-than-human-animal struggles are intrinsically bound. Those who fight a single-issue justice battle climb an endless ladder of oppressions, while those who can see the interconnected nature of various oppressions, human and more-than-human, get closer to the fundamental ills of human-animal society. The journalist Will Potter (2011) comments on what happens when multiple justice movements join forces:

> Their confluence is the redefinition of what it means to be a human being. These movements are not content with another recycling campaign and they do not want animals to have bigger shackles and longer chains. At their core, they challenge fundamental beliefs that have guided humanity for thousands of years, and that have for the most part remained unquestioned by prior social justice movements: that human beings are the center of the universe and our interests are intrinsically superior to those of other species and the natural world. (p. 245)

When issues of animal liberation are separated from other social justice issues, social injustice is promoted. It is evident that the siloing tendencies of academia and social justice movements have been ineffective in the vanquishing of various oppressions: class hierarchy, patriarchy, white supremacy, ableism, you name it. From her essay "In the Doing and the Being," Lori B. Girshick (2014) writes, "Any existing oppression tends to support the others because the framework of privilege operates through them all" (p. 54). The framework of privilege—a window through which to view the advantages of certain beings and the disadvantages of others—is an opportune mechanism for observing the power dynamics of groups and the linkages between oppressions.

Even when the linkages exist, we must be cautious in our comparisons. Although anthropocentric pressures may inspire us to make direct comparisons between human and more-than-human-animal struggles, it is unnecessary, can be seen as offensive, and can be a continuation of discrimination to those involved in the comparison. For instance, some animal advocates have made comparisons between human enslavement and more-than-human animal enslavement (Patterson, 2002). American slavery, for example, has been compared to the abuses of animal agriculture (Spiegel, 1988). And perhaps most infamous was PETA's (People for the Ethical Treatment of Animals) "Are Animals the New Slaves?" campaign, which the NAACP called racially insensitive (Brune, 2005). In regard to the PETA campaign, political scientist and race scholar Claire Jean Kim (2015) says in her book *Dangerous Crossings* that the analogy of human-animal slavery and more-than-human animal slavery "attempts to ground the argument for the moral considerability and grievability of animals upon the elision of race" (p. 207). While some situational likenesses may exist, it is disingenuous to make direct comparisons between species of animals or between different oppressed groups. The way different creatures experience the world varies wildly, and one cannot speak accurately from the perspective of another (even from another within the same species). There is a great deal of variability in social context as well. As several Black scholars and activists have pointed out, it is more constructive to analyze the similarities in struggles of oppression. Black social justice and animal-rights activist Christopher Sebastian (2014) puts it this way:

> Humans are animals. Whether or not you believe that we are conceived from a common ancestor with bonobos, we don't exist outside of the animal kingdom. So it's important to deconstruct the narrative that pits "us" against "them." Also, let's listen to the correct part of the conversation. This is not a comparison of human animals to nonhuman animals. This is a comparison of like systems of oppression. Whether talking about white humans and brown ones or horses and pigs, slavery is an abuse of power. (para. 6)

In her book *Afro-Dog*, author and scholar Bénédicte Boisseron (2018) also comments on comparisons between more-than-human animals and Black human animals specifically. She says:

> While questioning the animal-human divide is essential to animal rights activism, contesting the divide with a racial paradigm indeed carries the potential effect of reinscribing a discriminative approach that one had sought to reject in the first place. On the other hand, there is no denying that there are important parallels to be drawn between the rationale behind opposing animal oppression and that behind condeming discrimination against minorities. In both cases, it is a question of arbitrary divides.

The results of the abuses of power and discrimination described by Sebastion (2014) and Boisseron (2018) is privilege for the dominant groups and lack of privilege for the marginalized groups, whether human or not.

What is more, it is essential to note that privilege is complex. It is not a binary concept where you either have privilege or you do not. One can have privileges A, B, and C, but lack privileges D, E, and F, and on top of that, privilege A may interact differently with privilege F than E, for example, or one may have more or less of privilege A than another person. In her book *Powerarchy*, Melanie Joy (2019) says, "All of us straddle multiple realities, playing various roles within a given system. We all have some forms of privilege, and we all belong to some oppressed groups. (Because powerarchies comprise systems involving nonhumans, even people who belong to multiple oppressed groups nevertheless retain human privilege)" (p. 125). There is an interconnected, sometimes referred to as an intersectional, nature to systems of discrimination. Kimberlé Crenshaw (2015) coined the term intersectionality and suggests that it is a "way of thinking about identity and its relationship to power" (para. 5). In her conversations with Julia Feliz Brueck (2017) for the book *Veganism in an Oppressive World*, Margaret Robinson, an indigenous vegan and scholar, notes that intersectionality is "helpful for understanding how experiences of advantage and disadvantage are shaped by systems of privilege and oppression related to racialization, ability, gender, sexuality, class, and other categories" (p. 8). Much of the complexity stems from the multiple identities people possess and how they overlap in a variety of ways. Some scholars suggest that intersectionality may be too limiting in a discussion of species privilege. David Pellow (2014), for example, in his book *Total Liberation*, argues that because intersectionality "begins and ends with humans" it is "unnecessarily restrictive." He continues, " . . . one cannot fully grasp the foundations of racism, classism, ableism, heterosexism, and patriarchy without also understanding speciesism and dominionism because they are all ideologies and practices rooted in hierarchy and the creation of oppositional superior and inferior subjects" (p. 20).

No system of privilege, be it white, male, ability, human, or other can be entirely generalized to every individual in a particular group, for everyone has their own list of privileges based on the unique circumstances of each individual's life. Patrice Jones (2014), in her book *The Oxen at the Intersection*, emphasizes the importance of considering social circumstances, saying that "Everything humans do to animals or their habitats is done by humans in particular social, economic, and environmental circumstances—all of which have been shaped by sexism, racism, and other forms of oppression among human beings" (p. 67). If the authors were to create a list of our privileges, as McIntosh (1988) created a list of her own privileges, it would be from the perspective of our own experience and would not apply to every person that shares our social class, gender presentation, race, sexual orientation, or species status. Even so, readers can still observe list commonalities among similarly circumstanced individuals. Such is the case for human-species privilege. One of the main reasons to understand one's own privileges is to use the platform that those privileges grant to challenge the systems that produce these advantaged and disadvantaged realities. That is the responsibility of all of us: to transform existing power imbalances and shrink our own privilege where possible.

But it is hard to shrink privilege that we do not take note of, and human animals who occupy positions of power are disincentivized to change. This speaks to why white privilege goes unrecognized by so many white people and male privilege goes unrecognized by so many men. As the dominant cultural narrative, it masquerades as "normal," and most significantly it has permeated all our social and power structures. Linda Martin Alcoff (2007) comments in her contribution to the book *Race and Epistemologies of Ignorance*:

> One of the key features of oppressive societies is that they do not acknowledge themselves as oppressive. Therefore, in any given oppressive society, there is a dominant view about the general nature of the society that represents its particular forms of inequality and exploitation as basically just and fair, or at least the best of all possible worlds. It is very likely, however, that this dominant representation of the unjust society as a just society will have countervailing evidence on a daily basis that is at least potentially visible to everyone in society. (p. 48)

Bringing to light this "countervailing evidence" is an important first step in recognizing privilege and remedying power imbalances. Simply taking the time to reflect on dominant ideologies will reveal contradictory evidence. Although remaining largely unresolved today, dominant forces that create privileges such as class privilege, white privilege, male privilege, or ability privilege have been getting more mainstream attention and contemplation. In contrast, human privilege, the inherent privilege one is afforded just by being a human animal in this world, is left relatively unexamined in the popular discourse. This is not emphasized to belittle other unjust, dominant cultural forces, for all oppressive ideologies share an underlying relationship of abuse of power. Instead, this emphasis on human privilege in particular is to point out the lack of representation that ideas around species privilege are allowed.

Even left unexamined, human privilege is still visible in ways large and small. From climate destruction to grocery store trips, our everyday lives are an exercise in human privilege. We exist in a world designed and constructed for human use. Human animals wake up from slumber in a bed, the components of which may include: foam, which is a product manufactured from petroleum, a fossil fuel contributing to the unnatural warming of Earth and the destruction of innumerable wildlife habitats; wool, which comes from sheep, who are genetically engineered to grow never-ending fur for humans (this unceasing fur growth would kill them without human intervention); and steel, which is made from iron ore mined from the Earth, the production of which emits CO_2 into the atmosphere and utilizes coal heavily as an energy source. Many human animals eat breakfast made from the lives and secretions of other beings: most eggs, bacon, and milk products come from animals who live in CAFOs, where their lives are so heavily manipulated they in no way resemble anything close to natural. Human animals drive to work on roads, the construction of which decimates the natural world and disturbs so fiercely the lives of our wild neighbors, all the while literally paving the way for another significant contributor to climate destruction, automobiles.

The authors have identified ten privileges that are common advantages among human animals and common disadvantages among more-than-human animals:

1. We can pursue legal cases on our own behalf.
2. We can decide (for the most part) what happens to our bodies.
3. We can travel safely for great distances without being impeded by another species' infrastructure.
4. We have some protection against enslavement and exploitation.
5. We are surrounded by others who understand our emotions, desires, and needs.
6. We speak a language that is understood by those in power.
7. We cannot be commodified without our consent.
8. We do not have to live in ongoing fear of harm from unnatural forces.
9. Our species is a species considered worth saving.
10. We are referred to as "them" and not as "it."

This is not an exhaustive list of human privileges by any means but rather a representative sampling. A longer list was drafted at first, with more details that could be reducible down to the following themes: Justice (e.g., the justice system, rights, economic interests), Autonomy (e.g., sexual freedom, imprisonment, individual identity), Lifestyle (e.g., mental, physical, and social stimulation, family), Psychology (e.g., recognition of emotions and intelligence, pain and pleasure, understanding), and Environment (e.g., infrastructure, home, travel, safety). Each of these categories would benefit from more future development and research to be more impactful.

Lamentably, all this talk of unjust privilege is obliterated by the dominant view that our species privilege is in fact, a justifiable and earned advantage. The most common justification for elevating the interests of humans over more-than-humans is human intelligence. Humans often believe that our intellectual capabilities place us at the top of nature's ladder. However, we built the ladder ourselves and designed the evaluations on which all life should be measured. The environmentalist, philosopher, and author of *The Myth of Human Supremacy*, Derrick Jensen (2016), writes:

> . . . most of the scientific (and "common sense") arguments used to defend human supremacism (and the same is true for various scientific and "common sense" means that have been used to defend white or male supremacism) are tautological, in that humans are using themselves as the standard by which

> all others are judged. Here's another way to say this: humans choose human characteristics as the measure of what characteristics define superiority. (p. 17)

The method of measuring more-than-human animals against a human-animal standard purposely reinforces our own invented dominance. It is dangerously supremacist to say, these beings cannot do X thing; therefore, their interests are less valuable than mine—where X could represent recognizing oneself in a mirror, dreaming about the future, driving cars, doing mathematics, having white skin, walking, having money, and so on.

At the same time, this line of thinking ignores the richness of capabilities that exist outside the human world: the Japanese firefly squid uses bioluminescence to attract others (Barratt & Allcock, 2014); whitetail deer communicate through chemical signals (Doty & Müller-Schwarze, 2013); ravens can solve puzzles (Cory, 2016); and salmon can remember their home stream after traveling hundreds of miles into the ocean and back (Quinn, 2018). In the eighteenth century, Georg Christoph Lichtenberg (1990), best known as a physicist and satirist, wrote, "The most accomplished monkey cannot draw a monkey, this too only man can do; just as it is also only man who regards his ability to do this as a distinct merit. It is only human arrogance that is able to find beauty and perfection exclusively in those things human" (p. 6). It is imperative to recognize our human bias to alleviate our obsession with our own capabilities and equally value the capabilities of more-than-humans. This is an essential step in slashing the unjust hierarchy that maintains the human grip on power and in eliminating human privilege in its many forms.

A major mechanism that is woven through various forms of our species privilege is the economic system of capitalism, which has morphed into both a philosophical and political set of beliefs in some parts of the world. Historians still dispute the exact moment that capitalism became the dominant economic system in the Western world. However, many agree that capitalism's foundations were formed in the merchant trading systems of Europe and then expanded as city centers became more urbanized (Wood, 2016). Modern capitalism then emerged between the sixteenth and eighteenth centuries in Europe, with England and the Netherlands being major pioneers of both capitalism and colonialism. Both nations constructed trading companies—the East India Company and the Dutch East India Company being the most influential—that sent forth merchants and business people in search of obtaining any and all resources that could be extracted. Adam Smith (1776), an inaugural oracle of the merits of capitalism, wrote in his seminal work *The Wealth of Nations*, "Consumption is the sole end and purpose of all production; and the interest of the producer ought to be attended to, only so far as it may be necessary for promoting that of the consumer" (p. 152). It has always been understood that the driving force of capitalism is that of consumption which should benefit the producer of the good being consumed, whether those goods are the bodies of animals, Earth's resources, or people's labor.

The underlying and fundamental doctrine of capitalism is one of intense extraction and violence. That violence has manifested in the form of colonialism and the decimation of peoples as well as the intensification of anthropogenic climate destruction. Given these facts, the etymological origins of the word should come as no surprise. The word "capitalism" is derived from the Latin word *capitale* based on *caput*, meaning "head." "Head," in this instance, is literally referring to the head on one's body. *Caput* is also the origin of the words "chattel" and "cattle," which were labels given to beings considered to be movable property (Braudel, 1982). From its etymological beginnings, capitalism has disregarded the livelihood of those considered property. It is a system of have and have-nots, where beings are hierarchically categorized and valued, favoring humans over animals and ultimately favoring a few wealthy humans over everything else.

From its early history and etymological origins up to the present, capitalism has been a proponent of human dominance and supremacy. Capitalism's wind has been a perverse and destructive force, obliterating animal habitat and wreaking havoc on Earth's climate. As humans, particularly humans living in what are considered developed nations, we benefit from many of the immediate products of capitalism: we can visit one or two locations to buy most things we want and need; we can drive to a restaurant or grocery store and purchase foods from all over the world at low costs; and we can order anything imaginable online and have it shipped directly to our homes. Although we might marvel at the low prices of clothes, food, or electronics, these things come with a hefty and unseen cost to Earth. Or, as Robin Wall Kimmerer (2013) writes, "Your strange hunger for ease should not mean a death sentence for the rest of creation" (pp. 427–428). This is perhaps one of the largest privileges our species is afforded: to do and get what we please at the expense of others.

One of the most emblematic examples of our human privilege is the unnecessary consumption of animals. Again, these choices, particularly under the ideology of unregulated capitalism, come with an increasingly hard to ignore price. Animal agriculture is one of the leading causes of habitat destruction. Human demand for meat, dairy, and other products fuel an industrialized system that simultaneously raises animals for slaughter while destroying the habitats of others. In a 2018 report published by the World Wildlife Fund, the term "runaway consumption" was used to describe the unrelenting pressures put upon Earth by human demand. This consumption has not only put immense pressure on Earth but has also contributed to the extinction of many species. Since AD 1500, of all the species who have gone extinct, 75 percent were harmed by overexploitation, agricultural activity, or both. As of 2014, roughly 18 billion global hectares of Earth's surface were occupied for animal grazing while 15 billion global hectares were used as croplands (Barrett et al., 2018). Of those croplands, 36 percent were used to grow animal feed (Cassidy et al., 2013). This number has most certainly grown since 2014. In the driver's seat of this unceasing growth and destruction are the doctrines of capitalism. The wealth justifies an unfettered growth it provides producers and the low costs it supplies to consumers. The human demand and "runaway consumption" of animals as resources, contributing so enormously to climate and habitat destruction, is an ideology of cancerous human supremacy.

DEFEATING HUMAN-SPECIES PRIVILEGE

There is no single antidote to the disaster of human domination nor a single treatment to reduce our species privilege. Although this is the case, it is important to remember that, as Noam Chomsky (2013) notes, "The more privilege you have, the more opportunity you have. The more opportunity you have, the more responsibility you have" (N. Chomsky, personal communication, January 12, 2013). We have a unique and pressing responsibility to animals: to listen, respect, protect, and make amends for all transgressions against them. The responsibility we have is not imperative only because of our physical destruction and stolen potential of the more-than-human world, although these need to be equally recognized. As animals ourselves and members of biotic communities, we have a responsibility to *our* community; to give what we can, care where we are able, and promote justice for everyone, including more-than-humans.

The challenge is enormous. We must rectify the thousands of years of human supremacy and domination that has gifted our species with immense privilege. Furthermore, a solution must address more than our individual contributions. As Allan Johnson (1997) so succinctly put it, "The solution also has to include entire systems, such as capitalism, whose paths of least resistance shape how we feel, think, and behave as individuals, how we see ourselves and one another" (pp. 141–142). And ultimately, we must remember that similar hierarchical organizations link all struggles of oppression involving gender, sexuality, race, class, ability, or species. Taking all of this into account, the process for eliminating privilege is trifold, consisting of recognition, compassion, and catalyzation.

Recognizing privilege is a tall hurdle. Those with the most privilege also have the greatest power to affect change. One of the best tools for recognizing one's privilege is to listen. Listen without judgment to those who speak about injustice and those who stand up for those most vulnerable among us. And most importantly, take the time to listen to the voices of the oppressed, whether it is a protest chant, a whisper, or a language one does not speak. In addition to listening, a true, probing self-reflection is required. In our positions of privilege, we must determine our relationship with the more-than-human world around us. We must examine the groups that we belong to, the position of those groups within the dominant systems of power, and how we participate in those groups.

Through intensive listening and radical self-reflection, one's own human privilege comes to the fore. The cow tells us with loud cries when she's upset about the abduction of her newborn baby (Marchant-Forde et al., 2002). The red-bellied woodpecker tells us about warming climates as he moves irregularly northward from his southern home to seek out a mate (ESF, 2009). The orangutan families tell us that their homes and food have been stolen as their numbers dwindle to the level of critically endangered (WWF, 2020). The Toad Mountain harlequin frog tells us that our reckless transportation of species worldwide has paved the way for an apocalyptic fungus called Bd to kill 6.5 percent of *all* her amphibian brethren (Yong, 2019). We have to take the time to listen and reflect on how ourselves and the groups of which we are part are responsible.

Compassion is the next stage in defeating privilege. After real listening and reflection has taken place, compassion acts as an acknowledgment of and attention to the oppression of others. The trouble is that the normalization of oppression disowns compassion (Adams, 2016). In other words, it is difficult to exercise compassion for someone when their oppression is so normalized that it does not appear like they are being oppressed. A fishbowl on one's counter at home is so normal that we overlook the wild, richly social, and intelligent being who is being held captive inside it. This illustrates why the first steps of listening and reflecting are so important and need to be employed continuously, without end. To exercise compassion is to emphasize one's care and concern for others. Then, it is out of compassion that we should ask, what can I do to help?

This brings us to catalyzation, how we use the power we have in our positions of privilege to enlist in the battle against the preservation of injustice. This can come in many forms, but a willingness to break away from the status quo and take on thoughtful social risk is imperative (Johnson, 1997). We must launch our critiques from within our privileged groups, become allies with marginalized groups, and stand up against oppressive systems and ideologies. There is no consensus on the efficacy of any individual method of ideological reform, but the opportunities are plentiful and appear every day. For example, one might abstain from consuming animal products, volunteering with advocacy organizations, being open to having conversations about speciesism and human supremacy, or participating in social and political disruptions, to name just a few. Whatever methods for eliminating privilege one chooses, what is absolutely certain is that as human animals, we must challenge our own species privilege and transform it into true advocacy for more-than humans. This means actively fighting to end the long-standing stranglehold of human supremacy.

NOTES

1. The Phrase "preservation of injustice" originally comes from the writing of Dr. Martin Luther King Jr. in his 1963 "Letter From Birmingham Jail." In the letter, King asked, "Will we be extremists for the preservation of injustice, or will we be extremists for the cause of Justice?"
2. These examples originated in Peggy McIntosh's 1988 essay "White Privilege: Unpacking the Invisible Knapsack."

SELECTED BIBLIOGRAPHY

Adams, C. J. (2016). *The Carol J. Adams reader: writings and conversations 1995–2015*. Bloomsbury Publishing USA.

Adams, C. J. (1995). Living among meat-eaters: An interview with Carol Adams. *Satya: A magazine of vegetarianism, environmentalism, and animal advocacy*. https://caroljadams.com/living-among-meat-eaters-an-interview-with-carol-adams

Allcock, L. & Barratt, I. (2014). *Watasenia ccintillans*. The IUCN red list of threatened species. https://doi.org/10.2305/iucn.uk.2014-1.rlts.t163146a977074.en

Alcoff, L (2007). Epistemologies of ignorance: Three types. In Sullivan, S., & Tuana, N. (Ed.) *Race and epistemologies of ignorance* (pp. 39–57). SUNY Press.

Appelrouth, S., & Edles, L. D. (2008). *Classical and contemporary sociological theory: Text and readings*. Pine Forge Press.

Black, L. L. & Stone, D. (2005). Expanding the Definition of Privilege: The Concept of Social Privilege. *Journal of Multicultural Counseling and Development*, 33(4), 243–255. https://doi.org/10.1002/j.2161-1912.2005.tb00020.x

Boisseron, B. (2018). *Afro-Dog: blackness and the animal question*. Columbia University Press.

Braudel, F. (1982). *Civilization and capitalism, 15th–18th century: The wheels of commerce*. HarperCollins.

Brueck, J. F. (2017). *Veganism in an oppressive world: A vegans-of-color community project*.

Brune, A. (2005, October 5). PETA exhibit provokes anger from blacks. *Orlando Sentinel*. https://www.orlandosentinel.com/news/os-xpm-2005-10-05-peta05-1-story.html

Bruner, B. (2017). *Biocentrism in environmental ethics*. https://study.com/academy/lesson/biocentrism-in-environmental-ethics.html

Bunyasi, T. L. & Smith, C. W. (2019). *Stay woke: A people's guide to making all black lives matter.* New York University Press.

Cassidy, E. S., Foley, J. A., Gerber, J. S., & West, P. C. (2013). Redefining Agricultural Yields: From Tonnes to People Nourished per Hectare. *Environmental Research Letters.*

Chomsky, N. (2013, January 12). Noam Chomsky: The responsibility of privilege [Online Talk]. In *Talk to Al Jazeera*. Al Jazeera. https://www.aljazeera.com/programmes/talktojazeera/2013/01/201311294541129427.html

Cory, E. (2016). The Rooftop Raven Project: An Exploratory, Qualitative Study of Puzzle Solving Ability in Wild and Captive Ravens. *The University of Arizona.*

Crenshaw, K. (2015, September 25). Why intersectionality can't wait. *The Washington Post*. https://www.washingtonpost.com/news/in-theory/wp/2015/09/24/why-intersectionality-cant-wait/

Crosley-Corcoran, G. (2014, May 8). Explaining white privilege to a broke white person. https://www.huffpost.com/entry/explaining-white-privilege-to-a-broke-white-person_b_5269255

Doty, R. L., & Müller-Schwarze, D. (1992). Chemical signals in vertebrates 6. *Springer Science & Business Media.*

Du Bois, W. E. B. (1903). *The souls of black folk: Essays and sketches*. A. C. McClurg & Co.

Duin, J. (2012, May 5). The animal-rights movement graduates into an academic field. https://www.seattletimes.com/nation-world/the-animal-rights-movement-graduates-into-an-academic-field/

ESF. (2009, February 25). Birds move north with climate change. *Newswise*. https://www.newswise.com/articles/birds-move-north-with-climate-change

Girshick, L. (2014). In the Doing and the Being. In W. Tuttle (Ed.), *Circles of compassion: Essays connecting issues of justice* (pp. 54–62). Vegan Publishers.

Hansen, N. C. (2010). Rethinking Cross-Species Relations: Feminist Interventions. *Michigan Feminist Studies*, *23*(1). https://quod.lib.umich.edu/cgi/t/text/text-idx?cc=mfsfront;c=mfs;c=mfsfront;idno=ark5583.0023.103;rgn=main;view=text;xc=1;g=mfsg

Jackson, Z. I. (2020). *Becoming human: Matter and meaning in an antiblack world.* NYU Press.

Jensen, D. (2016). *The myth of human supremacy*. Seven Stories Press.

Johnson, A. G. (1997). *Privilege, power, and difference*. Temple University Press.

Jones, P. (2014). *The oxen at the intersection*. Lantern Books.

Joy, M. (2019). *Powerarchy: Understanding the psychology of oppression for social transformation*. Berrett-Koehler Publishers.

Kim, C. J. (2015). *Dangerous crossings*. Cambridge University Press.

Kimmel, M. S. (2018). *Privilege: A reader*. Routledge.

Kimmerer, R. W. (2013). *Braiding sweetgrass*. Milkweed Editions.

Lichtenberg, G. C. (1990). *Aphorisms*. Penguin Classics.

Malik, K. (2020, June 14). "White privilege" is a distraction, leaving racism and power untouched. *The Guardian*. https://www.theguardian.com/commentisfree/2020/jun/14/white-privilege-is-a-lazy-distraction-leaving-racism-and-power-untouched

Marchant-Forde, J. N., Marchant-Forde, R. M., & Weary, D. M. (2002). Responses of Dairy Cows and Calves to Each Other's Vocalisations After Early Separation. *Applied Animal Behaviour Science*, 78(1), 19–28. https://doi.org/10.1016/s0168-1591(02)00082-5

McIntosh, P. (1989). White Privilege: Unpacking the invisible knapsack. *Peace and Freedom Magazine.*

McIntosh, P. (2019). *On privilege, fraudulence, and teaching as learning: Selected essays 1981–2019*. Routledge.

Montford, K. S., & Taylor, C. (2020). Colonialism and Animality. In *Colonialism and Animality* (pp. 1–16). https://doi.org/10.4324/9781003013891-101

Nocella, A. J., Matsuoka, A., Socha, K., & Sorenson, J.(2014). *Defining critical animal studies: An intersectional social justice approach for liberation*. Peter Lang.

O'Brien, J. (2009). *Encyclopedia of gender and society.* SAGE.

Online Etymology Dictionary (2021). Privilege. In *Online etymology dictionary*. https://www.etymonline.com/search?q=privilege

Patterson, C. (2002). *Eternal treblinka: Our treatment of animals and the holocaust.* Lantern Books.

Pellow, D. (2014). *Total liberation: The power and promise of animal rights and the radical earth movement* (pp. 5–6). University of Minnesota Press.

Potter, W. (2011). *Green is the new red: An insider's account of a social movement under siege*. City Lights Publishers.

Quinn, T. P. (2018). *The behavior and ecology of pacific salmon and trout.* University of Washington Press.

Roberts, J. (2020, June 8). *White academia: Do better*. The Faculty. https://medium.com/the-faculty/white-academia-do-better-fa96cede1fc5

Salomon, D. (2010). From Marginal Cases to Linked Oppressions: Reframing the Conflict Between the Autistic Pride and Animal Rights Movements. *Journal for Critical Animal Studies*, *8*(1/2), 47–72.

Sebastian, C. (2014). Slavery. It's still a thing. https://veganpublishers.com/slavery-its-still-a-thing-christopher-sebastian-mcjetters/

Sebastian, C. (2020, July 6). Joe Biden, veganism, and the unbearable privilege of talking about privilege. https://www.christophersebastian.info/post/joe-biden-veganism-and-the-unbearable-privilege-of-talking-about-privilege

Spiegel, M. (1988). *The dreaded comparison: Human and animal slavery*. Mirror Books.

Sullivan, S. (2006). *Revealing whiteness: The unconscious habits of racial privilege*. Indiana University Press.

Taylor, P. W. (1981). The Ethics of Respect for Nature. *Environmental Ethics*, *3*. https://rintintin.colorado.edu/~vancecd/phil308/Taylor.pdf

Wolbring, G. (2014). Ability Privilege: A Needed Addition to Privilege Studies. *Journal for Critical Animal Studies*, *12*(2). https://www.ucalgary.ca/uofc/Others/CRDS/research/faculty/icasjustmine.pdf

Wood, E. M. (2016). *The origin of capitalism: A longer view*. Verso Books.

WWF. (2020). Orangutan species. *World Wildlife Fund.* https://www.worldwildlife.org/species/orangutan

WWF. (2018). Living planet report—2018: Aiming higher. *World Wildlife Fund.* https://c402277.ssl.cf1.rackcdn.com/publications/1187/files/original/LPR2018_Full_Report_Spreads.pdf

Yong, E. (2019, March 28). The worst disease ever recorded. *The Atlantic*. https://www.theatlantic.com/science/archive/2019/03/bd-frogs-apocalypse-disease/585862

Chapter Seven

Manufacturing the Line Between Brutality and Best Practice in the Animal-Industrial Complex

Ellyse Winter

INTRODUCTION

Nicolas Kristof (2015) wrote: "If you torture a single chicken and are caught, you're likely to be arrested. If you scald thousands of chickens alive, you're an industrialist who will be lauded for your acumen" (para. 1). This quotation was published in an article in the *New York Times*, written in response to a recent undercover investigation into a poultry supplier for Gordon Food Service—the largest private foodservice distributor in North America. This quotation mirrors the work of Ruth Harrison (1964) in her observation that while one person being unkind to an animal is generally considered cruelty, situations where large groups of people are unkind to animals for the sake of industry are generally sociopolitically supported. Conducted by Mercy for Animals—a nonprofit organization that aims to prevent cruelty to farmed animals and promote compassionate food choices and policies—the investigation revealed birds having their wings and legs broken as they were violently shackled upside down, frightened birds dragged through an electrified vat of water, birds having their throats slit open while still conscious, and conscious birds scalded to death in feather-removal tanks (Kristof, 2015). Particularly shocking for some was "the speed of the assembly line" which undoubtedly caused "workers to fall behind in ways that inflict agony on the chickens" (Kristof, 2015, para. 6). Mercy for Animals has conducted countless undercover investigations within farms and slaughterhouses across the United States and Canada. While some of these investigations have led to cruelty charges filed against individual workers, others—including the one mentioned above—have been analyzed by a third party and have been found to include no evidence of abuse but rather reveal "industry standard methods" of "humane" treatment and slaughter (Kristof, 2015). Consequently, it seems a boundary exists regarding violence in industrial animal agriculture, between those acts of violence that are criminalized and those that are normalized. Relying on the theoretical dimensions of critical animal studies, the purpose of this chapter is to argue that the line between brutality and best practice in industrial animal agriculture is meaningfully constructed in a way to maintain capitalist imperatives of productivity and profitability. In this chapter, capitalist logic is understood as a dominant ideology that that maintains power and the status quo in society (Gramsci, 1971). To demonstrate this argument, I will discuss the notion of violence as it pertains to animals within industrial animal agriculture. I will examine both the systemic and individualistic violence in industrial animal agriculture, paying particular attention to the Mercy for Animals investigation at Canada's largest dairy farm—Chilliwack Cattle Sales in British Columbia. Further, I will discuss how public reception of this investigation in particular, and others more generally, is ultimately bound to the individualistic and psychopathological conceptualization of violence that undergirds Canada's legal system (Flynn, 2001). In this way, this chapter positions Canada's legal system as a key social institution that maintains capitalist ideology, the power of the elite, and the socially constructed boundaries between both necessary and unnecessary harm and humans and animals. Finally, I will discuss the implications of recognizing violence as an anomaly and leaving intact the structural violence endemic to a capitalist and industrial system of animal agriculture. I anticipate this work being useful to scholars and activists alike, by offering an analysis of a landmark case of farm animal abuse in Canada and calling into question the broader implications of failing to truly take animals seriously as beings worthy of moral consideration in the context of legality and public consciousness.

DEFINING KEY TERMS

Two recurrent terms will be used throughout this analysis—capitalism and the animal-industrial complex. As such, the purpose of this section is to provide a working definition for both of these terms as they will be used throughout this chapter.

Capitalism

Capitalism is understood as both an economic and sociopolitical system that has come to shape all aspects of life (Fairclough, 2010). The two definitive characteristics of a capitalist economy are production for profit and wage labor, whereby the production of commodities is primarily done by private companies who aim to generate profit and use individuals who do not own the company but are given a wage in return for their labor (Stanford, 2008). These two characteristics have led to the emergence of broader patterns, including the drive to accumulate the greatest profit in the least amount of time, the necessity to grow, incessant competition in the marketplace, the urging of people to purchase and consume repeatedly, vast inequality between those who own private companies and those who do not, and the desire to achieve economies of scale, or the increase of output per worker to reduce the relative cost of production labor (Albritton, 2012; Adams et al., 2016; Magdoff & Foster, 2010; Stanford, 2008; Weis, 2012). Moreover, under capitalist imperatives, corporations operate with the desire to increase both the distance between the cost of production and the price the good is eventually sold for and the speed at which commodities are produced and ready to enter the market (Albritton, 2012).

As a particular form of capitalism, neoliberalism is thought of as more aggressive than previous kinds and is largely rooted in unfettered, free-market capitalism that is supported by the state (Stanford, 2008). Neoliberalism, which has been dominant since the late 1970s, revolves around the privatization of public resources and spaces, the reduction of labor costs and public expenditures, the elimination of environmental and safety regulations considered unfavorable to corporations, the transferring of governing responsibilities from the nation-state, and lower corporate taxation made possible through reduced public spending (Fairclough, 2010; Guthman, 2008a; Klein, 2014; Martinez & Garcia, n.d.; Stanford, 2008). While a neoliberal market is purported as the best means to stimulate economic growth and ultimately benefit everyone through the logic of trickle-down economics, the truth of the matter is that the benefits remain exclusive to an elite minority (Klein, 2014; Martinez & Garcia, n.d.).

As the dominant economic system, neoliberalism has also facilitated substantive change in other aspects of social life, including work, education, healthcare, value systems, and lifestyles (Fairclough, 2010). Neoliberalism depends on individuals being socialized into accepting greed, individualism, competition, exploitation, and consumerism as natural and positive characteristics for a flourishing society (Magdoff & Foster, 2010). In particular, the spirit of hyper-individualism encourages individuals to act primarily out of self-interest and emphasizes the agency of individuals over collective control

(Magdoff & Foster, 2010; Stanford, 2008). Moreover, individuals are encouraged to view society as meritocratic, whereby hard work and aptitude alone are thought to determine economic prosperity, with little attention paid to the structural forces that shape access to wealth and other resources (Magdoff & Foster, 2010). Taken together, the policies and practices associated with neoliberalism have contributed to an increasing income gap, economic insecurities, exploitation of labor, and environmental degradation (Fairclough, 2010; Martinez & Garcia, n.d.). For instance, the regulations that allowed multinational corporations to flourish with minimal constraints have also contributed significantly to increased greenhouse gas emissions and global warming (Klein, 2014).

ANIMAL-INDUSTRIAL COMPLEX

The production of meat, eggs, and dairy products within the United States and Canada is now largely dominated by an industrial model, generally characterized by the intensive confinement of a large number of animals and tight control over their breeding, feeding, and living conditions to minimize input and maximize output (Albritton, 2012; Food and Agricultural Organization, 2006; Hendrickson & James, 2005; Gunderson, 2011; Gunderson & Stuart, 2014; MacDonald & McBridge, 2009; Rossi & Garner, 2014; Rowe, 2011; Walker et al., 2005; Wiebe, 2012). Further, facilitated by government subsidies, production is now increasingly in the hands of the largest and most intensive systems, thus representing a shift in political and economic power from the family and community to corporate agribusiness and globalized markets (Mason & Finelli, 2013; Weis, 2013; Wiebe, 2012). Overall, this shift represents a change in how food is conceptualized and valued, from a physiologically and culturally nourishing life-good to a commodity for profit and trade in the marketplace (Wiebe, 2012). It has been argued that within this model, the purpose of livestock production "is *not to create food*, but *to make money*" (Gunderson, 2011, p. 261, emphasis in original). I will refer to this model of producing animal products and by-products as the animal-industrial complex. Similar to the prison-industrial complex and the military-industrial complex, the animal-industrial complex highlights the largely opaque and intersecting interests of the government, agribusiness corporations, and the economy that together result in the commodification and objectification of animals (Fitzgerald & Pellow, 2014; Noske, 1997; Twine, 2012). Further, conceptualizing this model as the animal-industrial complex elucidates how animal agriculture is deeply entrenched in a capitalist logic that depends on large-scale, highly technologized, and depersonalized systems of production for mass consumption and values profit over all else (Noske, 1997; Twine, 2012).

Although this analysis focuses primarily on the harm experienced by animals, it is important to recognize that humans and Earth are also impacted by the capitalist logic underpinning the animal-industrial complex. For instance, research and anecdotal evidence point to the deplorable working conditions and high injury rate experienced by slaughterhouse workers—a workforce made up of primarily racialized and low-income groups (Nibert, 2013; Oxfam America, 2016). Additionally, research illustrates the contributions that the animal-industrial complex makes to some of the most serious environmental problems, including greenhouse gas emissions, water pollution and depletion, land degradation, and biodiversity loss, far exceeds that of other industries (Food and Agricultural Organization, 2006; Oppenlander, 2013).

THEORETICAL FRAMEWORK

This project is rooted in the theoretical dimensions of critical animal studies and a sociology of violence that considers the systemic exploitation of animals. The purpose of this section is to outline the key tenets of this theoretical framework, including a consideration of the linkages to critical analysis more generally, the distinctions from other animal-based approaches, and the need to consider the plight of "food" animals in the sociological analysis of violence.

CRITICAL ANALYSIS

First, it is important to consider how the central objectives of critical animal studies as a discipline are similar to that of critical analysis and function as a branch of critical theory more generally. Critical analysis is broadly rooted in a concern with various forms of social injustice (Fairclough, 2010). Moreover, critical analysis involves the development of explanatory theory that aids in interpreting the root causes of such injustice and ultimately facilitates redress and emancipatory action (Fairclough, 2010). As a branch of critical analysis, critical animal studies is concerned with the entangled injustice experienced by animals, humans, and Earth, how this injustice is rooted in capitalism, and strategies for transformative action (Nibert, 2014). Like other critical approaches, critical animal studies aims to move beyond the production of theory for theory's sake to facilitate meaningful social action (Nibert,

2014). Overall, critical animal studies is rooted in a critical theory that questions power, domination, and the status quo.

DISTINCTION FROM OTHER ANIMAL-BASED APPROACHES

In contrast to other theoretical approaches related to the study of animals, including animal studies and human-animal studies, the field of critical animal studies challenges the notion of animals as objects without agency that are meant to be anatomically or theoretically dissected or examined by detached scholars (Nocella et al., 2014). In this way, critical animal studies recognizes the intrinsic value of animals and suggests that animal perspectives are no less worthy of consideration simply because they are not human (Nibert, 2014). Critical animal studies then contrasts with the scholarly tradition of examining animals without consideration of the violence and exploitation they experience or the researcher's own complicity in such systems of oppression (Nibert, 2014). Further, critical animal studies challenges positivist approaches to research (Nibert, 2014). As such, researchers are encouraged to clarify their own values and commitments according to the notion that all writing and research is political (Best et al., 2007; Nibert, 2014). Moreover, critical animal studies asserts that the animal-industrial complex, amongst other industries involving animal exploitation, is ultimately rooted in a logic of domination and a dichotomous relationship between culture and nature. As such, critical animal studies promotes justice for animals and aims to deconstruct and reconstruct the socially constructed binary oppositions between human and animal, culture and nature, civilization and wilderness, and other dominator hierarchies (Best et al., 2007; Nocella et al., 2014). In this way, a critical animal studies approach seeks to abolish the logic of domination and associated dichotomies, to create a meaningful and respectful notion of difference that does not facilitate domination (Warren, 1993b).

SOCIOLOGY OF VIOLENCE

The routine and normalized killing of animals for food is not typically an issue that has concerned sociologists of violence (Cudworth, 2015). First, some sociologists who research violence are resistant to studying animals out of a belief that this minimizes or undermines violence towards humans (Cudworth, 2015). Second, even those who do engage with violence against animals may disregard the plight of "food" animals and focus primarily on the maltreatment of "companion" animals (Cudworth, 2015). I place the words "food" and "companion" in quotations to indicate the socially constructed nature of these categories. For instance, Flynn (2001) applies a sociological analysis to violence against animals, yet premises his work on a definition of cruelty that excludes practices that are socially acceptable including "the humane killing of farm animals" (p. 72). By focusing exclusively on violence that is considered "socially unacceptable," such as the maltreatment of companion animals, Flynn does little to unpack the troubled logic behind the line that is drawn between justifiable and unjustifiable forms of violence against animals. This is particularly problematic considering that the farming of animals is the most significant social manifestation of human-animal relations (Cudworth, 2015). Consequently, the scale and reach of the violence against farmed animals makes tacitly or explicitly ignoring it within a sociology of violence particularly troubling (Cudworth, 2015).

Putting forward a sociology of violence that does consider the normalized and systemic killing of billions of animals for food urges an examination of where violence is embedded in everyday practices, constituted by and through social institutions, and manifests as a set of power relations (Cudworth, 2015). Within the context of the animal-industrial complex, it is therefore important to consider how the violence associated with breeding, growing, and killing practices are largely regulated and sociopolitically legitimized (Cudworth, 2015). Such a conceptualization of violence is important in emphasizing that the harming of animals transcends individual and socially prohibited actions, and is also institutionalized and socially accepted (Fitzgerald & Pellow, 2014; Porcher, 2011). It should also be noted that although I operationally distinguish systemic violence from individualistic violence, the primary purpose of this chapter is to take issue with the notion that there is a boundary between those acts of violence that are criminalized and those that are normalized. Moreover, I argue that this boundary is manufactured in a way to maintain the status quo of capitalist ideologies related to productivity and profitability.

RESEARCHER ASSUMPTIONS

This section explicitly identifies the assumptions, beliefs, and biases that I, as the researcher, bring to this particular project. As previously mentioned, one of the central tenets of critical animal studies is the rejection of the possibility of an objective or positivist academic analysis (Nibert, 2014). Rather, those engaging with critical animal studies are encouraged to clarify their values and political commitments to recognize that all theory and research is political (Nibert, 2014). As such, in keeping with a critical animal studies approach, I do not wish to present myself as neutral or apolitical in the context of this topic. It is therefore important for me to acknowledge that I have been vegetarian and later vegan for over ten years, partly in resistance to the practices of the animal-industrial complex as to be discussed in this project, but more generally as a *partial* and *incomplete* means of practicing non-injury and harmlessness to all living beings. As such, I have a personal and political investment in resisting the animal-industrial complex and considering the strategies of resistance most conducive to transformative change.

Beyond simply identifying as vegan, I believe it is also crucial for me to recognize how my various social identities impact my access to and engagement with veganism. I am deeply indebted to the work of scholars such as Dr. Breeze Harper (2010a/2010b/2010c/2011a/2011b/2013) and activists such as Lauren Ornealas for urging this recognition. In particular, I am mindful of the immense social privileges I experience as a white, settler, middle-class, cisgender, heterosexual, and able-bodied person and recognize how these positionalities are interwoven in my vegan praxis. First, when I considered making the change from an omnivorous to a veg[etari]an diet, I was able to easily locate resources and information to assist in this transition. Moreover, the assumptions and values implicit to the resources and information I accessed largely aligned with those of my own social location, or more specifically, they perpetuated whiteness as the norm and took for granted access to particular goods that may be associated with middle-class privilege. Second, my social class and geographic location have afforded me consistent access to plant-based staples, such as fruits, vegetables, grains, legumes, etc. and the ability to prepare and store such foods. Third, I have never been criticized for sacrificing cultural authenticity or rejecting my religion, ethnicity, or identity in my decision to abstain from animal products and by-products (Greenebaum, 2017; Robinson, 2013). While veganism does lie in contrast to my familial roots and traditions, it does not dismantle our sense of collective identity or impact particular entitlements, as my family's foodways have not been colonized. Finally, I have not been criticized for failing to conform to socially constructed gender expectations, or more specifically, been accused of being weak or inappropriately feminine for the choice not to consume animal products and by-products (Greenebaum, 2017).

SYSTEMIC VIOLENCE IN THE ANIMAL-INDUSTRIAL COMPLEX

Approximately 64 billion land animals are killed each year globally for food (Food and Agricultural Organization, 2006; Weis, 2013; Sorenson, 2010; Walker et al., 2005). However, death in and of itself is not the focus of this section, but rather the particular conditions experienced by such animals in life and death and how these conditions are shaped by a capitalist logic (Deckha, 2012). Shaped by capitalist values of profit and productivity, animals are viewed as commodities, often raised in desolate and restrictive environments, and forced to endure routinized forms of violence (Kim, 2011; Mason & Finelli, 2013; Rossi & Garner, 2014). For instance, methods of confining animals such as battery cages, veal crates, gestation crates, and tethering prohibit an animal from stretching his or her legs or wings, turning around, or lying down comfortably (Kim, 2011; Mason & Finelli, 2013; Rowe, 2011). In this way, Medero (2014) argues that an animal confined for the majority of his or her life is not alive, but rather "simply not dead" or kept perpetually "in a realm of not dying" (p. 209). Further, the overcrowding of animals often requires continuous anatomical and physiological manipulation to maintain the mass production of animal products and by-products (Mason & Finelli, 2013). For instance, to manage the biting, pecking, and fighting that can occur as a result of overcrowding and the disruption of social groups, pigs' tails and birds' beaks are frequently cut off (Mason & Finelli, 2013; Rossi & Garner, 2014; Rowe, 2011). Rather than addressing the underlying cause of such stress-related problems, animal bodies are mutated in order to maintain capitalist imperatives of productivity and profitability (Mason & Finelli, 2013).

Further, the animal-industrial complex relies on processes of reproductive manipulation to guarantee continuous impregnation and production of future animal products and by-products (Cudworth, 2010; Gillespie, 2014; Mason & Finelli, 2013; Rossi & Garner, 2014; Weis, 2013). For instance, dairy cows, like other mammals, produce milk following pregnancy and delivery (Berreville, 2014). As such, to initiate milk production, farmers often forcibly ejaculate bulls and impregnate cows using human hands, arms, and instruments (Bereville, 2014; Cudworth, 2015; Gillespie, 2014). Moreover, to accelerate reproductive cycles, and to prevent calves from consuming any of the milk intended for them that can instead be sold to humans, calves are often prematurely separated from their mothers and fed milk replacer or waste whole milk (Bereville, 2014; Mason & Finelli, 2013). As such, although a calf might nurse and run with his or her mother for approximately one year in nature, on many large-scale dairy farms the calf is typically removed from the mother shortly after birth (Mason & Finelli, 2013). In fact, this practice is built right into the National Farm Animal Council's (2009) *Code of Practice for the Care and Handling of Dairy Cattle* which states:

> Generally, dairy calves are separated from their mothers shortly after birth. There are benefits to both the calf and dam by allowing the pair to bond. Allowing the calf to spend a longer period of time with the dam may result in

> lowered morbidity and mortality in the calf; however, separation stress to both the cow and calf will be higher the longer they are together. (p. 26)

Anecdotal evidence from life-long dairy farmers has illustrated cows bellowing for their young for weeks after premature separation (Gillespie, 2014). Consequently, although industry-based and anecdotal evidence points to the negative impact that prematurely removing a calf from his or her mother can have, it is considered best practice—code for most profitable—to remove the calf shortly after birth. This psychological violence caused by separation is therefore an inherent product of an industrial system, wherein the demands of uninterrupted milk production result in an endless cycle of insemination, pregnancy, calving, calf removal, and lactation for cows (Berreville, 2014).

Moreover, the inability to express species-life behaviors is also considered a form of violence enacted on animals within the industrial complex and raises considerable ethical questions (Weis, 2012). In this way, the harm inflicted on animals within systems of industrial agriculture is not solely physical, but also stems from how animals are manipulated to live in systems that reflect human needs and economic priorities rather than their own natures and preferences (Anthony, 2012; Corman & Vandrovcova, 2014; Davis, 2004/2010; Weis, 2012). Such systems ignore the fact that animals are sentient beings capable of developing profound social relationships and possess emotional lives, preferences, desires, and innate tendencies that they would express in natural conditions (Davis, 2010; Corman & Vandrovcova, 2014; Cudworth, 2015; Medero, 2014; Kim, 2011; Nibert, 2013; Rossi & Garner, 2014; Weis, 2013). For instance, within the confines of battery cages, egg-laying hens cannot take a real dustbath, which acts not only as a cleansing activity but also as a social gathering (Davis, 2012).

Lastly, in an effort to increase turnover time, animals' lifespans are cut drastically short within systems of industrial agriculture (Weis, 2013). For instance, cattle can now reach commercial slaughter weight in eighteen months, pigs in as few as six months, and broiler chickens in only six weeks (Weis, 2013). As this time approaches, animals may be shipped long distances to slaughter without food or water, are frequently exposed to extremes of heat and cold during transport, and experience overcrowding, making them subject to suffocation and crushing (Berreville, 2014; Cudworth, 2015; Rossi & Garner, 2014; Rowe, 2011). According to a recent article published by CTV National News, Canada's livestock transportation rules are the worst in the Western world. These rules allow for pigs, chickens, and cattle to be transported between 36 and 52 hours without access to food or water and without minimum or maximum temperature regulations to protect the animals from harsh winters or extreme heat (Schulman, 2016). As a result, the Canadian Food Inspection Agency highlights that between two and three million animals die during transport every year (Schulman, 2016). Further, animals are often handled roughly during transport, particularly during the stages of loading and unloading where they may be corralled using electric prods (Rossi & Garner, 2014). Moreover, given the expected line speeds within industrial slaughterhouses that may not allow time for proper stunning, animals may be scalded, skinned, or dismembered while partly or fully conscious (Rossi & Garner, 2014).

Each of these implications for animals is closely linked to the capitalist imperatives of maximizing productivity and profits through the implementation of labor-saving and "more-efficient" technologies (Gunderson, 2011). More specifically, issues of confinement and overcrowding, anatomical and reproductive manipulation, and transport and slaughter reveal the methods in place for minimizing inputs and maximizing outputs, increasing the gap between the production costs and market prices, and decreasing the amount of time it takes to convert a live animal into a commercial good ready to be bought and sold in the marketplace (Albritton, 2012; Magdoff & Foster, 2010; Weis, 2012). Moreover, these issues draw attention how animals are transformed from living and feeling beings into machines (Gillespie, 2014; Kim, 2011; Sorenson, 2010; Stanescu, 2013). As legal property of their owners, every aspect of the machine is controlled as animals become cogs in the capitalist wheel of production whose bodies are not truly their own in life or in death (Deckha, 2010; Gillespie, 2014; Kim, 2011; Sorenson, 2010; Stanescu, 2013). As Stanescu (2013) poignantly states, "within factory farms it isn't just that we experience death that can't be called death, but also life that cannot be called life" (p. 153).

INDIVIDUALISTIC VIOLENCE IN THE ANIMAL-INDUSTRIAL COMPLEX

While systemic violence in the animal-industrial complex has referred to those acts of violence inherent to standard industry procedures, individualistic acts of violence refer to "exceptional cases of cruelty or gross animal welfare violations" (Gillespie, 2014, p. 1232) and those "individual acts of sadistic abuse [that] deliberately inflict pain on animals for no legally accepted purpose" (Sorenson, 2003, p. 380). As previously mentioned, although I distinguish systemic violence from individualistic violence, my aim is to problematize the notion that some acts of violence are legitimate and others are sadistic and suggest that the distinction is strategically manufactured in a way to maintain productivity and profitability. To contextualize the notion of individualistic violence in the animal-industrial complex, I will focus primarily on one case, although there is no shortage of existing cases.

In 2014, Mercy for Animals conducted an undercover investigation at Canada's largest dairy farm—Chilliwack Cattle Sales. Chilliwack Cattle Sales milks approximately 3,500 cows at its main location, compared to the average Canadian operation that runs 77 cattle (Hutchinson, 2014). The video footage captured during this investigation revealed workers viciously kicking, punching, and beating cows in the face and body with chains, canes, metal pipes, and rakes, including downed and trapped cows who could not escape the abuse. Many cows were shown to be suffering from open wounds, oozing infections, and painful injuries. Workers were poking and squeezing wounds, ripping clumps of hair out of cows' tails, and punching bulls in the testicles (Hutchinson, 2014). Moreover, the footage revealed workers using chains and tractors to lift sick and injured cows by their necks (Mercy for Animals, 2014). Furthermore, the formal complaint to the British Columbia Society for the Prevention of Cruelty to Animals (BCSPCA) and the Royal Canadian Mounted Police (RCMP) indicated that some employees laughed and made rude comments as they inflicted harm upon the cows (Hutchinson, 2014). This formal complaint included 14 incidents of alleged abuse against a worker, Brad Genereux, who "beat a cow who had recently given birth, as evidenced by the retained placenta hanging out of her uterus" and "attached milking equipment to three separate bulls' testes while they were trapped in the rotary [milking] parlor . . . [who] tried to kick away the machinery but could not" (Hutchinson, 2014, para. 14). The complaint also included allegations against a worker, Travis Keefer, who "repeatedly whipped cows trapped in parlor stall hocks," "jabbed a cow in the face with a metal pole," and "twisted a cow's tail until a 'pop' could be heard" (Hutchinson, 2014, para. 16). Another employee is cited 34 times in the complaint lodged by Mercy for Animals for "viciously beat[ing] two cows for over two minutes, holding the cane with both arms and winding up above his head, clenching his jaw with exertion . . . jam[ming] a cow in her sensitive genital region . . . [and saying] 'I just fuckin' hit that cow like 50 times'" (Hutchinson, 2014, para. 17).

The investigation led to a raid of the facility by law enforcement and the BC SPCA recommended Criminal Code Charges against the eight employees identified in the video for "willfully causing unnecessary pain, suffering, and injury to animals" (BC SPCA, 2014, para. 2). This was in fact a landmark case in that it was the first time that farm animal cruelty led to jail time in Canada. Individuals involved in the abuse received prison sentences ranging from 1 week to 60 days and prohibition from having custody or care of any animals (Hernandez, 2017). While this may seem like an insufficient sentence in light of the violence these animals endured, it sets legal precedent for taking the abuse of "food" animals more seriously. Additionally, Chilliwack Cattle Sales and one of its owners were convicted of animal cruelty and ordered to pay fines totaling almost $350,000 (Hernandez, 2017). The case also sparked outrage across Canada and mainstream media coverage by the *National Post*, Global News, CBC News, and *The Province* (Mercy for Animals, 2014). Jeff Kooyman, who co-owns the farm with his siblings, told CBC News (2014) that his family was devastated by the allegations and said: "The guys were going crazy . . . I couldn't imagine how people could do that to animals" (para. 16). Moreover, Kooyman insisted that the farm has zero tolerance for animal abuse, stating: "This is a family farm and this is not what we're all about . . . maybe I failed to instill the passion and love that we have into our employees" (CBC News, 2014, para. 20). Such comments speak to a larger pattern, whereby the outrage expressed by institutions when workers "unnecessarily" abuse animals attempts to ensure the public that overall animal welfare on industrial farms is sufficient.

Despite Kooyman's insistence that he and his family were unaware of the abuse and that this behavior is "not what [they're] all about" (CBC News, 2014, para. 20) others have suggested "the conduct is part of the culture at this facility and not simply the modus operandi of a rogue or mentally unstable individual" (Hutchinson, 2014, para. 2). For instance, the Mercy for Animals activist who conducted the undercover investigation was hired on the spot and started work the next day without having to provide a resume or references or undergo any form of training (Hutchinson, 2014). Particularly noteworthy was a comment that Brad Genereux, one of the terminated employees, posted to his Facebook page after the allegations: "It's pretty interesting seeing people put all the blame on 8 guys from a farm that's been training and operating in this way for years" (Hutchinson, 2014, para. 14). As such, it is important to consider the degree to which these forms of individualistic violence are bound to the broader industrial system. We must also question the degree to which individual farm workers have become victimized by the system and the dehumanizing nature of the work and have become manipulated by industry and societal discourses regarding animals.

CANADA'S LEGAL SYSTEM AND THE PERPETUATION OF VIOLENCE

The reception and consequences of the Mercy for Animals investigation into Chilliwack Cattle Sales, among other investigations conducted by Mercy for Animals, illustrates how Canada's legal system perpetuates an individualistic and psychopathological perspective of violence and leaves intact the systemic violence foundational to the animal-industrial complex (Flynn, 2001). I will rely on the Criminal Code of Canada, the Meat Inspection Act, the Health Inspection Act, British Columbia's Prevention of Cruelty to Animals Act, and the National Farm Animal Care Council Codes of Practice to juxtapose the significance of the Chilliwack Cattle Sales investigation with the significance of the violence inherent to standard industry procedures within the animal-industrial complex. Moreover, I will highlight that this significance is bound to concerns regarding productivity and profitability.

While societal attitudes toward our relationship with other animals are progressing, Canada's legal system still largely reflects outdated understandings of animals as property and mere machines without the capacity for pain, suffering, emotion, perception, or intention (Bisgould, King, & Stopford, 2001). As such, Canada's regulation of animal agriculture emphasizes preserving the value of animal products with little to no concern for the welfare of animals themselves (Bisgould et al., 2001). Consequently, it is important to "distinguish between regulations meant to protect animals and those meant to protect the products we make from them" (Bisgould et al., 2001, p. 3). For instance, Bisgould et al. (2001) highlight the frequent references in the legislation to the need for "humane" treatment of animals and the avoidance of "willful," "unnecessary," "undue," or "avoidable" pain and suffering and problematize the fact that these terms are not adequately defined and reinforce the notion that some degree of violence is in fact acceptable in the name of industry. For example, Section 139 of the Health of Animals Act (2015) states that "no person shall beat an animal being loaded or unloaded in a way likely to cause injury or *undue* suffering to it" (emphasis added, p. 87). Further, Section 140 of the Health of Animals Act (2015) prohibits the overcrowding of animals to transport that occurs "to such an extent as to be likely to cause injury or *undue* suffering" (emphasis added, p. 88). Moreover, Section 62 of the Meat Inspection Act (2014) states that "no food animal shall be handled in a manner that subjects the animal to *avoidable* distress or *avoidable* pain" (emphasis added, p. 60). Additionally, in particular reference to cattle, Section 445 of Canada's Criminal Code (2015) criminalizes one who "*willfully* kills, maims, wounds, poisons or injures cattle" (emphasis added, p. 441). This notion of "unnecessary," "undue," "avoidable," or "willful" suffering can thus be understood as those individual acts of violence against animals that are meant to deliberately cause pain without lawful purpose (Sorenson, 2003).

Furthermore, Bisgould et al. problematize the fact that many aspects of the daily existence of animals are unregulated and that governments have deferred a large portion of the authority to voluntary care standards created by the industry. The authors elaborate in saying:

> Given that the goal of industry is to earn the greatest possible profit, it is difficult to imagine how, in the absence of mandatory regulation, these Codes can provide meaningful protection to animals. If the standard is to simply do what everybody else in a competitive industry is doing, there is no incentive

> to consider the non-economic interests of animals. These, after all, can only require capital outlays which decrease profits. (Bisgould et al., 2001, p. 5)

This passage draws attention to the disparate situation of expecting meaningful strides in animal welfare to occur within an industry specifically, and within a capitalist society more generally, that maximizes productivity and profitability. Given that this report was published in 2001, it is important to acknowledge that the National Farm Animal Care Council has since released several revised Codes of Practice, intended to regulate the care and handling of farmed animals. For instance, The Code of Practice for the Care and Handling of Dairy Cattle was released in 2009 to replace the original dairy code released in 1990. A presentation published by the Dairy Farmers of Canada (2009) suggests that the revised code outlines industry requirements that go beyond recommended best practices and is said to illuminate Canada's dairy industry as "an active leader in animal care improvement" and Canada's dairy farmers as those who "care about their animals" and "invest research in animal care" (Dairy Farmers of Canada, 2009, p. 3). Following these romanticized statements regarding the welfare of cattle on Canada's dairy farms is the statement: "A comfortable cow is a productive cow" (Dairy Farmers of Canada, 2009, p. 3). Again, this demonstrates the importance of distinguishing "between regulations meant to protect animals and those meant to protect the products [and profits] we make from them" (Bisgould et al., 2001, p. 3). Moreover, despite these revisions, a lack of regulation and enforcement of these Codes of Practice still remains. Speaking directly to the revised Code of Practice for the Care and Handling of Dairy Cattle, the BC SPCA (2014a) highlights that "currently, there is no independent monitoring to ensure that dairy cattle are being cared for humanely" (para. 3). Moreover, the Codes of Practice have yet to be adopted into B.C. law, as in many other Canadian provinces (BC SPCA, 2014a). Further, many of the investigations conducted by Mercy for Animals, including the investigation conducted into Chilliwack Cattle Sales, were done after the revised codes had been published and still revealed the occurrence of individual and systemic abuse. Consequently, although the Dairy Farmers of Canada (2009) have suggested that the revised Codes of Practice for farm animals are meant to enforce minimum acceptable standards, they remain largely voluntary, and thus ignored, across Canada. Within British Columbia, for instance, only one dairy farm—Little Qualicum Cheeseworks—is currently SPCA Certified, meaning that they have been found to adhere to the Code of Practice for dairy cattle (BC SPCA, 2014a). Consequently, all others have yet to adopt the Code of Practice which only represents the bare minimum in terms of acceptable standards. In addition to protecting the products and profits accrued through the violence against farmed animals in industrial systems, it seems as though revisions such as those made to the Code of Practice for the Care and Handling of Dairy Cattle and other legal frameworks relevant to the animal-industrial complex are intended to ensure the comfort of human consumers regarding the sourcing of their animal products. In part, such policies serve as an attempt at manufacturing consumer docility and ignorance regarding the conditions behind the production of meat, dairy, and eggs.

Consequently, the reception and consequences of the investigation into Chilliwack Cattle Sales demonstrates a focus on dealing "with individuals who deliberately inflict pain on animals for no legally accepted purpose" (Sorenson, 2003, p. 380). As previously mentioned, in light of the video footage and the formal complaint released by Mercy for Animals, the BC SPCA (2014b) recommended Criminal Code charges against the eight employees identified in the video for "willfully causing pain, suffering and injury to animals" (para. 2). Consequently, the legal system has deemed the kicking, punching, and beating of cows in the face and body and the use of chains and tractors to lift sick or injured animals by their necks as "willful" violence and suffering. While I do not disagree that these particular acts of violence did cause "willful" or "unnecessary" suffering, I would suggest that the systemic acts of violence including intensive confinement, the physiological and anatomical manipulation of farmed animals' bodies, of transportation of slaughter, continuous artificial ejaculation and insemination, premature separation of newborn animals from their mothers, and the denial of species-life behaviors also cause "willful" and "unnecessary" suffering, given that alternative foods and agricultural practices are possible (Bisgould et al., 2001; Sorenson, 2003). More specifically, Bisgould et al., (2001) argue that:

> Many, if not all of the practices by which animals are turned into food could be considered to be violations of [the Criminal Code] in that they cause pain, suffering or injury to animals for an ultimate purpose which is not "necessary" in any true sense of the word. Relying on animals for food may be done for reasons of custom, habit, or preference, but it cannot be considered "necessary" in most parts of Canada. (p. 12)

Consequently, the words "willful," "unnecessary," "undue," or "avoidable" within Canadian legislation regarding animal agriculture would more accurately be replaced with "unproductive" or "unprofitable" in reference to the pain and suffering inflicted on animals in the animal-industrial complex. The systemic acts of violence such as the physiological and anatomical manipulation of farmed animal bodies or the premature separation of newborn animals from their mothers allow the industry to maximize productivity and profitability. Whereas, the kicking, punching, and beating of cows in the face and body and the use of chains and tractors to lift sick or injured animals by their necks do not, and perhaps even briefly decrease productivity and profitability in instances where these acts of violence are recorded and lead to negative publicity and the temporary uneasiness of the consumer. Ultimately, the reason that the eight employees were terminated and faced criminal charges is because they were caught causing "unprofitable" and "unproductive" harm to animals. As outlined by Bisgould et al., activities that are institutionally abusive, standard practice, and commonly done are not within the realm of Canada's legislature regarding animal agriculture.

IMPLICATIONS

Up to this point in the analysis, I have argued that the line between normalized and criminalized violence within the animal-industrial complex is meaningfully constructed in a way to maintain capitalist imperatives of productivity and profitability. Examining the legal reception of an undercover investigation that took place at Chilliwack Cattle Sales in British Columbia, I have positioned Canada's legal system as a key social institution that perpetuates an individualistic conceptualization of violence, maintains capitalist ideology and the power of the elite, and leaves intact the structural violence endemic to the animal-industrial complex. I will consider the social landscape for and broader implications of this legal framework and discuss possibilities for transformative social change. It is important to consider the interplay between capitalist production, cultural norms, and laws that perpetuate the animal-industrial complex and our reliance upon it. While the focus of this work has been on understanding the legal system as an institution that maintains the boundary between necessary and unnecessary harm and capitalist imperatives within the animal-industrial complex, it is crucial to consider that the legal system does not exist in isolation from other social forces, and to therefore recognize the complex reciprocity between social institutions and social attitudes to facilitate transformative change.

DISTANCE BETWEEN PRODUCTION AND CONSUMPTION

To begin, it is important to situate this legal framework within the context of an increasing distance between the producers and consumers of food, facilitated by an industrial food system (Albritton, 2012). With fewer people involved in food production, the industrial food system is premised on a drastically different relationship with animals and Earth and both a spatial and conceptual distance between the production and consumption of food

(Anthony, 2012; Gross, 2011; Hudson & Hudson, 2003; Knezevic, 2012; Weis, 2012/2013). A consequence of this distance is that the socioecological implications of the animal-industrial complex are largely hidden from society and obscured by market strategies, leaving consumers with limited knowledge about exactly what is involved in the food products they purchase and consume (Greenebaum, 2017; Gross, 2012; Hudson & Hudson, 2003; Knezevic, 2012; Weis, 2012/2013). I argue that it is, in part, this distance that allows for the systemic exploitation of animals within the industrial complex to be maintained. Not only are the socioecological implications of the animal-industrial complex largely hidden from society, but our understanding of food production generally and animal agriculture more specifically are further veiled by industry promotions designed to hide the violent reality of industrial farming. For instance, society has become inundated with the ruralized and romanticized labelling and advertising of animal products (Mason & Finelli, 2007). Billboards, television, and Internet advertisements, and food packaging commonly feature rolling hills, country homes, small red barns, grazing cattle, and animals roaming freely and thus perpetuate an image of farm life as rustic and serene. Glenn (2004) highlights one example in particular—the Happy Cows advertising campaign launched by the California Milk Advisory Board in October 2000—which included television, radio, and billboard ads and merchandise for children and adults that featured "healthy, clever, and funny animals enjoying their easy lives and happily consenting to 'contributing' their share to the 'family' business" (p. 73). Particularly troubling, is that this campaign is being credited in part for advancing California's dairy industry ahead of Wisconsin's and vastly increasing profitability (Glenn, 2004). Glenn (2004) also highlights the industry's use of "doublespeak" as a discursive strategy, whereby one is "intentionally misleading by being ambiguous or disingenuous" (p. 64). For instance, the industry has recommended using the euphemism family farm rather than factory or high intensity farm, despite the tremendous size and corporate ownership of these facilities (Glenn, 2004). Interestingly, this is evidenced in light of the abuse allegations against Chilliwack Cattle Sales, as Jeff Kooyman—the co-owner of the largest dairy farm in Canada—insisted that "this is a family farm and this is not what we're all about" (CBC News, 2014, para. 20). In this way, consumers engage with a food object that is largely divorced from the socioecological implications behind it, are discouraged from seeking additional context, and may thus have difficulty recognizing and addressing the resultant implications (Hudson & Hudson, 2003; Rowe, 2011; Sage, 2011). Consequently, given that the adverse effects of the animal-industrial complex are purposely hidden or minimized within public consciousness, the Mercy for Animals investigations are crucial for "removing the veil" (Hudson & Hudson, 2003) and illustrating the reality of the animal-industrial complex as starkly different from the discourses perpetuated by the industry.

HUMAN-ANIMAL BINARY

The socially constructed boundary between necessary and unnecessary harm lends itself to an analysis of other socially constructed boundaries that facilitate the exploitation of animals. As such, it is important to locate the legal framework within the context of the socially constructed binary between humans and animals and to consider how this boundary is meaningfully constructed to maintain the power of humans. Such contextualization is in keeping with a critical animal studies approach which argues that the animal-industrial complex, amongst other industries involving the exploitation of animals, is ultimately rooted in a logic of domination and a dichotomous relationship between human and animal (Best et al., 2007; Nocella et al., 2014). In the human-animal binary, humans are considered superior to animals on the basis of uniquely possessing arbitrary characteristics such as civility, rationality, and moral agency (Fitzgerald & Pellow, 2014; Warren, 1993a). Critical animal studies scholars argue that this binary between humans and animals is socially constructed, which is not to suggest that species differences do not exist, but that the conception of and value attached to humans and animals is rooted in particular social, historical, and cultural contexts and used to justify exploitation (Warren, 1993a). While many have argued for the socially constructed nature of gender and racial difference, whose naturalness at one point was believed to be objective fact, humanity generally remains uninterrogated as a socially constructed category (Deckha, 2006). We can begin to understand the human as a socially constructed category by considering how understandings of humanity have been, and still can be, exclusive of some humans (Deckha, 2006; Harper, 2011a; Ko, 2015). The category of human is thus understood as socially constructed in a way that marginalizes both animals and particular groups of humans (Deckha, 2006). I argue that this socially constructed boundary between humans and animals is an important part of the social landscape within which cases such as the abuse at Chilliwack Cattle Sales persist. Being socialized into accepting this boundary as natural allows for a justification of systemic violence committed in the name of industry and self-interest. These boundaries allow us to distance ourselves from animals, feel comfortable and complacent in their exploitation, and are reinforced by social institutions such as the legal system, which consider animals as property and offer the bare minimum in moral consideration. Consequently, the human-animal binary, stemming largely from the colonial legacies of European imperialism, calls for critical interrogation (Armstrong, 2002; Deckha, 2008b; Rowe, 2016).

AFFIRMATIVE RESPONSES TO INJUSTICE

Understanding the connection between the economy, societal values, and the legal system in an effort to facilitate meaningful resistance calls for an understanding of the distinction between affirmative and transformative responses to injustice. Where affirmation "aims at correcting inequitable outcomes without disturbing the underlying framework that generates them," transformative remedies are aimed at "correcting inequitable outcomes precisely by restructuring the underlying generative framework" (Fraser, 1997, p. 23). A legal system that criminalizes particular forms of violence but not others within the animal-industrial complex represents an affirmative response to injustice in that it allows consumers to focus their gaze on the individual, rather than on the systemic acts of violence that farmed animal bodies are subjected to in everyday practice. The individual "sadist" is implicated and the violence is written off as an anomaly within the system, meanwhile the brokenness of the entire capitalist and industrial system of agriculture is left intact and further legitimatized.

Moreover, mainstream discourses surrounding resistance of the animal-industrial complex often rely on statements such as, "if slaughterhouses had glass walls, everyone would be vegetarian" or "if people only knew where their food came from, they would make different choices." Although useful in the way they speak to the disconnect many North Americans have from the production of the meat, dairy, and eggs they consume, I argue that such sentiments are overly simplistic and represent affirmative responses to injustice. Through their investigative work, Mercy for Animals has attempted to make the walls of farms and slaughterhouses glass and lift the veil of ignorance that surrounds the production of meat, eggs, and dairy products and yet many have come and gone in the national spotlight without any substantial consequences and the vast majority of Canadians continue to consume the products and by-products of the animal-industrial complex. For instance, cases such as the one described in the introductory paragraph above, wherein abuse was revealed at a poultry supplier for Gordon Food Service, have been reviewed by third party auditors and found to simply illustrate industry standard practices (Kristoff, 2015). Taken together, the continued consumption of animal products and by-products and legal indifference towards many undercover investigations, reveal that attempts at simply making the walls of the animal-industrial complex glass are insufficient in leading to meaningful change. Such attempts demonstrate an overreliance on the capitalist value of individualism—both in the sense of only problematizing egregious acts of individual violence and in expecting individual changes in behavior alone to facilitate meaningful change. This emphasis on individualism falls short of transformative resistance in the way it leaves intact the broader social forces that have created an industrial food system and contributed to our reliance upon it.

Further, these individualist sentiments and affirmative responses to injustice are premised on an unintelligible mass of people simply unaware of the socioecological implications of the animal-industrial complex, who, once made aware, would alter their consumption choices in favor of what has been deemed more ethical and sustainable, and that through principles of supply and demand, a more ethical and sustainable food system would flourish (Alkon & Agyeman, 2011; Almassi, 2011; Guthman, 2008a, 2011; Weis, 2013). First, it is problematic to assert that those who purchase and consume foods produced via the animal-industrial complex are fundamentally less knowledgeable or ethically inclined (Guthman, 2011; Wrenn et al., 2015). A focus on personal culpability ignores the collective power and institutional support of the animal-industrial complex and the structural conditions—including neoliberal and capitalist policy—that contribute to a reliance upon it and limit access to alternative foodways (Wrenn, 2015; Wrenn et al., 2015). In this way, I problematize that individualist sentiments within resistance discourse reify a banking model of education, whereby individuals are considered empty containers lacking any knowledge of the animal-industrial complex and spaces of resistance must impose knowledge on an ignorant mass (Corman & Vandrovcova, 2014; Freire, 1996).

Overall, I argue that a focus on individual culpability alone, in terms of both the legal system criminalizing individual acts of violence and resistance efforts promoting individual behavioral or attitudinal change, represents an affirmative response to injustice. Such affirmative responses are problematic in that they leave intact and further legitimize the underlying capitalist ideology and human-animal binary that drives the animal-industrial complex and the conditions for violence and exploitation. For instance, the use of the words "willful," "unnecessary," "undue," or "unavoidable" in regard to the pain and suffering of animals within Canadian legislature, reinforces the notion that some amount of suffering and pain is "necessary" and therefore acceptable in the name of commerce (Bisgould et al., 2001; Sorenson, 2003). Regardless of how we conceptualize the relationship between law and popular consciousness—be it that the law shapes popular consciousness or popular consciousness shapes the law—both conceptualizations would involve both the law and the masses believing that a certain degree of violence against animals is acceptable in the name of satisfying taste, dietary protein, and vitamin requirements. Coupled with discursive strategies such as "doublespeak"

(Glenn, 2004), misleading advertisements (Mason & Finelli, 2007; Glenn, 2004), and legislative policies that aim to romanticize the industry's concern for animal welfare, the consumer may be able to buy into the general acceptability of certain forms of violence and that his or her "animal food comes to them without distress or suffering" (Bisgould et al., 2001, p. 3). It is for this reason that I call for an understanding of the interplay between capitalist production, cultural norms, and laws that perpetuate the animal-industrial complex and our reliance upon it to facilitate transformative change.

TRANSFORMATIVE RESPONSES TO INJUSTICE

Moving forward, I question what it would take for a transformative remedy aimed at "correcting inequitable outcomes precisely by restructuring the underlying generative framework" (Fraser, 1997, p. 23) to occur. This concern is informed by a critical animal studies approach, which calls for moving beyond theory for theory's take to facilitate meaningful social action (Nibert, 2014). What would it mean to call into question the underlying generative frameworks of capitalism, as well as the cultural norms and social institutions that produce and maintain the animal-industrial complex and our reliance upon it? What would it mean for the animal-industrial complex if we did in fact start to recognize issues of confinement, the physiological and reproductive manipulation of farmed animal bodies, methods of transportation and slaughter, premature separation of newborn animals from their mothers, and denial of species-life behaviors as violent?

Given that critical animal studies urges us to consider our own complicity in systems of exploitation (Nibert, 2014), I often think about my personal responsibility to challenge the violence endemic to the animal-industrial complex. In this pursuit, I consistently waver between empowerment and immobility as an individual. Given a theme of this work has been challenging dichotomous thinking, I suppose I need to consider the possibility of both existing simultaneously. I argue that as individuals we do have a responsibility to be aware and cease support of exploitative industries and practices, while also recognizing that "the perfect is the enemy of the good," that the implications of neoliberal, capitalist, racist, and colonial logic and policies create varying levels of access to "ethical consumption," and call into question the capacity for any consumption to be ethical under capitalism. To this end, I consistently remind myself that just because I cannot do everything does not mean I should not do anything and thus need to recognize the value of altering my attitude, behaviors, and consumption patterns in ways that do not support the exploitation of animals.

However, we must also avoid overestimating the ability for individuals alone to create transformative change within an inherently broken system. We must recognize the extensive power and support backing these institutions that have contributed to our reliance upon them and consider that a focus on individual action alone treats a symptom rather than the disease. As such, on a collective level, transformative change would involve challenging the epistemologies of ignorance regarding the animal-industrial complex that are actively produced for purposes of domination and exploitation (Sullivan & Tuana, 2007). It would mean challenging the mythical, philosophical, religious, and scientific forms of knowledge that have been used to justify human superiority and the violence and exploitation of animals for the purpose of our consumptive habits (Gianetto, 2013). I think, most importantly, it would mean implicating systems rather than individuals as the perpetrators of violence in the animal-industrial complex and putting forward a sociology of violence that recognizes and contests the "necessary," normalized, and systematic killing of animals within the animal-industrial complex (Cudworth, 2015). In this sense, critical animal studies provides a useful framework for unpacking the logic that produced and maintains the animal-industrial complex, offering a critique of capitalism, dominator hierarchies, and socially constructed boundaries. Part of destabilizing this logic is challenging levels of profit and productivity that compromise justice for animals, as well as for humans and Earth, and recognizing cases such as the abuse at Chilliwak Cattle Sales as part of the price paid for inexpensive and widely accessible animal products and by-products. Moreover, we must recognize legality as distinct from morality and understand that our social institutions are flawed and largely human-centered. Unpacking this logic also involves critiquing hyper-individualism and exploitation as natural and beneficial facets of our society and recognizing that it is these values that allow us to accept that some form of harm against others is acceptable. We accept some form of harm as necessary when we say we cannot imagine a life without cheese and believe our right to agency as individuals takes precedent over a responsibility to or concern for the collective. To this end, we must critically interrogate convenience, taste, and tradition as defining what constitutes "necessary" harm in a context where individualism and exploitation are naturalized. We must recognize that just because this is the way it has been for many years, or because we feel we are reliant on an industrial food system to feed the world, it is possible to imagine and cultivate a system outside of this. It is possible to redefine who counts as worthy of moral consideration as we have seen such boundaries deconstructed and reconstructed throughout history. Overall, the fear and selfishness that keeps the powerful complacent in the maintenance of the status quo cannot be accepted as justification.

I do not mean to trivialize these solutions, as I do recognize that altering ideologies and epistemologies regarding human-animal relations is not an easy task. However, we have seen Indigenous communities thrive without reliance on the animal-industrial complex, we have seen other individuals resist the animal-industrial complex by altering their consumption habits, and we have seen other groups develop a critical pedagogy through documentaries, literature, blogs, protests, university programs and courses, etc. that resist the animal-industrial complex and the underlying generative frameworks that sustain it. We have seen efforts made at disrupting the discourse of food as a commodity and instead positioning food as a human right and both a physiologically and culturally nourishing life-good (Knezevic, 2012; Wiebe, 2012). In this endeavor, critical food pedagogies have challenged the anonymity and commodification associated with an industrial food system in favor of a community food economy that lessens the distance between producers and consumers (Gross, 2011). This has involved the creation of counterhegemonic possibilities within the food system, such as farmers' markets, community gardens, urban agriculture, community supported agriculture, school gardens, food co-operatives, and food-based education (Barndt, 2012).

To this end, I see part of my role as a self-reflective educator and researcher as employing critical pedagogy and planting seeds for transformative change within my praxis. Here I will discuss two key strategies that I employ as a postsecondary educator in the discipline of sociology: (1) balancing pedagogies of discomfort with pedagogies of hope and (2) facilitating opportunities for students to think critically about our relationships with animals as socially constructed. Regarding the first strategy, in my teaching of both critical animal studies and introductory sociology courses, I always preface the course with the following quotation:

> When your views on the world and your intellect are being challenged and you begin to feel uncomfortable because of a contradiction you've detected that is threatening your current model of the world or some aspect of it, pay attention. You are about to learn something. (Drury, n.d.)

I explain to students that they are likely going to encounter moments of discomfort throughout the course, where the content will upset them or challenge formerly held attitudes and behaviors. I outline that the common reaction we have when we experience these moments of discomfort is to turn away or reject this new information and encourage them to instead work to navigate within this tension—while still prioritizing personal well-being—as it is often within these moments where growth and transformation occur. For me personally, it was the discomfort that came along with being shown the undercover investigation footage from Chilliwack Cattle Sales as a student in a critical animal studies course that made me immediately switch from vegetarianism to veganism. I used to justify my consumption of dairy and eggs based on the idea that death was not involved in the production of these goods—which I later learned is not in fact true, given the relationship between the dairy and veal industries, the disposal of male chicks, and the premature slaughter of spent animals. As a pedagogy of discomfort, videos such as this pushed me to consider that death is such a small part of the violence enacted on animals and that this violence extends far beyond physical pain to also include psychological pain. This pedagogical moment helped me to understand that justice for animals is incomplete when we focus exclusively on the conditions of their death and not on the constraints on and possibilities for their lives. In this sense, I feel it is also important to facilitate pedagogies of hope, which for me includes an understanding of animal behavior outside of systems of industrial animal agriculture. Part of this involves (1) destabilizing the idea that the lives of animals on industrial farms are natural, (2) learning about animal behavior or spending time at farm sanctuaries and witnessing animals in their natural state to recognize animals as sentient beings who possess innate tendencies and preferences they would display in natural conditions, and (3) contrasting the lives they would live under natural conditions with the violent reality of the animal-industrial complex. Taken together, I understand these three steps as creating a balance between pedagogies of discomfort and pedagogies of hope to plant seeds for transformative change and destabilize the logic that drives the animal-industrial complex and our reliance upon it.

Regarding the second strategy, in my teaching of both critical animal studies and introductory sociology courses, I provide opportunities for students to think critically about how our relationship with animals is socially constructed in an effort to destabilize the human-animal binary and hierarchy. I will now explain one particular activity I often use in this pursuit. The purpose of this activity is to urge students to consider their perceptions of various animals and to think about the social structures and processes that have contributed to these perceptions. Additionally, this activity is meant to encourage students to critically interrogate the shared meanings and understandings that have created societal norms in terms of their attitudes and behaviors towards animals that appear to be "natural" and are taken for granted. Working in small groups, I have students create a table with the following headings: (1) animals we love, (2) animals we eat, (3) animals we wear, and (4) animals we hate. Based on what is typical in North America, I ask students to come up with as many animals as possible for each category. It is of course important to remind students that there will be variation in terms of which animals go into which category based on the individual, but I urge them to consider the "norm" in North American/Western culture. After doing this, I ask students to consider the following questions: (1) How did I learn which animal belongs in each category? What social processes and structures contributed to this understanding (i.e., family, school, church, media, peers, etc.)? Try to think of specific examples where this knowledge was explicitly or implicitly conveyed, and (2) Imagine for a moment that you have come into contact with a being from another planet who is unfamiliar with our societal customs. How would you explain to him/her why the chart looks the way it does? I generally record the answers to each stage of this activity in a Google Doc in an effort to increase interactivity and make the file available to students after the activity is complete. Overall, this activity draws on important sociological concepts of culture, socialization, social constructionism, and seeing the strange in the familiar and encourages students to consider the fact that they are not born with particular attitudes or behaviors towards animals. Rather, we learn these attitudes and behaviors over time by interacting with others and with social structures and processes. Overall, this activity helps to destabilize the generative framework of the human-animal binary that in part produced and sustains the violence inherent to the animal-industrial complex.

CONCLUSION

The purpose of this chapter has been to consider how the reception and consequences of a Mercy for Animals investigation into Chilliwack Cattle Sales in British Columbia reinforces an individualistic and psychopathological conceptualization of violence against animals in the animal-industrial complex and simultaneously legitimizes the systemic acts of violence that are inherent to the industrial model. I have suggested how this conceptualization of violence is bound to the Canadian legal system, and ultimately seeks to protect the value of animal products in order to maximize productivity and profitability, with little to no concern for the welfare of the animals themselves. Moreover, I have argued that the focus on individual acts of violence within the animal-industrial complex represents an affirmative response to injustice that does little to disrupt the underlying generative framework of a capitalist and industrial system of animal agriculture and thus reinforces this system and particular forms of violence as legitimate (Fraser, 1997). Lastly, I have outlined individual and collective suggestions that I believe align with a transformative response to injustice and thus challenge the underlying discourses and epistemologies of ignorance that have allowed the animal-industrial complex to remain the dominant model of animal agriculture and the consumption of meat, dairy, and eggs to remain as part of the typical North American diet (Fraser, 1997; Rossi & Garner, 2014; Sullivan & Tuana, 2007).

SELECTED BIBLIOGRAPHY

Adams, M., Hopkins, L. E., & Shlasko, D. (2016). Classism. In M. Adams & L. A. Bell (Eds.), *Teaching for diversity and social justice* (3rd ed.) (pp. 213–254). Routledge.

Albritton, R. (2012). Two great food revolutions: The domestication of nature and the transgression of nature's limits. In M. Koc, J. Sumner, & A. Winson (Eds.), *Critical perspectives in food studies* (pp. 89–103). Oxford University Press.

Alkon, A. H., & Agyeman, J. (2011). Introduction: The food movement as polyculture. In A. H. Alkon, & J. Agyeman (Eds.), *Cultivating food justice: Race, class, and sustainability* (pp. 1–20). MIT Press.

Anthony, R. (2012). Building a sustainable future for animal agriculture: An environmental virtue ethic-of-care approach within the philosophy of technology. *Journal of Agricultural and Environmental. Ethics, 25*(1), 123–144.

Barndt, D. (2012). Catalyzing creativity: Education and art feed the food justice movement. In M. Koc, J. Sumner, & A. Winson (Eds.), *Critical perspectives in food studies* (pp. 65–84). Oxford University Press.

Berreville, O. (2014). Animal welfare issues in the Canadian dairy industry. In J. Sorenson (Ed.), *Critical animal studies: Thinking the unthinkable* (pp. 186–207). Canadian Scholars' Press.

Best, S., Nocella, A. J., Kahn, R., Gigliotti, C., & Kemmerer, L. (2007). Introducing critical animal studies. *Journal for Critical Animal Studies, 5*(1), 4–5.

Bisgould, L., King, W., & Stopford, J. (2001). *Anything goes: An overview of Canada's legal approach to animals on factory farms* (pp. 1–65). Animal Alliance of Canada. http://www.animalalliance.ca/wp-content/uploads/2011/07/report-Anything-Goes.pdf

British Columbia Society for the Prevention of Cruelty to Animals [BCSPCA]. (2014a). The welfare of dairy cattle: The BC SPCA is helping to make a change. *BC SPCA: Speaking for Animals*. http://www.spca.bc.ca/welfare/campaign-issues/the-welfare-of-dairy-cattle.html

British Columbia Society for the Prevention of Cruelty to Animals [BCSPCA]. (2014b). BC SPCA recommends charges of animal cruelty against eight employees of a Chilliwack dairy farm. *BC SPCA: Speaking for Animals*. http://www.spca.bc.ca/news-and-events/news/cwk-dairy-farm-investigation.html

Canadians for the Ethical Treatment of Food Animals [CETFA]. (2011). *Welfare issues in the egg industry* (pp. 1–14). http://www.getcrackingcruelty.ca/wp-content/uploads/2011/12/Welfare-Issues-in-the-Egg-Industry.pdf

Cassuto, D. (2007). Bred meat: The cultural foundation of the factory farm. *Law and Contemporary Problems*, *70*(1), 59–88.

CBC News. (2014). Chilliwack Cattle Sales to fire 8 workers caught on tape abusing cows. http://www.cbc.ca/news/canada/british-columbia/chilliwack-cattle-sales-to-fire-8-workers-caught-on-tape-abusing-cows-1.2670098

Corman, L. & Vandrovcova, T. (2014). Radical humility: Toward a more holistic critical animal studies pedagogy. In A. J. Nocella, J. Sorenson, K. Socha, & A.

Matskuoka (Eds.), *Defining critical animal studies: An intersectional social justice approach for liberation* (pp. 135–157). Peter Lang.
Cudworth, E. (2015). Killing animals: Sociology, species relations and institutionalized violence. *The Sociological Review*, *63*(1), 1–18.
Cudworth, E. (2010). "The recipe for love"? Continuities and changes in the sexual politics of meat. *Journal for Critical Animal Studies. 8*(4), 78–100.
Dairy Farmers of Canada. (2009). *The New Code of Practice*. http://www.dairyfarmers.ca/what-we-do/animal-health-and-welfare/faq
Davis, K. (2012). The mental life of chickens as observed through their social relationships. In J. Smith & R. Mitchell (Eds.), *Experiencing animal minds: An anthology of animal-human encounters* (pp. 13–29). Columbia University Press.
Davis, K. (2010). Chicken-human relationships: From procrustean genocide to empathic anthropomorphism. *A Journal of Archetype and Culture*, *83*(1), 255–280.
Davis, K. (2004). A tale of two holocausts. *Animal Liberation Philosophy and Public Policy*, *2*(2), 1–20.
Deckha, M. (2012). Toward a postcolonial, posthumanist feminist theory: Centralizing race and culture in feminist work on nonhuman animals. *Hypatia*, *27*(3), 527–545.
Deckha, M. (2010). The subhuman as a cultural agent of violence. *Journal for Critical Animal Studies, 3*(3), 28–51.
DeGrazia, D. (1996). *Taking animals seriously*. Cambridge University Press.
DeGrazia, D. (n.d.). *Animal rights: A very short introduction*. Oxford University Press.
Fairclough, N. (2010). *Critical discourse analysis: The critical study of language* (2nd ed.). Routledge.
Fitzgerald, A. J. & Pellow, D. (2014). Ecological defense for animal liberation: A holistic understanding of the world. In A. J. Nocella, J. Sorenson, K. Socha, & A. Matskuoka (Eds.), *Defining critical animal studies: An intersectional social justice approach for liberation* (pp. 28–50). Peter Lang.
Flynn, C. (2001). Acknowledging the "zoological connection": A sociological analysis of animal cruelty. *Society & Animals*, *9*(1), 71–87.
Food and Agricultural Organization of the United Nations. (2006). Executive Summary. *Livestock's long shadow: Environmental issues and options* (pp. xx–xxiv).
Fraser, N. (1997). *Justice interruptus: Critical reflections on the "post-socialist" condition*. Routledge.
Freire, P. (1996). *Pedagogy of the oppressed*. Continuum.
Gianetto, E. R. A. (2013). Notes on a metamorphosis. *Society & Animals*, *21*(1), 75–89.
Gillespie, K. (2014). Sexualized violence and the gendered commodification of the animal body in Pacific Northwest US dairy production. *Gender, Place & Culture*, *21*(10), 1321–1337.
Glenn, C. (2004). Constructing consumables and consent: A critical analysis of factory farm industry discourse. *Journal of Communication Inquiry*, *28*(1), 63–81.
Gramsci, A. (1971). *Selections from the Prison Notebooks*. International Publishers.

Greenebaum, J. B. (2017). Questioning the concept of vegan privilege: A commentary. *Humanity & Society, 41*(3), 355–372.

Gross, J. (2011). Constructing a community food economy. *Food and Foodways, 19*(3), 181–200.

Gunderson, R. (2011). From cattle to capital: Exchange value, animal commodification, and barbarism. *Critical Sociology, 39*(2), 259–275.

Gunderson, R., & Stuart, D. (2014). Industrial animal agribusiness and environmental sociological theory. *International Journal of Sociology, 44*(1), 54–74.

Guthman, J. (2011). "If they only knew": The unbearable whiteness of alternative food. In Alkon, A. H., & Agyeman, J. (Eds.), *Cultivating food justice: Race, class, and sustainability* (pp. 309–330). MIT Press.

Guthman, J. (2008a). Neoliberalism and the making of food politics in California. *Geoforum, 39*(3), 1171–1183.

Guthman, J. (2008b). Thinking inside the neoliberal box: The micro-politics of agro-food philanthropy. *Geoforum, 39*(3), 1241–1253.

Harman, E. (2011). The moral significance of animal pain and animal death. In T. Beauchamp & R. Frey (Eds.), *The Oxford handbook of animal ethics* (pp. 726–737). Oxford University Press.

Harper, A. B. (2013). Vegan consciousness and the commodity chain: On the neoliberal, afrocenric, and decolonial politics of "cruelty free." http://www.sistahvegan.com/wp-content/uploads/2013/03/harperpdftelfordupdates.pdf

Harper, A. B. (2011a). Connections: Speciesism, racism, and whiteness as the norm. In L. Kemmerer (Ed.), *Sister species: Women, animals, and social justice* (pp. 72–78). University of Illinois Press.

Harper, A. B. (2011b). Vegans of colour, racialized embodiment, and problematics of the exotic. In A. H. Alkon, & J. Agyeman (Eds.), *Cultivating food justice: Race, class, and sustainability* (pp. 221–238). MIT Press.

Harper, A. B. (2010a). "Race as a feeble matter" in veganism: Interrogating whiteness, geopolitical privilege, and consumption of "cruelty-free" products. *Journal of Critical Animal Studies, 8*(3), 5–27.

Harper, A. B. (2010b) Introduction: The birth of the sistah vegan project. In A. B. Harper (Ed.), *Sistah vegan: Black female vegans speak on food, identity, health, and society* (pp. xii-xix). Lantern Books.

Harper, A. B. (2010c) Social justice beliefs and addiction to uncompassionate consumption. In A. B. Harper (Ed.), *Sistah vegan: Black female vegans speak on food, identity, health, and society* (pp. 20–41). Lantern Books.

Harrison, R. (1964). *Animal machines: The new factory farming industry*. Ballantine Books.

Hendrickson, M. K., & James, H. S. (2005). The ethics of constrained choice: How the industrialization of agriculture impacts farming and farmer behavior. *Journal of Agricultural and Environmental Ethics, 18*(1), 269–291.

Hernandez, J. (2017). 3 men in Chilliwack cattle abuse scandal get jail time. *CBC News.* https://www.cbc.ca/news/canada/british-columbia/3-men-in-chilliwack-cattle-abuse-scandal-get-jail-time-1.4121997

Hudson, I., & Hudson, M. (2003). Removing the veil? Commodity fetishism, fair trade, and the environment. *Organization Environment, 16*(4), 413–430.

Hutchinson, B. (2014). Canada's largest dairy farm crippled by abuse allegations from undercover animal rights worker on his first mission. *The National Post*. http://news.nationalpost.com/2014/06/20/canadas-largest-dairy-farm-crippled-by-abuse-allegations-from-undercover-animal-rights-worker-on-his-first-mission/

Joy, M. (2009). *Why we love dogs, eat pigs, and wear cows: An introduction to carnism*. Red Wheel/Weiser.

Klein, N. (2015). *This changes everything: Capitalism vs. the climate*. Simon & Schuster.

Knezevic, I. (2012). Labels and governance: Promises, failures, and deceptions of food labeling. In M. Koc, J. Sumner, & A. Winson (Eds.), *Critical perspectives in food studies* (pp. 247–259). Oxford University Press.

Ko, A. (2015). 3 reasons black folks don't join the animal rights movement—and why we should. *Everyday Feminism*. http://everydayfeminism.com/2015/09/black-folks-animal-rights-mvmt/

Kristof, N. (2015, March). To kill a chicken. *New York Times*. http://www.nytimes.com/2015/03/15/opinion/sunday/nicholas-kristof-to-kill-a-chicken.html?_r=2

Martinez, E., & Garcia, A. (n.d.). What is neoliberalism? A brief definition for activists. http://www.corpwatch.org/article.php?id=376

MacDonald, J. M., & McBridge, W. D. (2009). *The transformation of U.S. Livestock agriculture: Scale, efficiency, and risks*. United States Department of Agriculture. https://www.ers.usda.gov/webdocs/publications/44292/13802_eib43fm_1_.pdf?v=41055

Mason, J., & Finelli, M. (2007). Brave new farm. In L. Kalof & A. Fitzgerald (Eds.), *The animals reader: The essential classic and contemporary writings* (pp. 158–170). Berg.

Magdoff, F., & Foster, J. B. (2010). What every environmentalist needs to know about capitalism. *Monthly Review, 61*(10), 1–30.

Medero, D. (2014). Spinning the pig: The language of industrial pork production. In J. Sorenson (Ed.), *Critical animal studies: Thinking the unthinkable* (pp. 208–215). Canadian Scholars' Press.

Mercy for Animals. (2014). Dairy's dark side: Criminal cruelty exposed at Canada's largest dairy factory farm. http://canadadairy.mercyforanimals.org/

Mercy for Animals. (2015). Rescued dairy cow remembers stolen babies, hides calf. *The MFA Blog*. Mercy for Animals. http://www.mfablog.org/rescued-dairy-cow-remembers-stolen-babies

Minister of Justice. (2014). *Meat Inspection Regulations* (pp. 1–121). Government of Canada. http://laws-lois.justice.gc.ca/PDF/SOR-90-288.pdf

Minister of Justice. (2015a). *Health of Animals Regulations* (pp. 1–171). Government of Canada. http://laws-lois.justice.gc.ca/PDF/C.R.C.,_c._296.pdf

Minister of Justice. (2015b). *Criminal Code* (pp. 1–1176). Government of Canada. http://laws-lois.justice.gc.ca/PDF/C-46.pdf

National Farm Animal Care Council. (2009). *The code of practice for the care and handling of dairy cattle* (pp. 1–67).

Nibert, D. (2014). Animals, immigrants, and profits: slaughterhouses and the political economy of oppression. In J. Sorenson (Ed.), *Critical animal studies: Thinking the unthinkable* (pp. 3–17). Canadian Scholars' Press.

Nibert, D. A. (2013). *Animal oppression & human violence: Domesecration, capitalism, and global conflict.* Columbia University Press.

Noske, B. (1997). *Beyond boundaries: Humans and animals.* Montreal, QC: Black Rose Books.

Oppenlander, R. A. (2013). *Food choice and sustainability: Why buying local, eating less meat, and taking baby steps won't work.* Langdon Street.

Oxfam America. (2016). Lives on the line: The human cost of cheap chicken. *Oxfam Research Report.* https://www.oxfamamerica.org/static/media/files/Lives_on_the_Line_Full_Report_Final.pdf

Porcher, J. (2011). The relationship between workers and animals in the pork industry: A shared suffering. *Journal of Agricultural and Environmental ethics*, *24*(1), 3–17.

Robinson, M. (2013). Veganism and Mi'Kmaq legends. *The Canadian Journal of Native Studies, 33*(1), 189–196.

Rossi, J., & Garner, S. (2014). Industrial farm animal production: A comprehensive moral critique. *Journal of Agricultural and Environmental Ethics*, *27*(1), 479–522.

Rowe, B. D. (2011). Understanding animals-becoming-meat: Embracing a disturbing education. *Critical Education*, *2*(7), 1–25.

Safran Foer, J. (2009). *Eating animals*. Little, Brown and Company.

Sage, C. (2011). *Environment and food.* Routledge.

Sapontzsis, S. (1987). *Morals, reason and animals*. Temple University Press.

Sayers, D. O. (2014). The most wretched of beings in the cage of capitalism. *International Journal of Historical Archaeology*, *18*(3), 529–544.

Schulman, M. (2016). Canada's livestock transportation rules "worst in Western world." *CTV News.* http://www.ctvnews.ca/canada/canada-s-livestock-transportation-rules-worst-in-the-western-world-advocate-1.2820563

Stanford, J. (2008). *Economics for everyone: A short guide to the economics of capitalism*. Fernwood Publishing.

Sorenson, J. (2010). *About Canada: Animal rights* (pp. 9–22). Fernwood Publishing.

Sorenson, J. (2003). "Some strange things happening in our country": Opposing proposed changes in anti-cruelty laws in Canada. *Social & Legal Studies*, *12*(3), 377–402.

Stanescu, J. (2013). Beyond Biopolitics: Animal Studies, Factory Farms, and the Advent of Deading Life. *Phaenex: Journal of Existential and Phenomenological Theory and Culture*, *8*(2), 135–160.

Sullivan, S., & Tuana, N. (2007). *Race and epistemologies of ignorance*. University of New York Press.

Twine, R. (2012). Revealing the "animal-industrial complex": A concept and method for critical animal studies? *Journal for Critical Animal Studies, 10*(1), 12–39.

Varner, G. (1994). What's wrong with animal by-products? *Journal of Agricultural and Environmental Ethics*, *7*(1), 7–17.

Walker, P., Rhubart-Berg, P., McKenzie, S., Kelling, K., & Lawrence, R. S. (2005). Public health implications of meat production and consumption. *Public Health Nutrition, 8*(4), 348–356.

Warren, K. (1993a). Introduction. In M. E. Zimmerman (Ed.), *Environmental philosophy: From animal rights to radical ecology* (pp. 253–267). Prentice Hall.

Warren, K. (1993b). The power and promise of ecological feminism. In M. E. Zimmerman (Ed.), *Environmental philosophy: From animal rights to radical ecology* (pp. 320–341). Prentice Hall.

Weis, T. (2013). *The ecological hoofprint: The global burden of industrial livestock* (pp. 1–12). Zed Books.

Weis, T. (2012). A political ecology approach to industrial food production. In M. Koc, J. Sumner, & A. Winson (Eds.), *Critical perspectives in food studies* (pp. 104–121). Oxford University Press.

Wiebe, N. (2012). Crisis in the food system: The farm crisis. In M. Koc, J. Sumner, & A. Winson (Eds.), *Critical perspectives in food studies* (pp. 155–170). Oxford University Press.

Wrenn, C. L. (2015). *A rational approach to animal rights: Extensions in abolitionist theory.* Palgrave Macmillan.

Wrenn, C. L., Clark, J., Judge, M., Gilchrist, K. A., Woodlock, D., Dotson, K., . . . Wrenn, J. (2015). The medicalization of nonhuman animal rights: Frame contestation and the exploitation of disability. *Disability & Society 30*(9), 1307–1327.

Chapter Eight

Animal Rescue on Facebook

About the Rescuer or the Rescued?

Tatjana Marjanovic

PART ONE

Introduction

Scholars have long been telling stories about dogs and many other animals: domesticated, tamed, wild; animals in circuses and captivity; service dogs; companion animals and those in the meat industry. Some of these stories have been written in a most engaging manner with every page oozing with affection (e.g., Caesar, 2009). No animal is thought too small or insignificant, and the circle of love and compassion has been widened to include more and more animals as our fellow creatures (e.g., Squier, 2009). Voices have been given to whales (e.g., Warkentin, 2009) and experimental animals (e.g., Mayer, 2009). Animated animals, such as penguins and raccoons (e.g., McFarland, 2009), and those that make headlines, especially dogs (e.g., Onion, 2009) and horses (e.g., Scott, 2009), are also researched with a keen interest. Animals are as frequent protagonists in literary works as they are in academic writing, and one such example is a critical re-reading of Anna Sewell's *Black Beauty*, which places "the suffering animal at the center of the narrative" (Nyman, 2016, p. 66) and "promotes a view of the animal as having access to knowledge and agency" (ibid., p. 76). Last but not least, analyzing the way humans speak of animals often corresponds to the way animals are treated by humans (e.g., Durham & Merskin, 2009).

To these accounts and many more we can now add a story of animal rescue on Facebook, where we look at how human protagonists speak to and of each other and, of course, the animals who need them. Abstract categories are infrequent visitors to these pages, as "we simply must remember that we are thinking about embodied individuals living their lives entangled with humans and their own wider environment" (Taylor, 2012, p. 40). It is only fair to say that both verifiable sources and personal accounts are employed to help the reader better understand the context of animal-human coexistence in the city of Banja Luka, the country of Bosnia and Herzegovina, and most of the Balkans region.

A Note on the Personal Tone of the Essay

My personal involvement in the matter means that the description of animal rescue on Facebook as a specific sociocultural context is mostly based on anecdotal evidence: I share with the reader my own experience and that of the people I have interacted with, providing examples that best capture that experience. I have been following animal rescue Facebook pages on a daily basis since 2011, normally devoting between half an hour and a couple of hours a day to this activity alone. As the number of posts I have accessed is measured in thousands, this exposure has enabled me to observe some recurring patterns and draw some conclusions from them.

I will not always strive to make my presence in this paper less conspicuous, as the style of academic writing would have it. I do not present figures, or draw charts, or refer to any one section of the law. Paradoxically, it is by telling more stories and relying on fewer citations that I hope to give more visibility to both people and animals who have been denied it in their daily struggle made up of giving and receiving help. Although the story will later take a linguistic turn, the reader should know from the start what not to expect from this rather testimonial piece.

Animal Rescue on Facebook and in Real Life

The following are some of the more visible Facebook groups, communities, and pages in Bosnia and Herzegovina, as well as Serbia, Croatia, and Montenegro: Šapa u srcu—Zampa nel cuore, Udruženje građana *Kerber* Banja Luka, Udomljavanje životinja Banja Luka, Help Animals Banja Luka, Projekat sterilizacija i kastracija Banja Luka, Nahranimo zajedno naše ulične pujde (NZNUP) BiH, *Av Mau* Sarajevo, Životinje jer mi brinemo Mostar, Pomoć životinjama/Helping Paws Mostar, Udruženje za spašavanje i zaštitu životinja *Šapa* Zenica, Pomoć napuštenim životinjama Kozarska Dubica, Napuštene šapice Mrkonjić Grad, Udomljavanje životinja Kotor Varoš, SOS šapice Gradiška, Udruženje za zaštitu životinja *Aska* Bijeljina, SPAS—Udomljavanje životinja/Adopting Animals Prijedor, Udruženje prijatelja životinja *Šapa u ruci* Trebinje, Udruženje za brigu o životinjama grada Beograda *Beta*, Udruženje *Beta* Zaječar, Društvo za zaštitu životinja *Spaske* Kraljevo, Pomoć napuštenim životinjama Valjevo, Udruženje za zaštitu životinja *Spans* Novi Sad, Mirijevo—napuštene i izgubljene životinje, Organizacija za prava i zaštitu životinja *Orpak* Kruševac, Anima Subotica, Ruka šapi Odžaci, Prijatelji životinja Podgorica, Udruga *Šapa u srcu* Ogulin, Udruga za zbrinjavanje napuštenih i ozlijeđenih životinja Poreč, Udruga *Pobjede* Osijek, etc.

The list is far from complete and in need of regular updating and editing as some of the existing groups either cease to be active or for some reason choose to operate under a different name; some new ones are created, too. There are big cities represented in the list, and there are small towns that even some of the regional animal lovers may not be entirely familiar with. The names of the pages themselves identify the most threatening conditions for animals in need as well as the areas of human intervention: lend a helping hand to these abandoned and injured animals, feed them, try to save them from harm, rehome them, alert the community and provide assistance in case of an emergency, or simply show that you care.

Overall, the number of towns and cities in the region with at least one animal rescue group on Facebook seems to be steadily growing; the bigger the place, the higher the odds of the number going up. Sometimes, and especially in small and comparatively rural places where animals have extremely low visibility and receive little to no compassion, it is usually an informal group of animal lovers, sometimes only a couple of them, that do the thankless task of saving what can be saved. They often fight losing battles, keeping their supporters and followers duly informed of the culls, deaths, fatal injuries, road kill, cruelty and abuse that thousands of unwanted dogs and cats have to endure in their short stay in the world that either ignores them or tries to do them harm. Sometimes the volunteers, which is how the ones administering the pages often identify themselves, can do little more than procure one meal a day, which they bring to the sites with the largest concentration of the town's canine and feline populations. Although they may receive some financial support and donations in food and other supplies from the community of animal lovers following their activities, these volunteers do the work which no-one else in their town wants to do—street dogs and cats as well as those who care about them are often reduced to the status of pariah across the region.

It is beyond doubt an emotionally taxing life for everyone involved in animal rescue in the region. Human-animal studies scholars use the term compassion fatigue, which describes "the fatigue felt by shelter workers, animal welfare volunteers, veterinarians, and others who work in the caring professions" (DeMello, 2012, p. 27). Similar emotional responses can be experienced by anyone following animal rescue Facebook pages in their town and region, but also globally, as these pages are frequented by individuals of all races and nationalities brought together by their love of animals. An urgent post can draw so much attention on Facebook that the result will be the saving of a life. Many more animals will unfortunately not live long enough to see the happy ending animal lovers hope and pray for.

Even the position of a follower can be extremely trying as one is routinely confronted with images of sick and dying animals; those poisoned and convulsing in agony before they are finally allowed to find peace in death; those taking their last breath before being discovered in subzero temperatures, their spines severed, their legs broken, their paws cut off; those left to die in the middle of the road after their exhausted little bodies give one last faint heave to show they will be dead soon but are still not.

There are those who believe that no-one deserves to go unloved, so choose to love them instead, cry with and for them, if that is the only thing they can do. Many openly express their feelings in Facebook posts and their sadness seems both genuine and profound. Some make their status updates all about animals, others react to them. Some use real names, others feel less exposed under an alias. We cannot know how many watch and cry in silence, without posting comments and sad emoticons.

There are animal rescue supporters who do more than feel the pain of the suffering: they feed, spay, donate, foster, and so on. Animals are often fed and attended to on location, which is clearly not enough but might be preferable to, for example, an agonizing death in an overcrowded public shelter, either by hunger or illness. Extremely cold winters or hot summers are the times when animal lovers assemble makeshift cardboard houses and make other necessary provisions for their homeless canine and feline denizens. Although too few to save all who need saving, such individuals deserve the credit they do not always get.

Many spend their own resources along with their time, forever keeping quiet about their endeavors, of which the animal-loving Facebook community will know nothing. I have met such individuals, some of whom choose not to go public because they feel that kind of exposure may not be morally right: their love of animals and their need to assist are almost visceral, which is why they believe it should remain as private as possible. I have read stories and seen photos of men and women who have moved to remote villages and committed themselves to a life of isolation and deprivation just so they could look after a greater number of abandoned animals, mainly dogs, than the law would allow them to do in urban areas.

Two Weeks of Animal Rescue on Facebook

By way of illustration, I have compiled what may loosely be dubbed an activist's diary of fourteen select entries, each depicting a Facebook post felt to be the most disturbing of all those accessed on any one day during a period of two weeks. Only location is provided before each entry, and each entry is basically a rendition of the original post. No sources are revealed, and nor are the dates when the posts were made; however, the entries share the same timeline with the corpus that was compiled for the linguistic analysis carried out in the second part of the paper. Another reason why the references are missing is that there is no telling whether the events depicted in all the posts were real or invented, whether they were accurately reported or embellished. But even in their incomplete form, the entries convey an important message: whatever their factual status, they cannot but represent a psychological reality to someone who is emotionally invested in the matter.

Day 1: Sarajevo, Bosnia and Herzegovina

A male dog was hit by a car and left for dead. Whimpering in pain, he still wagged his tail, injured but clearly alive. Nobody pulled up to move him to the side of the road or take him to the vet. It took a quarter of an hour for a few local animal rescue volunteers to arrive on the scene only to find the dog reduced to a pulp on the tarmac, which was the exact wording of the original post. The dog was not difficult to spot on the road, according to the activists who saw the aftermath and documented it by posting several graphic photos and videos on Facebook.

Day 2: Niš, Serbia

A boy in his late teens is posing next to railway tracks with a big smile on his face and looking pleased with himself while at his feet lies the body of a medium-to-large-sized dog cut in half. No background to the story is provided but the graphic photo is causing an upheaval amongst the animal-loving Facebook community. One of the possible scenarios is that the boy tied the dog to the tracks and waited for the train to run it over.

Day 3: Sjenica, Serbia

A rescuer is filming a pack of dogs abandoned in what looks like wasteland, although her live commentary suggests that there is a neighborhood with houses and their occupants nearby. A few dogs in the video are eating the remains of a dead one, its carcass fully exposed and half of it already gone.

Day 4: Belgrade, Serbia

The owner of a florist shop in the vicinity of a cemetery saw a dog lying, possibly sleeping, in the driveway of his shop. The man got into his van, started it, and ran the dog over. The dog was injured and could not get up, screaming with pain. The man then went back and forth with his van, each time further crushing the body of the still living dog. The cries coming from the dog and the degree of mutilation were such that one of the eyewitnesses put the dog out of its misery using his bare hands. The driver was reportedly never prosecuted.

Day 5: Zenica, Bosnia and Herzegovina

The post features the photo of a man identified by name and surname along with the caption "dog rapist" underneath. The man was allegedly seen raping a dog in the street and the incident was reported to the police by one of the eyewitnesses. Neither the eyewitness nor the commenters were hopeful that the criminal act would be taken seriously by the police.

Day 6: Vršac, Serbia

A series of photos taken at the local pound show emaciated dogs with protruding rib cages in the same enclosure with half-eaten corpses of several other dogs. Some are missing the lower part of the body, others the upper—including the head. The photos are graphic to the point that it becomes almost irrelevant whether they were taken in Vršac or any other place in the world.

Day 7: Jablanica, Bosnia and Herzegovina

A woman has learned about a dog stranded on the ledge of a lake damn for almost three months. Bosnia and Herzegovina has a continental climate marked by harsh winters with temperatures going well below zero, especially during the night. The dog is completely exposed to the elements, with nothing but concrete and water surrounding it. The photo below the text of the post shows the dog's position highlighted with blue ink. The dog has survived that long thanks to some of the maintenance workers throwing pieces of bread down the cliff, which is about 80 meters high.

Day 8: Sarajevo, Bosnia and Herzegovina

In a series of photos with captions, a man holds a blood-covered butcher's knife and on the ground next to him lies a white beheaded animal with its legs cut off. The man, probably in his early thirties, poses with a grin on his face and offers inexpensive services of slaughtering stray dogs. He specifies the price at seven convertible marks (the local currency equivalent to around three and a half euros) a piece, adding that house calls are also available. It is understood that the mutilated animal in the photos is a goat.

Day 9: Zavidovići, Bosnia and Herzegovina

Two dogs died, and another was dying an agonizing death in the backyard of a kindergarten. It was Friday night and there were no on-call veterinarians available to either assist or euthanize the dying dog. Several video clips and photos show the dog seizing and vomiting blood, its paws and knuckles stripped to the bare bones with friction against a concrete surface on which it was lying. It was reported that the dog was agonizing for hours before passing away. In all three cases the suspected cause of death was poisoning.

Day 10: Banja Luka, Bosnia and Herzegovina

Seven abandoned puppies found impromptu shelter in what looked like an old, battered tent in a densely populated neighborhood. It is assumed that the puppies were brought there by their mother, who would leave them alone every time she had to roam the streets in search of food. On one such occasion someone set fire to the tent while the little ones were inside, and only one survived.

Day 11: Banja Luka, Bosnia and Herzegovina

A small dog weighing only seven kilos had a litter of three. She was fed and looked after by a group of animal lovers from the neighborhood, who even provided a dog house to keep the little family warm. The post ends on a tragic note with all the babies killed at only three weeks old. What happened to their mother remains unknown.

Day 12: Smederevska Palanka, Serbia

A paralyzed dog is filmed dragging his hind legs as another dog walks alongside him barking. With December temperatures well below zero, there is a risk of the dog freezing to death. The video shows suburban surroundings with densely packed houses and enclosed yards, yet the paralyzed dog is out on what looks like a gravel road with no shelter in sight. The post makes a reference to a woman who feeds him, but he has apparently neither been taken in nor taken to the vet. It is reported that the dog has been in that condition for three weeks already.

Day 13: Somewhere in Slavonia, Croatia

A photo was taken of a puppy standing by the side of the road in the freezing cold. By the time the word spread and help was on the way, it was already too late. The puppy froze to death during the night and was found lying in the snow where the photo had been taken, supposedly by someone driving through the Slavonia region.

Day 14: Sarajevo, Bosnia and Herzegovina

A litter of nine and their mum were roughing it in the mountain woods surrounding Sarajevo. A group of animal activists from Slovenia learned about the dogs through their contacts and tried to alert as many local rescuers as possible. It took the Slovenian volunteers a week to organize a plan of action so the family would have foster homes to go to after they were relocated from the woods. As the Slovenians were unable to obtain local assistance in a timely manner, all the little ones were eventually found dead. The assumption was that they were killed either by humans or other animals.

Between the Law and Public Opinion

Too many stories are recounted of pet dogs being poisoned in their own backyards, or bludgeoned to death by a next-door neighbor, or shot in cold blood by an animal hater (e.g., "Vlasnica psa," 2014). Some are made public and sometimes they also contain disturbing photos or footage (e.g., "Komšija mu otrovao psa," 2018). Bosnia and Herzegovina has had an animal welfare law (Zakon o zaštiti i dobrobiti životinja of 2008) in effect for over a decade but it seems to be in place only to protect the hygiene of communal living at the expense of animals by removing them from the streets.

Bosnia and Herzegovina is very much like other countries where the humane treatment of animals is not a well-established tradition and, as such, it is very different from countries that regard animals as sentient beings and that strive for the highest possible standards of animal welfare. A good legislative example may be the United Kingdom as the first country in the world to implement laws protecting animals. As early as in the nineteenth century, in 1822, an Act to Prevent the Cruel and Improper Treatment of Cattle was passed by Parliament (BBC, n.d.). It is interesting to note that there is also the Protection Against Cruel Tethering Act, passed in the UK in 1988 (BBC, n.d.). By comparison, in Bosnia and Herzegovina it is commonplace to see dogs living their entire lives chained outside.

As animal welfare is not a priority in a country such as Bosnia and Herzegovina, the law tends to be applied loosely: even when killings are reported, it is exceptionally rare to hear of a perpetrator being punished for the crime committed, especially if the victim is a street dog (e.g., "Prijeti mu robija," 2020). There is no public outcry to remedy the injustice, and a few protesting voices are not loud enough to make a lasting difference. Examples can be found in the way the animal welfare law is implemented, as well as in the way animals are treated in everyday life.

When I feed a scruffy-looking, sickly, emaciated dog out in the street, I often see passers-by of all ages, including mothers with young children, crossing the street or looking the other way instead of using these encounters as a learning opportunity for their young ones. But even more harmful than the invisibility of homeless cats and dogs is the local community's intolerance of them. Volunteers who feed abandoned animals in their neighborhoods occasionally complain of verbal and, in more extreme cases, physical abuse by one or more local residents. Many such confrontations happen for much the same reason: if volunteers leave food, the animals tend to stay in the neighborhood and they are not wanted there. The belief that animals living on the street are dirty and spread disease appears to be so deeply rooted in the minds of the local population that even those who mean no harm are often seen petting their canine and feline neighbors with their shod feet instead of their hands.

On the other hand, I sometimes see pedigree dogs, clean, fluffy, preferably small and white, faring much better and being treated with more benevolence and acceptance by passers-by. A similar tendency is observed on Facebook pages dedicated to animal rescue: the adoption of a pedigree dog or cat usually happens quickly and effortlessly due to a number of competing home offers. By contrast, street dogs are generally seen as a nuisance that should be kept out of sight and away from humans. News and television outlets add to the hardship of abandoned animals by taking part in the general hysteria that sometimes acts as an overture to dog-catching raids (e.g., "Psi lutalice napadaju prolaznike," 2017). I have been feeding street dogs for over a decade and have never come close to being bitten. Most dogs are wary or fearful, some simply shy, but very few are downright aggressive.

One of the places where dogs are brought to be kept out of sight is the only existing public shelter in Banja Luka. It is perhaps not a coincidence that it is located next to a landfill. I have been there only once but the images will haunt me forever: sick, dying, emaciated dogs everywhere, packed like sardines in a tiny enclosure with not nearly enough shelter to protect them all from the sun or the cold, with basically no human supervision and no veterinary treatment. I could see many dogs dying of illness and injuries inflicted by other dogs at the shelter. I also understood that they were selectively spayed and neutered due to the cost, so some continued to mate there. Taking photographs was strictly forbidden, but the few that were taken surreptitiously are in keeping with my experience of the place at the time.

Since my visit to the shelter in 2013, the management has made a slight move in the cyberspace by displaying a dozen or so photos of dogs for adoption (Grad Banja Luka, n.d.), and it has received some media attention promoting its activities such as vaccination and similar vetting procedures (e.g., "U prihvatilištu 140 pasa," 2018). However, some of the major challenges remain, such as relocating the existing shelter and building new facilities that will meet the minimum standards required. Transforming the image of the shelter would be the next crucial step in the process. For example, one of the employees there proved to be most cooperative and helpful when I contacted him in 2019 asking for help with a dog. It is unfortunate that the employee resigned from his job at the shelter soon afterwards as individuals like him could help to give the place a new face of compassion and civility and restore some of the trust lost along the way.

At the moment, animal lovers and activists can do little as the city has a full grip on the shelter and has so far remained deaf to their pleas. Letters of protest are written but seldom answered; after my visit to the shelter I also posted a letter to the former mayor but never received so much as a single line in return. It may have never reached the mayor, or perhaps it ended up in a rubbish bin as soon as his aides read the opening lines. It was a very important letter, though.

Some Contradictions and Controversies Surrounding Animal Rescue on Facebook

It is no coincidence that no party is referred to by their name or alias as the focus is on the way they act and the kind of message they send to the world at large. There is also no need to further promote individuals in the animal rescue Facebook community that have come close to acquiring celebrity status on account of their massive following measured in thousands. Such rescuers are mostly unaffiliated and use their personal Facebook accounts to communicate to their followers. They themselves have extremely high visibility, but their many helpers can easily become an amorphous mass in the process. That is how money gets paid into the account, a trip to the vet is organized with all expenses covered, and a foster welcomes another dog. In other words, we often do not know who the good people are because they are kept in the background and out of sight. A linguistic analysis will show how credit can be withheld from benefactors, helpers, and supporters by making them anonymous; as we unmask such conduct we also remain hopeful that it is not the dominant mode of practice in the animal rescue world. It would not be fair to the many who do the difficult rescue work selflessly enough not to seek praise and approval, but it needs to be exposed as something that in the long run goes against the very animals we are trying to help.

There are scores of lone helpers who work alone precisely because they have become disillusioned with organized animal rescue. Often when they make comments on Facebook, their bitterness and disappointment come through with cold clarity. Very few friendships and alliances last long in this world, and sooner or later most break apart and put on the much uglier face of hostility and intolerance. Quarrels and disputes are commonplace, and so is judgmental behavior. Foul language is a regular feature of exchanges in which one course of action or lack thereof receives public admonishment in a most severe form. For example, taking a photo of an abandoned dog or cat and sending it to an animal rescue group is bound to receive more criticism than taking no action at all. It is quite clear that some animal lovers have zero tolerance to the breach of the finders keepers rule, i.e., you must take with you the stray animal you find. Instead of encouraging and inspiring others, such uncompromising attitudes only seem to result in novice rescuers simply disappearing from the animal rescue scene for good. It might help to remind ourselves that animal rescue is but "an attempt to recognize and extend care to others while acknowledging that we may not know what the best form of care is" (Weil, 2012, p. 17).

On the other hand, going it alone, which in this case means trying to help animals in need single-handedly, is extremely difficult, if not entirely impossible. It imposes severe limitations on one's efforts in assisting homeless animals, so that one can only provide food and water, makeshift shelter, or one-off visits to the vet in extreme circumstances. Street dogs are a migratory species and it is customary for them to travel miles in the course of a single day. Hundreds and thousands are injured or killed by cars on a yearly basis, and if they are sick, they often cannot receive regular veterinary treatment because they do not stay in one place long enough.

Another reason why some animal lovers may feel discouraged about taking part in organized rescue work is the community's rampant contradictions. For example, foster care as a crucial step in the process of rehoming is always a matter of some controversy. Whereas most local fosters only keep dogs on commercial terms and with a fixed monthly or daily rate, some still do the same job free of charge. Some have comparatively high visibility, others mostly stay out of the public eye. Some have made fostering their only source of income, others do it on the side. Some bring the animals inside, others keep them outside. Some take good care of their fosters, others starve them to death.

And yet another hotly contested issue in animal rescue relates to a set of rehoming policies preferred by some but violently opposed by others. It is common parlance that good homes are impossible to find in the country, and that promised dog land is always abroad. Although this assumption is not unreasonable, it is often compounded by what accompanies the transport of an animal to a foreign country. The costs are substantial, as they include a huge amount of paperwork (e.g., passport and the likes of health and veterinary inspection certificates), along with the unavoidable vetting and transportation fees. A couple of hundred euros per animal is the going rate, which is why those in the opposite camp argue that all that money would not be needed were the animals adopted within the country.

Overall, animal rescue communities across the region claim to rely entirely on donations in their work. Those that form ties with an affiliated animal charity abroad stand a better chance of receiving more substantial as well as regular assistance, but there is no way of knowing how generous the donations are. Transparency is not exactly a prominent feature among some of them, which means not only making the receipt of donations inaccessible to their followers but also withholding credit to the benefactors. This practice will be further addressed in the linguistic section of the paper.

Financial matters are not the only controversial aspect of international adoptions. Especially disturbing are allegations that homeless dogs are exported (i.e., sold) by the truckload to pharmaceutical labs and military facilities in the western part of Europe (e.g., Preradović, 2019). This is by far the greatest worry, but even the way animal transport is arranged can be a cause for concern: some animals travel cramped and stressed in the boot of a car to get to their new families in Germany or Austria, for instance, while others are handled with care or entrusted to specialized companies that transport newly adopted dogs across Europe. Nonstandard pet transport normally incurs a higher degree of risk, such as when a dog suffered a heat stroke in the car and died. Unfortunately, this is not the only time a rescue did not make it to its adopter alive.

Even when a rescue dog or cat makes it across the border, we may never hear of them again. Some adopters keep in touch, but other rescues disappear from our lives forever and we never know whether they are alive or dead. This might be less of a problem for the rescuers who do not foster animals themselves on the assumption that less emotional hazard is involved in finding an international home for their protégés in circumstances where the two have not spent enough time together to make the parting a traumatic experience.

There are times when animal rescue becomes a community so rife with conflict that many decide not to be a part of it. Scams and frauds involving money are frequent occurrences, too: though often with lack of evidence, every now and then new rescuers are accused of receiving ample donations and spending the money on themselves rather than the animals on whose behalf the donations were received. The animals are said to be starving and dying, the allegedly corrupt rescuer buying state-of-the-art gadgets, for instance. The ending is usually inconclusive, accusations random, insults grave, with a lot of confusion created in the animal rescue community and serious trust issues raised. By way of illustration, a web portal writes of a couple based in Germany who generously supported animal rescue efforts in Bosnia and Herzegovina until they realized that some individuals and rescue groups in the country used the suffering of animals for personal gain ("Donatori iz Njemačke," 2015). Again, the animals are the ones who suffer the most in these private wars as many international supporters back out soon afterwards. Whether the rescuer is guilty or not, the damage is done as soon as doubt creeps in.

PART TWO

Some Preliminaries

The idea behind introducing linguistic features to the story is to see how they dovetail with the anecdotal evidence presented in the previous passages. A linguistic analysis strives to expose and provide more solid evidence for some of the communicative practices involving animal rescuers and their supporters. The focus is on the language of select Facebook posts, and the goal is to uncover some of the linguistic forms and functions that promote the rescuers, either self-proclaimed or affiliated with an animal rescue group, but marginalize both their supporters and animals featuring in the posts. The rescuers' own involvement is foregrounded as a matter of course, and the presence of others backgrounded through the use of clause patterns and word forms such as the ones described in the following passages.

The analysis carried out is strictly qualitative, and the hope remains that what it reveals is not the dominant way of communication in the animal rescue community depicted here. All the Facebook posts included in the study were originally written in Serbian and collected in the course of a fortnight between March and April of 2017. The Facebook posts I daily read on animal rescue pages were narrowed down through a process of self-selection (i.e., appropriate size and content presentation) to a micro-corpus of texts coinciding with orthographic sentences. Rather than analyze each post in its entirety, I chose to focus on segments that give linguistic embodiment to the related practices of the promotion of self and withholding credit to others.

The linguistic devices described in this section of the paper show how language can become strategic in expressing bias. To this end, I translated into English and used for illustrative purposes select sentences from the corpus. Although the source language was Serbian rather than English, I remained committed to a functional approach based on English (e.g., Halliday, 1985; Halliday & Matthiessen, 2004; Bloor & Bloor, 2004; Downing & Locke, 2002). I either focused on what is similar in the two language systems or relied on some of the basic theoretical tenets that are not considered language-specific. Whenever possible, I also retained a terminological bias towards English to honor the theoretical model which supported the analysis. Finally, I tried to combine the two systems by adding those language-specific features not found in English whenever I thought the analysis would benefit from such inclusion. Most of the study was grounded in the functional approach briefly sketched out in the following section, while the treatment of the noun phrase, notably headwords and their determiners, drew from a more general structural framework (e.g., Quirk et al., 1985).

Agency and Systemic Functional Grammar

Agency is an essential concept in this study, and understanding whether it is expressed or concealed, strong or weak, requires a look at what systemic functional grammar (SFG) calls the ideational metafunction (e.g., Bloor & Bloor, 2004, pp. 10–11). Of the three metafunctions, the ideational one is believed to be the most relevant in this case as it helps us to make sense of the world we live in. It is concerned with how our ideas of the world, the way we see and experience what is inside and around us, are expressed in linguistic terms. That world of ideas and experiences is populated with processes, participants, and circumstances (e.g., Halliday & Matthiessen, 2004, pp. 168–305).

There are material processes, those of doing, where agency may be expressed very strongly (e.g., *the volunteers are cleaning the kennels*). Then there are mental processes, those related to cognition and sensing, which espouse an inward-driven kind of agency (e.g., *Tatjana loves all animals*). There are also relational processes, which can result in especially weak agency of identification, attribution, or possession (e.g., *that rescuer has a heart of gold*). There are other processes, too (e.g., existential, verbal, behavioral, etc.), but they are not as common as material, mental, or relational ones.

Each process chooses its preferred set of participants, some of which have been given almost self-explanatory names: material processes notably have Actors, Goals, Scopes, and Recipients; mental processes basically have Sensers and Phenomena; and relational ones have, among others, Carriers and Attributes. Actors are doers or agents in the most direct sense of the word; the rest are much more attenuated or relegated to complementary roles of that to which the process extends, as is the case with the more physically oriented Goal (e.g., *the fence* in *the neighbor is fixing the fence*) or by definition the more abstract Scope (e.g., *a bath* in *the dogs are having a bath*). Furthermore, not all material processes imply the same amount of agency: for instance, biological processes belong in the material group but to say that someone has had a litter cannot be likened to the fully intentional agency of someone rescuing a blind dog and her six puppies.

Agency and Clause Structure

Passives are especially conspicuous structures in clause as representation, which harks back to the ideational metafunction, since they are a convenient linguistic device for concealing agency (e.g., *the kennels are being cleaned* leaves us with only one participant, *the kennels* as Goal, while the slot of Actor remains unoccupied). Passivization is not the only device with the potential to obscure agency (Fowler, 1991, p. 78); nominalization is very fruitful in that respect, too (p. 79). Serbian also abounds in impersonal structures (Piper & Klajn, 2014, pp. 433–436) and pronominal passives (p. 185), both of which can be used to bypass agency.

The role of the passive in the animal rescue pages analyzed here is mostly to communicate that animals are the victims of human negligence, irresponsibility, and abuse. Such use of the passive is understandable considering the rate of animal abandonment in the region, which is rampant. Dogs and cats are thrown out routinely, especially females when they get pregnant or have a litter, but also senior and sick animals, animals that have grown too big, animals that their former owners leave behind when they move house or when they go on holiday, or simply animals that their former owners have had enough of. They are dumped out of cars too far from home to be able to find their way back, or left by the side of the road, either a busy motorway or one that is used very sporadically. They are left to die in deserted, uninhabited places with no human presence in sight. They are thrown into skip bins, entire litters in plastic bags tied tightly to make sure they cannot make their way out. As expected, few are lucky enough to be rescued.

The passives in (1) and (2) below are illustrative of ellipsis in that they only contain the Serbian participles *odbačeni* and *ostavljen* without the auxiliaries *su* and *je*, respectively. One of the effects is that they almost read like headlines, urging the reader to fill in the blanks and aiming to provoke a reaction.

(1) Tipično za ovaj kraj, odbačeni u hrpu smeća.[1]

(2) Živ pas ostavljen kao da je riječ o običnom smeću.[2]

Human agency is deleted most likely because the perpetrators are unknown; acts of abandonment are commonly performed out of sight to avoid responsibility and social stigma. As for the abandoned animals in (1) and (2) above, their agency is taken away by the humans who got rid of them as if they were unwanted or broken objects. The references to rubbish, either metaphorical or literal, serve as powerful symbols of their perceived value in society. The passives in (1) and (2) may also be interpreted as an attempt to show how helpless and vulnerable animals are when they are victimized by humans.

The black dogs in (3) are condemned by humans who do not want to adopt them because of their color, except that human agency is implicit in this case. Black dogs are generally known to be less adoptable as a result of prejudice, among other things. The reference to money is most likely a plea for financial assistance, but the wording may also imply that black rescues become a liability after a while. It seems that both lexis and social stigma have conspired against these dogs, silencing their agency in the process.

(3) Crni psi su i dalje osuđeni na život u prihvatilištu, koji košta.[3]

Sometimes the passive can be used to conceal human agency that is beneficial to animals, as in the case of undisclosed donations in (4) and uncredited assistance in animal rescue efforts in (5). It is always inspiring and uplifting to read about good deeds performed by animal lovers that have not been reduced to a nameless status. Posts that are less transparent or withhold such information altogether, on the other hand, are always something of a letdown and can rightfully arise suspicion in the reader.

(4) Prevoz je plaćen zahvaljujući vašim donacijama.[4]

(5) Pokupljen je sa ulice još prije tri mjeseca.[5]

Pronominal passives perform the same role in Serbian as participial passives do in English, to which they also add a general feeling of actions performed routinely. In (6) the reader is expected to assign agency to the locally funded dog-catching company. In (7) we are reminded, somewhat dryly and laconically, of the brutal truth that not all dogs can be saved. The pronoun *all* is another acknowledgment that there are too many animals not lucky enough to be saved by anyone. I am not sure whether it is a feeling of desperation or cold-blooded common sense that emanates from this dooming six-word comment in Serbian.

(6) Psi se kupe svaki dan.[6]

(7) Ne mogu se svi ni spasiti.[7]

In the English rendition of (8), the gentle giant plays a part in the semantic role called Existent, which, as the name suggests, is clearly lacking in agency. On the other hand, the original caption in Serbian does not express the idea of existence at all; instead, it makes the process a relational one focusing on possession, i.e., *the gentle giant has a solution.* What is unusual about it is that this metaphorical expression of possession in Serbian once again obscures whatever real agency is involved in the story, i.e., the reader is none the wiser about what the solution is or who has come up with it.

(8) Nežni div ima rešenje.[8]

There is a lot of implied information in (9), too: the puppy that the post is about is a Possessor in a relational process again, from which we can only understand that a dog has been brought into a warm room by someone who happens to be a student. That is the only fact conveyed to the reader, while the rest of the post is made to sound more poignant than factual. In addition, the closing line has an alarming sound to it, as if the student will only keep the puppy inside for the night.

(9) Večeras ima toplu korpicu i sigurnost studentske sobice, a sutra . . . Sutra je već novi dan pun neizvjesnosti.[9]

Another relational process, this time focusing on attribution, is found in (10). The female dog featuring in the update posted online is recovering from surgery, but the dog's agency in a material process has been replaced with the role of Carrier in a relational process. The Attribute, *in recovery from spaying surgery*, features the nominalization *recovery*, which derives from the process *to be recovering*. The nominalization implies that the dog is somewhere where she can be monitored instead of being left to her own devices, but the information that has been deleted is where exactly, who has made it possible, and whether someone has paid for it or volunteered to take her in free of charge.

(10) Trenutno je na oporavku od sterilizacije.[10]

The processes in (11) and (12) are also of a relational kind featuring attribution, and both tell very sad stories: the Attributes are the prepositional phrase *in the public shelter* and the adjective *dead*, and the Carriers are *he*, a very sweet dog, and *most* (of the dogs), respectively. Relational processes imply a small degree of agency and suggest that animals, generally speaking, are but victims of circumstances. Relational processes are also stative and resultative, i.e., their job is simply to express states of being and not foreground the processes leading to them.

(11) Jako je umiljat ali nažalost je završio u azilu.[11]

(12) Nažalost, većina završi mrtva.[12]

A mixture of relational and material processes in (13) and (14) expose the social and linguistic contexts conducive to the assignment of different semantic roles to humans and animals, which helps to better understand the life of an animal living rough in Bosnia and Herzegovina. The material process in the subordinate clause opening the sentence in (13), active in Serbian but rendered passive in English, is followed by the relational process of attribution in the main clause, which suggests that the dog's fearfulness is a result of the treatment he has received from humans—with very few exceptions, too, judging by the expression *almost everyone*.

(13) Pošto ga gotovo svi proganjaju, jako je plašljiv i nemoguće ga je uhvatiti.[13]

(14) Nije ničija, nađena nekidan, odveli je kući, okupali, izgleda kupili i ogrlicu, i vratili nazad.[14]

There is a total of five material processes in (14), four of which are active in Serbian but rendered passive in English on account of thematic progression, which keeps this sequence of clauses consistent in being about a dog. The perspective remains clear in both wordings, Serbian and English, just as it remains sadly clear that the fate of nobody's dog whose home is the street is always a gamble: alive now and gone the very next minute. The opening clause with a relational process of possession makes for a pessimistic introduction, which is unfortunately echoed in the way the sentence ends, only this time through a material process: she is nobody's dog and there is no happy ending, only a series of four related events that may have given the dog a chance to feel what it is like to belong to someone, get a bath, and wear a collar. Human agency remains implicit in the original wording, too, despite four active material clauses in a sequence: in all four of them the Actor is merely encoded in the verb, i.e., not even pronominalized.

Mental processes, although one of the three major verbal categories, are comparatively rare in the animal rescue posts analyzed here. The only context in which they appear with more regularity is the formulaic expression *s/he needs a home*, the Serbian equivalent of which is *potreban dom*. The wording in (15) below has a funnier twist on the caption and allocates more (mental) agency to the Senser. Otherwise, animals are much more often assigned the semantic role of Phenomenon, while that of Senser customarily entails human referents, as in (16). This update contains four different processes, the first two of which are material with deleted agency; the third process is material with agency assigned to the animal referent, possibly in an attempt to obfuscate human responsibility; and the last one is mental with *her*, the dog, as Phenomenon and *no-one* as Senser in the fatalistic clause *no-one wants her*.

(15) On je odlučio da sebi sam nađe dom.[15]

(16) Sklonjena s ulice, sterilisana, ali nažalost opet mora na ulicu, niko je ne želi.[16]

Material processes with animals as agents, when they occur in the posts, support comparatively weak agency mostly tied to biological and other outcomes that do not entail any more "doing" than is already found in some relational processes, for instance. It is the meaning of the verb that makes all the difference, for material processes realized by lexical verbs such as *hit* and *kick* are undeniably more action-oriented than those containing lexical verbs such as *wait* and *stay* in (17) and (18), respectively. Although the waiting almost translates to a state of being in (17), there is reason to hope for a happy ending as beautiful dogs generally stand a better chance of getting adopted.

(17) I ovaj ljepotan na ulici čeka svoj dom.[17]

(18) Oni ostaju dok im ne presude.[18]

Both clauses in (18) are active in Serbian, but the first one, *they stay*, is seen as temporally contingent on the second, *until they are sent to death*. The English passive deletes human agency and keeps the pronominal reference *they*, the dogs, thematic in both clauses. It matches closely enough the caption in Serbian as human agency is not made explicit in the original text either: the subject of the second clause is encoded in the verb and presumably used with reference to those in charge of the public shelter. Both processes are material, too, but only the Actor in the second clause, whether pronominal or deleted, determines the fate of the Actor in the first clause.

The material processes in (19), (20), and (21) all have biologically determined Actors: those living, those dying, and those giving birth to their young. However, it seems that even such involuntary processes are conditioned by human mediation: the dogs in (19) are living their last days on earth because they will be killed; the cat in (20) will die if humans do not save her; and the news of the abandoned dog in (21) having her babies on the street is a matter of some urgency. All three only entail agency in the context of bare and conditional existence, and what becomes of these animals is really in the hands of humans. To let nature run its course, especially in the case of (20) and (21), most likely means to let them succumb to an illness or freeze to death, among other things.

(19) Oni žive svoje zadnje dane.[19]

(20) Ova maca će uginuti ako je neko ne spasi.[20]

(21) Odbačena skotna kujica se oštenila.[21]

What these and other examples suggest is that animal agency is generally weak, and that animals are viewed as being dependent on humans, who in turn need to assist them in their survival and ease their suffering. However, human agency is also largely subdued, not only in cases where humans are the doers of good deeds but also where they fail to provide assistance or, even worse, harm the animals around them in a number of ways, e.g., by abandoning them, shooting at them, persecuting them, and so on.

It is hard to say which is more harmful to animals: withholding credit to those who care for and help animals or protecting by silence those who do them harm. Fear and legal repercussions are the likeliest of motives for the latter; the former, I believe, has mostly to do with vanity, lack of awareness, or sheer carelessness. Whichever of these may be true, it is unpardonable if it prevents more animals from living better lives.

The Vagueness of Nominal and Pronominal Forms

Apart from processes and participants, nouns and pronouns can be put at the service of underspecification and information loss, both regarding humans and animals. Nouns that are either general or common, and pronouns that are either indefinite or personal—counterintuitive as it may sound—are very good at concealing the identity of their referents.

The general noun *people* in (22) is premodified by the adjective *good*, but the reader will never know who the good people are. As no names are provided, the good people from the post only exist as an abstraction whose realness requires a leap of faith.

(22) Zahvaljujući dobrim ljudima dobila je bar to, sigurnost od ulice i redovne obroke.[22]

It is not clear from the context of (23) whether the same general noun, *ljudi*, which translates to *people* in English, is definite or indefinite. Without more context to disambiguate the reference, it could be either since postverbal position alone is not enough to render the noun semantically definite. This kind of indeterminacy may even be a deliberate choice, and the only difference between the nominal expressions in (22) and (23) is the absence of a premodifier in the latter.

(23) Odneće ih ljudi i ostaviće ih ko zna gde.[23]

Of course, no anonymous praise is given for getting rid of puppies, but the point is that even deeds that are not praiseworthy are kept in the dark. There may be several reasons for this but the following two are especially prominent: not knowing the identity of the agent or not feeling confident about naming them, possibly out of fear. Anonymity has a dual role in animal rescue posts on Facebook: it makes both good and bad deeds less visible, along with their doers.

The indefinite pronoun *someone* in (24) strikes a similar chord, although in this context it is clear that the act of finding the puppies was temporally distanced from the act of leaving them in different locations; moreover, it is speculative whether the latter was committed by one or more individuals and whether it was done strategically or accidentally. In this case, the underspecification is clearly a product of not knowing what really happened.

(24) Pronađeni su juče, neko ih je rasijao po gradu, vjerovatno ih ima još.[24]

Although the negative pronoun *no-one*, which translates to *niko* in Serbian, does a similar job in (25), the difference is that the negative pronominal meaning further reinforced by the emphatic adverb *even*, which translates to *ni* in Serbian, carries with it more judgmental undertones. The mention of a restaurant may also have something to do with provoking an emotional response.

(25) Niko iz restorana ne želi ni da ih nahrani.[25]

The plural pronoun in (26) is indefinite, which does not tell us who the followers, supporters, and helpers are since they remain nameless.

(26) Hvala svima koji prate, podržavaju i pomažu moj rad, koji su uz mene i moje krznene prijatelje.[26]

In Serbian, where nominal heads do not require determination (i.e., articles), indefiniteness is sometimes expressed through numerals functioning as indefinite pronouns (Piper & Klajn, 2014, p. 114), as is the case with *jedna* in (27). The clause in Serbian is active, its English rendition passive, but the latter has yielded a word order almost identical to that of the original clause.

(27) O njenoj sestrici brine jedna predivna mlada porodica.[27]

It is clear that whoever has made this post on Facebook knows who the wonderful young family is, but for some reason decides to keep their identity from the rest of us who will read the post. The same effect is produced by the use of plural pronouns, as well as third person singular ones, when no prior identification has been made to justify the ensuing pronominal reference.

In the case of (28) the plural pronoun *they* has a rather general reference; for all we know, the referents may or may not be real, they may or may not exist. Their almost fictitious status seems to be at odds with a repetitive use of the pronoun: they certainly feature too prominently to be denied a more explicit form of identification. Although one's privacy is not to be taken lightly, there is no easily justifiable reason to hide or marginalize an act of kindness. Those behind it may not need public recognition but that does not mean that they should not receive it. Some acknowledgment in that direction may encourage more people to do good and inspire others to follow suit (even if it means starting a competition in doing good deeds!).

(28) Obećali su da će ga tražiti i probati dovesti nama. Kažu da ga svaki dan traže.[28]

Giving preference to common nouns over proper names can obscure both positive and negative actions. A general noun with animate reference keeps the identity of the woman in (29) undisclosed, and the negatively connoted indefinite noun in (30) also has a vague referent. Why the man's identity is not revealed may have to do with an unreliable information source, or even fear. On the other hand, why the identity of the woman in (29) should be kept secret is much harder to understand, unless the offer comes with a price tag attached to it.

(29) Dobila sam ponudu za foster, žena bi se odrekla posla i bila uz štence 24 sata.[29]

(30) Još iste noći kad su pronađene uginula je zbog zlotvora koji navodno tako redovno izbacuje štence.[30]

Sometimes the implications are of a political kind, as in (31), with the rescuer alluding to the party she believes to be responsible for the dire state of unwanted animals in her town. In this case it is clear that she hesitates to point the finger of blame and allocate responsibility with more precision out of concern for her own safety. It is common for local and regional public shelters to fall within the jurisdiction of the leading political party, of which one can be reminded in a number of subtle and less subtle ways. Some rescuers have had their work sabotaged, their Facebook accounts disabled, and some have even received calls from the police. The same concerns are expressed and the same apprehension felt in (32), although this time the general pronoun *they* gives way to the indefinite pronoun *someone*, which becomes *neko* in Serbian.

(31) Sve je išlo kako treba dok nisu došli oni.[31]

(32) Sve ovo neko uporno pokušava da negira i skloni sa strane.[32]

Last but not least, even animal lovers can contribute to this atmosphere of anonymity and irrelevance, and even when they make references to animals themselves. I am not sure that this is always or ever done by design, but such wordings surely do not highlight the uniqueness and importance of the animal that the post is about. In (33), for example, a young girl reports the existence of a stray animal to her local animal rescue community on Facebook by using the indefinite pronominal adjective *neki* (Piper & Klajn, 2014, p. 113). It is true that she accompanies it with a term of endearment, *ćuko*, along with a photo, but the announcement still reads too casually, as if it was not meant to be taken very seriously.

(33) Ovo je neki ćuko kojeg sam juče vidjela u mojoj ulici.[33]

In general, the use of indefinite nouns and pronouns, along with other nominal and pronominal forms which do not help the reader to identify their referents, indicates that there is a lot of missing information in the animal rescue posts analyzed here. Neither bad nor good deeds are addressed with nearly enough clarity, and the motives are more or less the same ones pointed out in the section dealing with agency, i.e., mostly fear and vanity. I strongly believe that an increase in transparency might do wonders and inspire scores of enthusiastic animal lovers to close ranks and do more good for the suffering animals, who need their human advocates and helpers more than ever. A combination of self-promotion and withholding credit is not the way to get there, and hopefully those who consider themselves rescuers will begin to understand how much harm it can do.

CLOSING REMARKS

Animals are ever more at the mercy of humans with whom they share their habitat, and their very existence in Bosnia and Herzegovina and most of the Balkans region is becoming more threatened by the day: they are thrown off bridges and into rivers, clubbed to death, burned alive, blown up with explosives planted inside their mouths, split in half with axes, decapitated, hanged, and more (e.g. "Objesila psa pred djetetom," 2019). I have seen footage and read stories about unthinkable atrocities committed against man's best friend, which call for many more papers and many more voices raised in protest.

It is comforting to know that the animal rescue Facebook community is one of those voices. The community could do even more good if it avoided some of the practices that are perceived as less desirable and encouraged those that are known to have positive effects. The recommendations below are not listed in order or preference or priority, while the imperative form is used as a reminder of the importance of dialogue and understanding in the community, as well as a symbol of interaction and cooperation among its members. Those who care about the well-being of animals understand the need for this checklist.

Remember that those involved in animal rescue experience varying levels of frustration on a daily basis, so show compassion and have patience in your dealings with each other. Bear in mind that language matters, both when we talk to each other and about the animals who need us, so try not to use words that may offend or belittle anyone. Express gratitude for every act of kindness, however small, and be careful of overreacting when you think that not enough has been done. Give credit where it is due but protect the anonymity of those who do not want their identity to be revealed. Teach by example and raise awareness about the needs of animals, both on Facebook and in real life. Talk about animals with respect and be their voice by telling their stories and sharing them with others. Acknowledge the receipt of donations in money and food and commend publicly every other kind of assistance.

The change that animal lovers like myself hope to see is more people working together to alleviate the suffering of animals in our town, country, and region. We hope to see more people feeding and petting the animals they now pass by in the street as if they were invisible. Above all, we want the animals to finally be acknowledged, and not forever shunned; we want them to be protected from danger and harm and to feel safe around humans. We want to see their helpers stand united, and not always divided. We want every human effort in helping animals in need to set an example for others to follow.

NOTES

1. Typical for this area, discarded in a pile of rubbish. (All translations by Tatjana Marjanović.)
2. A live dog left behind like a piece of rubbish.
3. The black dogs are still condemned to a life in the shelter, which takes money.
4. The trip has been paid for thanks to your donations.
5. He was picked up off the street as long as three months ago.
6. Dogs are collected every day.
7. They cannot all be saved after all.
8. There is a solution for the gentle giant.
9. Tonight s/he has a warm little basket and the safety of a student dorm room, and tomorrow . . . Tomorrow is yet another day filled with uncertainty.
10. Currently she is in recovery from spaying surgery.
11. He is very sweet but has unfortunately ended up in the public shelter.
12. Unfortunately, most end up dead.
13. As he is maltreated by almost everyone, he is very fearful and impossible to catch.

14. She is nobody's dog, was found the other day, taken home, given a bath, apparently even bought a collar, and then returned to the street.

15. He has decided to find his own home.

16. Taken off the street, spayed, but unfortunately she has to go back to the street, no-one wants her.

17. This beautiful boy in the street is also waiting homeless.

18. They stay until they are sent to death.

19. They are living their last days.

20. This kitty will die if someone does not save her.

21. The discarded pregnant dog has had her babies.

22. Thanks to good people she has got at least that, safety from the street and regular meals.

23. People will take them and leave them who knows where.

24. They were found yesterday, someone scattered them across town, there are probably more.

25. No-one from the restaurant even wants to feed them.

26. Thank you to all who follow, support and help with my work, who are there for me and my furry friends.

27. Her little sister is being looked after by a wonderful young family.

28. They promised to look for him and try to bring him to us. They say they look for him every day.

29. I have received a foster home offer, the woman would give up her job and look after the puppies 24/7.

30. The same night they were found, she died because of an evil man who allegedly makes a habit of getting rid of newborn puppies.

31. All went well until they came.

32. Someone keeps trying to deny all this and keep it out of sight.

33. This is some pup that I saw in my street yesterday.

SELECTED BIBLIOGRAPHY

BBC (n.d.). *Ethics guide: Animal welfare legislation.* Retrieved September 22, 2017, from http://www.bbc.co.uk/ethics/animals/defending/legislation_1.shtml

Bloor, T., & Bloor, M. (2004). *The functional analysis of English.* London: Arnold.

Caesar, T. (2009). *Speaking of animals: Essays on dogs and others.* Leiden/Boston, MA: Brill.

DeMello, M. (2012). *Animals and society: An introduction to human-animal studies.* New York, NY: Columbia University Press.

Donatori iz Njemačke optužuju bh. "zaštitnike životinja" za zloupotrebu pasa i profiterstvo. (2015, April 16). Saff. http://saff.ba/donatori-iz-njemacke-optuzuju-bh-zastitnike-zivotinja-za-zloupotrebu-pasa-i-profiterstvo/

Downing, A., & Locke, P. (2002). *A university course in English grammar.* London/New York, NY: Routledge.

Durham, D., & Merskin, D. (2009). Animals, agency, and absence: A discourse analysis of Institutional Animal Care and Use Committee meetings. In S. E. McFarland & R. Hediger (Eds.), *Animal agency: An interdisciplinary exploration* (pp. 229–247). Leiden/Boston, MA: Brill.

Fowler, R. (1991). *Language in the news: Discourse and ideology in the press.* London/New York, NY: Routledge.

Grad Banja Luka. (n.d.). *Prihvatilište za pse*. Retrieved April 27, 2020, from http://www.banjaluka.rs.ba/gradjani/prihvatiliste-za-pse/?sr_pismo=lat

Halliday, M. A. K. (1985). *An introduction to functional grammar*. London: Edward Arnold.

Halliday, M. A. K., & Matthiessen, C. (2004). *An introduction to functional grammar*. London: Hodder Arnold.

Komšija mu otrovao psa: Moje dete je odraslo uz Lili, a sad je umrla u najgorim mukama (uznemirujući video). (2018, August 8). Kurir. https://www.kurir.rs/vesti/srbija/3099483/komsija-mu-otrovao-psa-moje-dete-je-odraslo-uz-lili-a-sad-je-umrla-u-najgorim-mukama-uznemirujuci-video

Mayer, J. (2009). Representing the experimental animal: Competing voices in Victorian culture. In S. E. McFarland & R. Hediger (Eds.), *Animal agency: An interdisciplinary exploration* (pp. 183–205). Leiden/Boston, MA: Brill.

McFarland, S. E. (2009). Dancing penguins and a pretentious raccoon: Animated animals and 21st century environmentalism. In S. E. McFarland & R. Hediger (Eds.), *Animal agency: An interdisciplinary exploration* (pp. 89–103). Leiden/Boston, MA: Brill.

Nyman, J. (2016). Re-reading sentimentalism in Anna Sewell's *Black Beauty*: Affect, performativity, and hybrid spaces. In J. Nyman & N. Schuurman (Eds.), *Affect, space and animals* (pp. 65–79). London/New York, NY: Routledge.

Objesila psa pred djetetom: Žena ispitana u policiji zbog brutalnog ubijanja životinje. (2019, April 1). Srpskainfo. https://srpskainfo.com/objesila-psa-pred-djetetom-zena-ispitana-u-policiji-zbog-brutalnog-ubijanja-zivotinje/

Onion, R. (2009). Sled dogs of the American North: On masculinity, whiteness, and human freedom. In S. E. McFarland & R. Hediger (Eds.), *Animal agency: An interdisciplinary exploration* (pp. 129–155). Leiden/Boston, MA: Brill.

Piper, P., & Klajn, I. (2014). *Normativna gramatika srpskog jezika*. Novi Sad: Matica srpska.

Preradović, Lj. (2019, September 29). Otimaju pse iz Srbije i koriste ih kao pokretne mete! *Novosti*. https://www.novosti.rs/vesti/naslovna/hronika/aktuelno.291.html:821273-Otimaju-pse-iz-Srbije-i-koriste-ih-kao-pokretne-mete

Prijeti mu robija: Uhapšen serijski trovač pasa iz Jajca, otrovao 35 životinja. Faktor. (2020, April 8). https://www.faktor.ba/vijest/prijeti-mu-robija-uhapsen-serijski-trovac-pasa-iz-jajca-otrovao-35-zivotinja/78253

Psi lutalice napadaju prolaznike. (2017, September 30). ATV. https://www.atvbl.com/banjaluka-psi-lutalice-napadaju-prolaznike

Quirk, R., Greenbaum, S., Leech, G., & Svartvik, J. (1985). *A comprehensive grammar of the English language*. London: Longman.

Scott, S. R. (2009). The racehorse as protagonist: Agency, independence, and improvisation. In S. E. McFarland & R. Hediger (Eds.), *Animal agency: An interdisciplinary exploration* (pp. 45–65). Leiden/Boston, MA: Brill.

Squier, S. (2009). Fellow-feeling. In T. Tyler & M. Rossini (Eds.), *Animal encounters* (pp. 173–196). Leiden/Boston, MA: Brill.

Taylor, N. (2012). Animals, mess, method: Post-humanism, sociology and animal studies. In L. Birke & J. Hockenhull (Eds.), *Crossing boundaries: Investigating human-animal relationships* (pp. 37–50). Leiden/Boston, MA: Brill.

U prihvatilištu 140 pasa: Ove godine udomljena 52 ljubimca. (2018, July 28). Frontal. https://www.frontal.ba/novost/92992/u-prihvatilistu-140-pasa-ove-godine-udomljena-52-ljubimca

Vlasnica psa: Našeg labradora je otrovao komšija. (2014, January 21). Mondo. https://mondo.rs/Info/Drustvo/a654209/Vlasnica-psa-Naseg-labradora-je-otrovao-komsija.html

Warkentin, T. (2009). Whale agency: Affordances and acts of resistance in captive environments. In S. E. McFarland & R. Hediger (Eds.), *Animal agency: An interdisciplinary exploration* (pp. 23–43). Leiden/Boston, MA: Brill.

Weil, K. (2012). *Thinking animals: Why animal studies now?* New York, NY: Columbia University Press.

Zakon o zaštiti i dobrobiti životinja, *Službeni glasnik RS, br. 111/2008*. Retrieved April 27, 2020, rom https://www.paragraf.ba/propisi/republika-srpska/zakon-o-zastiti-i-dobrobiti-zivotinja.html

Chapter Nine

Women, Nonhuman Animals, and the Notion of Marginalization in Bengali Literature

Swatilekha Maity

INTRODUCTION

The presence of animals in the mainstream literary platform is articulated through a deep-rooted dynamic between language and power that is steeped within a monolithic paradigm. Pearson and Weismantel (2010) suggest animal's position within the history of the Western literary canon is problematic because the entirety of Western metaphysics rests on dependency on linguistic abilities. Much has been written from a Critical Animal Studies (CAS) about the harms of focusing on Western metaphysics in literature for understanding animal consciousness (Shapiro & Copeland, 2005; Palmeri, 2020). From this perspective, it is interesting to observe how the presence of animals in literature creates a power dynamic among characters of varied sociocultural and gender backgrounds. As Cixous (2008) has noted, literature and the very act of writing is fundamentally interwoven with the gendered notions of power dynamics. Perceived from this aspect, writing is essentially a male domineering act, where women writers need to create their own literature by writing "through their body." Following the point, raised by Elizabeth Behnke, I intend to view the relation between animals and women as a form of "interanimality" (Behnke, 1999). She continues that according to Merleau-Ponty, "the human-animal relation is not a hierarchic one characterized by the 'addition' of rationality to a mechanistically conceived animal body, but a lateral relation of kinship" (Behnke, 1999). This relationship of kinship should be explored in relation to women's position in society and animals' involvement in the scenario. In terms of politics and CAS praxis, mainstream culture is androcentric culture itself and the oppression of animals is interlinked with the oppression based on gender and racial dynamics. Anthropocentricism emerges from an ideology which prioritizes itself with the narrative of dominance, that is centered around gendered and speciesist violence and ensures the continuation of this process in the society. The logocentric and androcentric aspect of civilization translates itself into mainstream literature, which, according to Ursula Le Guin's poignant observation is a platform where animals, women, and children are "obscure matter upon which civilisation erects itself phallologically" (Le Guin, 1988).

This analysis does not follow a chronological pattern, but rather maps the journey of the female protagonists and nonhuman animals to demonstrate how the evolution of the self and empowerment underscores a plethora of identity formation in its nascent stage. Short stories from male authors such as Tarashankar Bandyopadhyay, Sarat Chandra Chattopadhyay, and Rabindra Nath Tagore cover a range of subjects including gender, spatiality, and inclusion using interdisciplinary literary approaches. Most of the stories selected, are situated in colonial India and provide a provocative insight into women's contemporary sociohistorical milieu in society. There is an encompassing range of women characters that have varied economic, educational, and sociohistorical backgrounds. These texts present the social construction of women during a time when a woman's character and moral standards were implicated by social positioning. Some of these women characters endured ostracization and were defiant through deliberate and self-willed actions. In this way, these women characters emerge as outcasts in a predominantly androcentric, elitist society. Furthermore, the nonhuman animals enter into a heterogeneous yet mutually reciprocating dialogue, which underscores this "shared experience" of marginality. This analysis also focuses on how dominant literary metaphors used by Euro-American ideologies preface animals as inferior to humans, alongside women of color and other marginalized individuals within colonial and postcolonial India (Sabloff, 2001).

The analysis presented in this chapter gradually moves from a narrative of marginality into a position of centrality, which correlates to the situation of women and animals. Interestingly, nonhuman animals experience oppression, stigmatization, and a downtrodden existence symbiotically with women. Two of Sarat Chandra Chattopadhyay's stories, which include *Mahesh* (Sinha, 2004; Sinha, 2016) and *Bilashi* (Sinha, 2004), are noteworthy because they emphasize the marginalized, disenfranchised section of society and depart from the literary trends that prioritized the privileged over the disenfranchised, powerful over the silenced. The first part of this analysis centers on understanding disability and gendered identities in Sarat Chandra Chattopadhyay's *Mahesh* and Rabindra Nath Tagore's *Subha*. The alienation that both humans and nonhumans endure with their depth of communication, extends from the natural world to develop more consideration and sensibility toward each other. Using this framework of shared understanding, Tarashankar Bandyopadhyay's stories are explored to study a realistic co-existence of human beings and animals. In his works, some characters are conscious of their social difference, causing them to attune themselves toward their inner nature rather than external societal conditioning.

The second part of this chapter will address femininity with animality in the stories *Bilashi* by Chattopadhyay and Tarashankar Bandyopadhyay's *Bedeni* (*The Gypsy Woman*), *Nagini Kanyar Kahini* (*Tale of the Snake Girl*), and *Nari o Nagini* (*The Woman and the Serpent*). These stories highlight marginalization in divergent ways; the characters are subaltern survivors of a highly hostile society. Similar analyses have been arisen by CAS scholars including Kelly Svoboda's (2021) investigation of the exploitation of nonhuman animals and women within the novel of *The Handmaid's Tale* along with Sarah D'Stair's (2021) analysis of how nonhuman animals and other marginalized individuals are perceived within utopian British culture in the novel *Proud Man.* Both of these texts seek to deconstruct the anthropocentric and heterosexist ideologies surrounding the treatment of nonhuman animals but they do so within a Western framework. This chapter goes beyond traditional Western analysis to provide cultural insights into Indian perspectives related to nonhuman animal liberation and politics in literature. The three texts analyzed in this chapter provide counter narration to women's docility and nonhuman animal's struggle by creating their own subversive and radical narratives. This chapter focuses on the convergence of human and animal consciousness, and its effects on the characters. The third part of this chapter deals with the centrality of women characters and their defiant and righteous acts of recognition and solidarity with nonhuman beings in the narrative.

THE HUNGER, THE INDIFFERENCE, AND SHARED UNDERSTANDING IN HUMAN-ANIMAL BONDING

Sarat Chandra Chattopadhyay believed in an inclusive ideology, which has been reflected in all his works. His stories, novels, essays are peopled with the vagrants, the destitute, and those often forgotten and despised in colonial India. In his works the principal characters are fishermen, snake charmers, prostitutes, tramps, sharecroppers whose identities are rooted in prejudice of caste and religious persecution. *Mahesh* is a study in human-animal bonding in a fundamentally materialistic, cruel world, in which the subjugated animals are pitted against the subjugated human beings. What is noteworthy about this story is the centralized positioning of the animal subject. *Mahesh*

(*The Drought*) is a story about one family of father, daughter, and their dearly loved bull named Mahesh.

Gafoor is the weaver who resides in Kashipur in the midst of deplorable poverty with his ten-year-old daughter Amina. Given the sociocultural background of the story, they emerge as the outcasts as they are the only Muslim family residing in a predominantly Hindu village. From the very beginning of the story, the hierarchy is established in the narrative through Gafoor's interaction with the other characters; when contextualized within a locale dominated and controlled by religious politics and power, *Mahesh* asserts a testament of voicing the marginalized. When Gafoor falls ill with fever, the bull, Mahesh is tied out in the open sun, without food or water, left alone lest he becomes a nuisance to the neighbors. Neighbors of higher castes know that Gafoor cannot take Mahesh out to greener pastures, but they refuse to offer assistance and instead jeer at him with foul words. Regardless, Gafoor loves Mahesh and does not hesitate to do everything in his capacity to make his life comfortable. Furthermore, Amina's relationship with Mahesh establishes itself as one of those deeper bonds which transcends the threshold of species and verges on becoming sibling camaraderie. Mahesh emerges as the character, who stands there, literally as well as metaphorically to take in all the blames for the failure of human characters; he symbolizes with his silent presence the collective yet silenced populace, in whose lexicon, living is synonymous with never-ending tolerance with no route to retaliation.

Through the lens of mainstream literary criticism, one might consider Mahesh to be the embodiment of a downtrodden individual, whose central purpose is to live for others, internalize their pain, humiliation, and systematic denial. Mahesh emerges as the character who stands there, literally and metaphorically, to represent humanity's failures. But when explored from a critical animal studies perspective, Mahesh performs a pivotal role in the story. By acting according to his inherent impulses and initiating a course of events, Mahesh forces other characters to act accordingly. Mahesh is not only the passive recipient of human emotions with its range of cruelty to compassion; he is also an acting agent who dictates his own presence. When perceived from this angle, Mahesh's literary presence becomes a sacrificial motif, relatable to the Derridean perspective on animal presence in the domestic space (Danta, 2018). From the psychological as well as symbolical perspectives, Mahesh's last gaze appropriates the essentially exclusionary aspect of an anthropocentric worldview, which thrives on the scapegoat mechanism (Girard, 1988).

Dwelling in a village populated by the Hindu majority, Amina and Gafoor had to encounter much bullying due to their caste and religion. Some of the tormenting was involved goading the family to sell Mahesh to the nearby market for a possibly cruel purpose. Manik Ghosh, another character whose respect for bovines stemmed from a religious yet hollow, unsympathetic worldview, was said to take him to the Dariapur pen, as Mahesh intruded into his garden out of excruciating hunger. Chattopadhyay accentuates Gafoor's love for his Mahesh against the stark contrasts of Manik Ghosh and Tarkaratna, whose apparent respect for bovine animals stems from a strictly religious perspective. Gafoor's interactions with Mahesh underscores the pervasive force of shared hunger and excruciating uncertainty of their own existence. Their collective deprivation and hunger symbolize their systemic marginalization based on caste, religion, and species. It is interesting to point out that if we trace the course of animal rights as a movement in India, it becomes evident that the laws and legislative decisions were made to ensure the compassionate way of dealing with animals. A sweeping overview of the legislative proceedings of this time, demonstrates the emphasis on cattle, horses, and elephants, as they were more directly linked to the economic worth in contemporary time.

The direct correlation of animals with property was underscored by the proceedings related with cruelty to animals during colonial India. Several incidents were documented where the direct references to the incidents link the animal subjects with compensation and material worth. On the other hand, under the agricultural system of that time, we see that small farmers and sharecroppers were directly under the power and influence of the landlords, who functioned as the intermediate agents between these farmers and the colonial administration. There are multiple instances, which demonstrate the extent of these powerful landlords in their villages and in some cases including their own subordinates. Mahesh's own precarious position was accentuated with Gafoor's own vulnerability in the hands of these powerful people. This vulnerability is poignantly showcased in the process of Mahesh's relegation to a profit-worthy, tangible, labelled object in the eyes of people like the Muslim buyer. In the eyes of these Hindu characters as well as Gafoor's Muslim acquaintances, the process of transformation of a sentient, autonomous being to a mode of profit and objectification is linear and abrupt. The Muslim buyer indifferently interjects "only the skin is worth selling" (Sinha, 2016). Cornered down by the landlord, with intolerable pangs of hunger, Gafoor is compelled to decide between selling his dearly loved Mahesh and recuperating economically or staying together with Mahesh rooted in the traumatic existence of their shared quotidian life. Gafoor's act of killing Mahesh subliminally articulates his attempt to liberate Mahesh from this clutch of vicious existence, and in this way, this act of killing also verges onto an act of self-destruction. In the very last part of the story after the abrupt, climactic demise of Mahesh in the hands of Gafoor, the readers were made to fathom the equivalent position of women and animals in the contemporary period of economic crisis. The story takes place during colonial India during a time of drought and famine. Hunger becomes a significant motif in the story with the evocative imagery of emaciated Mahesh, empty bowl and the gesture of sharing food across principal human characters and their beloved bull.

Although occurring in a slightly different timeframe, famines in Bengal during the Second World War dominates the literary imagination of the time. The narrator tells us that, the areas around jute mills were equally unsafe for women, whose honor and safety could be compromised. In a word, the jute mills in the urban areas are the spaces, which are as antagonistic to women as the village was for Mahesh (Arnold, 1980). The expendability of women as well as animals is consolidated with just one line, which showcases the capacity of predominantly androcentric society to devalue its animals and women subjects. This notion of materializing women as well as animals into expendable instruments, which can translate into objects of essentially tangible, countable worth, is itself a process of denying these individuals their own selfhood. By situating animals and women outside, the mainstream, patriarchal society actually ensures a position of systematic subjugation. By performing an indifference to these autonomous beings, the contemporary society maintained a power dynamics, relegating women and animals to a fundamentally marginalized position.

The mutually responsive and complementary relationship between women and animals point towards the bond of solidarity in an undermining society. In Rabindra Nath Tagore's short story *Subha*, we come across the eponymous protagonist, whose marginalization is multilayered stemming from a gendered as well as a disabled position. This story captures the "rite of passage" of Subha during her adolescence years. Tagore constantly juxtaposes the two opposing ways of interpreting Subha's representation; the human characters, including Pratap's view of her as a silent observer, whose identity is defined by a lack, is countered by her depiction as an interactive subject with other nonhuman beings and nature itself. Here in this story, this lack is her inability of utterance, which denies her entire mode of communication. On the other hand, her rendition according to the omniscient narrator's perspective clarifies her position as an active and capable participant with her two domesticated cows, named Sarbbashi and Panguli, the goats and the kitten. This story hinges on a crux of ability or disability of articulation. It is an important point of departure from *Mahesh*, as here the incomprehensibility of nonverbal communication eludes the grasp of majority of the human beings, yet animal companions succeed. Tagore writes, "Whenever she heard any words that hurt her, she would come to these dumb friends out of due time. It was as though they guessed her anguish of spirit from her quiet look of sadness" (Tagore, 1918). The story centralizes the animal presence by prioritizing this animal communication over the human ones, which fails to decipher the nonverbal communication of Subha. The animals enter into an interspecies communication with Subha and they undermine the essentially anthropocentric perspective of Subha as incapable of articulation. These animals inhabit a space of marginality, a niche that only grants them a position to serve humans and thus they are forced into a vicarious existence; by aligning them with the eponymous protagonist of the story, the narrator facilitates a centralized space for these animals in an interconnected, mutually reciprocative relationship beyond the comprehensibility of able-bodied, patriarchal anthropocentric societal conditioning. Seeing Subha's narrative from this angle, the story embodies the "collaborative aspect of nonhuman animals, nature and disabled human beings" in Eco-ability ideology (Nocella II et al., 2019). Alex Woloch maintains that the minority of characters in terms of importance can be traced through the qualitative presence in the narrative (Woloch, 2003). Considering this stylistic aspect, animals in this story are marginal, yet their ability of reciprocation and understanding a human subject creates a foray of centrality in the narrative. The space shared by the eponymous character with these nonhuman beings underscores her own position of peripherality in androcentric point of view which characterizes itself through its exclusion of difference, in terms of gender, ability, and species. It also asserts narrative of interspecies companionship beyond the patriarchal cultural conditioning.

THE WOMEN CHARACTERS AND THE CONVERGENCE OF MULTISPECIES CONSCIOUSNESS

Starting with *Manasamangal-kavya*, the snake charmers have occupied an ambiguous position in the literary landscape of Bengal. By eliciting the populace's voyeuristic curiosity, they incorporate a position of their own agency in a ritualized, forbidden yet psychologically provocative existence of a specific, marginalized community. The proximity with reptiles gives these people a unique rendition in the eyes of the populace who exercise curiosity, suspicion, and discernment. Seeing from this aspects Sarat Chandra Chattopadhyay's *Bilashi* (*The Snake Charmer's Daughter*), and Tarashankar Bandyopadhyay's *Nari o Nagini* (*The Woman and the Serpent*) and *Nagini Kanyar Kahini* (*Tale of the Snake Girl*) are studies in the marginalized community in colonial Bengal. What makes these stories stand out in animal studies and its discourses, is a specific stylistic rendition, which positions women characters at the axis of the story with their reptile companions in a position, oppressed in a multidimensional way. These stories expose a history of ostracization in the colonial India, in terms of space, race, and gender.

In *Bilashi*, we encounter characters who inhabit with nonhuman beings in the outskirts of civilized, educated urban populace. The notion of space is crucial to determine the hidden threads of human-animal interaction. In *Bilashi*, Chattopadhyay takes the readers into the lives of snake charmers or *bediyas*. It is a story on the poignancy of human love, vulnerability, and incomprehensibility of life. In this story, we find Mrityunjay and Bilashi as the human characters, who share a strange relationship with animals, more specifically with reptiles. Behind the veneer of love between Mrityunjay and Bilashi, we find a spirit of defiance against the casteism of the contemporary time. Mrityunjay, an upper caste man, fell in love with Bilashi, a lower caste woman from an ostracized community, as she served him and helped him to survive during his life-threatening sickness; he embraced not only Bilashi, but also her way of life, which was nonconformist and to a great extent, relegated to the level of transgression in comparison to the contemporary casteist, orthodox society. The narrator in the story, never lets us forget the magnitude of this relationship in terms of societal pressures and stigmatization. Mrityunjay's impulsive decisions are subtly interlinked with his upbringing in a hierarchically superior level of the society, which is distanced and distinct in terms of animal-human co-habitation. Hailing from an upper-caste and economically affluent family, Mrityunjay's knowledge of these reptiles lacks a certain level of intimacy and depth. Bilashi's multiple attempts to dissuade Mrityunjay from engaging with the dangerous game of snakes, underscores her all-too intimate knowledge of these nonhuman beings; her personal experience of proximity with these reptiles, does not allow her the idealistic yet distanced perspective towards them. The closure is borne out of her experience of being rooted in a way of life, that revolves around the co-existence of snakes and human beings. This co-existence is dependent, yet it also ensures a sense of respect towards these animal subjects.

This respect is taken onto another dimension, where the snakes are not only respected, but can also be regarded as the equals of human beings. In the works of Tarashankar Bandyopadhyay, the women characters are ostracized but they are unabashed and defiant in terms of asserting their own unique individuality to the world. There are several stories by Tarashankar which draw upon a rich source of oral tradition of Rarh Bengal, the central region of Bengal. In his works, the red soil of this region, the arid landscape of this specific locale, the hostility of nature is extended on to the human characters. His works expose a justifiable ambivalence in terms of human-animal relationship, as the proximity of contact and the lived experience of the natural world with all its diversities and difficulties, engender a polarized notion of emotional responses towards animals' bodies. The characters are conditioned to view them more on the equal plane with a sense of caution as well as subtle admiration than as beings waiting to be sympathized. In his story named *Bedeni* (*The Gypsy Woman*), the crudities of Shambhu are counterpoised by the sensuousness of Radhika. The torture inflicted on the tiger by Shambhu underscores a deep-rooted cruelty and disrespect to the animals. The co-habitation with a goat, a monkey, and a few of the snakes fails to soften Radhika's empathy towards these animals. Their presence in the story seems to function as the source of Radhika and Shambhu's material profit. Like the tiger of Shambhu, these animals' sole existence is relegated to the level of corporeality, measurable in strictly economical worth. Radhika has been directly compared with serpentine attributes of charm, grace, and a certain sense of ruthlessness. Bandyopadhyay's handling of her character betrays a sense of admiration which emerges from fear of the capable and confident women. The female desire is explored from an ambiguous point of view, which aligns destruction and manipulation with the exercise of feminine desire in a structurally parochial vision.

His *Nari o Nagini* (*The Woman and the Snake*) takes this concept of human beings' relationship with animals to a more problematic level. It is a story about Khonra Sheikh and his wife Zobeda and his pet snake, whom he named as Bibi. The narrative centers around Khonra's attempts to humanize the snake, an act which is problematic in multiple ways. Seen from this aspect, Bibi's position in the story is subjugated by an essentially anthropocentric, male-centered perspective. The part of the story which portrays his act of marriage to the snake, involves a certain level of disregard for the animal subjects on their own autonomous, independent selfhood. His humanizing attempts of the reptile creature by forcefully putting the nose ring on her and marking her with vermilion is an act of imposing femininity on to the body of the snake. It is an act which incorporates a certain amount of cruelty and violence on the creature's body. In discussing the position of dogs in Dickens's *Great Expectation*, Ivan Kreilkamp notes, how the domesticated animal's position is problematized due to their association and dependence with human beings (Kreilkamp, 2007). The story makes an important observation on how the animal in the human society, shares a dually marginalized position by sharing the space with subaltern outcasts, the disfigured and the ostracized. From a linear reading of the narrative, it may seem that the feeling of discernment and later, deep hatred expressed by his wife, Zobeda towards Bibi, is the conventional maneuvering pattern of instigating one oppressed against the another. But when read in the context of the story itself, it emerges that the power dynamics is very ambiguous here, as the story recurrently dwells on Zobeda's role as a capable person, stronger of the two. Khonra himself constantly points out his own dependence on Zobeda. His admiration towards his wife stems from a respect interwoven with gratitude for her. Seen from this level, his act of equating his pet snake as a potent rival of his wife can be his way of demonstrating the inherent identification with the animal subjects. This identification is transformed in a way, which influences even Zobeda's perspective towards Bibi. The overtly sexual jealousy felt by Zobeda towards the snake, articulates the dangers of this identification, which transcends the barriers of interspecies contact. The humanization on creaturely existence gives rise to a range of arguments in this context. It is inconclusive as the readers are left to decipher the emerging centrality of the two alternatives, the woman and the snake.

In the other story of Tarashankar Bandyopadhyay, *Nagini Kanyar Kahini* (*Tale of the Snake Girl*), we find the opposite form of internalization in the female psyche. This story is noteworthy as, it creates a matrix of multiple dimensions, the convergence of oral and folk tradition along with the rewriting of Hindu purana and the consequence of internalization of animal consciousness in human psyche. In this story, both the female characters are conditioned to internalize the animality in themselves. An animality which they strive to preserve against their personal, individual, corporeality. In her analysis of this story, Pritha Kundu has shown, how this story can be read from three distinct perspectives, "anthropological, psychological and mytho-critical" (Kundu, 2013). Kundu maintains that, Shabala and Pingala, the two women represent two differing renditions of individual spirit; "Shabala leaves the community to avenge the murder of her lover while Pingala ritualizes herself so keenly that she becomes the community" (Kundu, 2013). The story exercises the grasp of the orality on individual level, as their community demands them to forego their natural passions by imposing certain serpentine attributes. Pingala's increasing fear of her own desire is a deep-rooted conditioning of her collective consciousness, which systematically ensures the internalizing process of animality in herself. Kundu maintains that the story appropriates the power dynamics of the mainstream, canonical Hindu myth by reframing them in an essentially "subaltern" narrative. With this observation, I would like to include that it also performs another process of coercion too. It is interesting how Bandyopadhyay maneuvers the significance of olfactory senses in terms of aggression, sexual awakening and the cognizance of primal instincts. By associating smell and fragrance with the awakened femininity and animality of creaturely existence, Bandyopadhyay creates a space for the politicization of female body. Even without the direct corporeality of their presence, Bibi in *Nari o Nagini* asserts her identity through her smell; Pingala's fear emerges from her apprehension of her suppressed sexuality. It was a fear which was manipulated by Gangaram, the corrupt chieftain to make her distraught with her own guilt. The story ends with the return of Shabala as a Muslim snake charmer's wife and thus ends in a promise with the reappropriation and rewriting of the masculinist, elitist mainstream Hindu myth itself.

THE JOURNEY OF THE EMPATH IN THE CONTEXT OF WOMEN'S GROWING AWARENESS TOWARDS NONHUMAN BEINGS

From the narratives of marginalized women and their silent yet deep-rooted bonding with animal characters, the stories by Rabindra Nath Tagore take a different turn. It is very difficult to draw an outline of the references to every animal presence in his works, as his entire compendium of works are numerous. His poems, stories, and novels are peopled with animal characters, yet they are marginalized. Going by the sheer multiplicity of these animal subjects, it is very tempting to refute their positions of minority, yet when studied deeply, these stories underscore a different power dynamic in a fundamentally male-dominated worldview. It is not only the latent yet powerful and mutual understanding that betrays itself in human-animal bonding in his works. Rather it is the expository power of these animal-human bonding, which showcases the variant stages of species identification in relation to the women's integration in a male-dominated, and mostly heterosexual relationships. In the early part of this chapter, I have discussed the shared identifiability of women characters with their companion animals. The human-animal bonding in Tagore's women characters is inversely connected to their position in heterosexual relationships. In *Samapti* (*The Conclusion*), Mrinmayi's newly awakened love for her husband Amulya, makes her absent minded to her pet squirrel, and to that extent, that even his death fails to create a significant repercussion in her. Mrinmayi's love for the flora and fauna of her surroundings is rendered as an articulation of the independent streak in her character, which is unconventional in the role of a romantically inclined girl. The rite of passage in her life ensures the increasing distance between her and the natural world with all its animals, birds, and trees. These deeper influences of patriarchal intervention are potently reflected through her utter indifference to the pet squirrel. The episode with the squirrel is an important pointer of her transformation from a girl, who is confident in her ability to synchronize with the natural world to a home loving, conformist young wife. Seen from this aspect, the squirrel who is only mentioned a few times in the story performs an integral purpose in addressing the women's relationship with animals. In another novel, *Chaturanga* (*Four Chapters*), Sreebilas notes how Damini becomes increasingly indifferent to the pet eagle and the mongoose, when Sachis left for a few days. These subtle hints in various works of Tagore are inconclusive and ambiguous on a multidimensional aspect.

On the other side, the strong women characters demonstrate a more conspicuous affinity in their relationship with animals. In this part of the chapter, I will argue that the rising autonomy in women's identity can be traced to their awakened compassion and solidarity towards animals. In this part, I would like to argue that the growing awareness for the animals and a bond of solidarity with them, are symptomatic of assertion of female autonomy which compels a pluralistic, inclusive purview of the "other." In this context, the argument of Charles Peek, Nancy Bell, and Charlotte Dunham underscores women's empathetic understanding of "Structural oppression" (Peek et al., 1996). Looking at stories, like *Anadhikar Prabesh* (*Trespass*) and *Strir Patra* (*A Wife's Letter*), the strength and defiance of women's perspectives raise questions against the injustice and alienation of the animals in their domestic space. The notion of space plays an important role in underlining the politicization of gendered power dynamics, which acts out in the domestic space during colonial Bengal. Their course and action of life suggest the heightened sensitivity and cognizance of their own autonomous identity in connection to the animal consciousness. Unlike the story *Trespass*, *A Wife's Letter* does not address the animal presence directly in their central narrative yet this image of a silently suffering, bonded animal to be sacrificed to satiate human hunger and desire for power, is reiterated through the entire story. *A Wife's Letter* is an account of Mrinalini, whose decisions transcend the liminality of domestic space and initiates a journey into the larger backdrop of a more volatile, politically turbulent social milieu. Seen from this perspective, *A Wife's Letter* has been regarded as one of the most potent narratives of feminism in Indian literature. Mrinalini's compassion and identification with the underdogs and the marginalized is a recurrent motif in her life. Her love and support of Bindu, the dark-skinned, orphan girl, her active support to her brother whose involvement in the extremist community against the colonial establishment, underscores the journey of self-identification with the dispossessed and the struggles to express it with the entirety of her existence. In this story, what is striking is the place of animal consciousness, as it intervenes into a narrative of woman's liberation. In the narrative, there is a poignant observation of domestic space as a both debilitating and suffocating arena for both women and animals. The empathetic and individualistic streak in Mrinal's character comes out in her observation of domesticated bovine presence, who are subjected to an indifferent cruelty in their quotidian lives. She remembers how the domesticated cows have been subjected to absolute indifference and utter disregard. Her experience in the household, as a woman in that cloistered space is symptomatic of the experience of these animals, equable and parallel. In the course of the story, this micro narrative is transformed into a testament of the polyphonic voices of the oppressed. Mrinalini writes that the very first memory of this household, was the animals in the cowshed and the graphically evoking negligence of people towards them; she voices her strong and deep-rooted connection with these animals, as only they reminded her of her exiled motherland, her native village. The two cows with their three calves stood to her not as animals, but as compatriots in their mutually exclusive longing for open, green spaces and shared experience of sheer indifference which verged on to cruelty. Mrinalini took time to tend these animals and often supplied them with food stealthily, as these cows were forced to wait longer in their captivity in a square, enclosed insufficient spaces. It is noteworthy how all the other family members including the women, never granted a room for consideration of these animals and exercised verbal cruelty in the form of mockery and insults to Mrinalini for her extending empathy to the animals. Mrinalini's identification and solidarity with these domesticated animals hints at her consequent empathy for the disenfranchised, which later exposed itself through her unflinching support of Bindu and her brother, Sarat. Throughout the entire narrative the image of the tortured neglected cows, will haunt the story; on the day of her avowal to wear the sarees made of coarse materials like Bindu, her refusal to conform to the family's dictatorial practice expresses itself through her feeding of the cows in the courtyard. A similar real-life incident occurred to Joanne, one of the interviewees of Emily Gaarder, who notes in one of her articles, that women's higher levels of animal advocacy emerge from an "empathy based on shared inequalities" (Gaarder, 2011). There is another reference to a sheep given by the tenants of the estate for this specific purpose, to the household, when Mrinalini discovered Bindu, after the latter's marriage to an insane man, in the coal-shed. The very language expressed by Mrinalini is a potent articulation of the monstrous hunger and domination, which other animals and women undergo in a consuming patriarchal society. She writes, "The tenants of your estate had given you a sheep to feast on; I saved it from the fire of your hunger and kept it in one corner of the coal-shed on the ground floor. I would go and feed it grain first thing in the morning. I had relied on your servants for a day or two before I saw that feeding the animal was less interesting to them than possibly feeding upon it" (Gupta, 2002). Later, when married to an insane husband, Bindu came to Mrinalini for a safe shelter, Mrinalini stood up against the entire household to save her from the impending tortures. Very poignantly, Mrinalini has compared Bindu's position with that of a cow about to be slaughtered at the hands of a cleaver. Mrinalini writes, "I didn't know where my strength came from, but my mind would not accept the idea that for fear of the police I would simply hand her over—hand over to the butcher himself the calf that had come running from the cleaver, afraid for her life, to seek shelter with me" (Gupta, 2002). It is interesting to note here, that this poignant turn of the story underscores the politics of carnism with gendered identity, which was established by Carol Adam's seminal work, *The Sexual Politics of Meat*; she argued that consumption of meat is rooted in the industrial socioeconomic culture, which relegates women as well as animals to the status of unthinking, unfeeling objects, ready to be consumed (Adams, 1990).

The comments of the British doctor regarding the inner chambers of this household reaffirms the equivalent negligence and cruelty perpetrated on the animals as well as the women in their shared existence in a claustrophobic, unsanitary, enclosed spaces. The domestic space is a prison house for women, in whose lexicon it is comparable to the enclosed pen of the animals, where they are kept before the slaughter. Mrinalini's distinctive resolution of never returning to twenty-seven no, Makhan Baral Street, places her as one of the earliest feminists in Indian literature and in the same line with the early well-educated and radical women in her time. Her journey is relevant in tracing the first feminists in colonial India (Forbes, 2005).

From Mrinalini's identification with the plight of the domesticated animals, my chapter will focus on the notions of empathy and compassion in respect to the societal factors, the caste, privilege, and the notion of purity. The short story *Trespass*, dwells on a climactic moment in the life of Jaykali Devi, who is portrayed as a stern, matron like character, in the story. Her dedication to maintain the elaborate rituals, the purity of the sanctified space is brought out with her ritualistic worship of the Radhanath temple. The narrative focuses on her single-minded dedication to the temple and unambiguously depicts her concept of purity through her maintenance of the temple space. The story starts off with the punishment of her nephew, for attempt to pollute the temple space. The writer unambiguously posits the character of Jaykali in a web of casteist narrative. From the beginning, Jaykali Devi's notion of caste in relation the purity has been cited in the story. When a pig enters into the course of the narrative, the readers are made to witness a different discourse at the center. While being hunted by the domes, a section of lower caste people, a pig enters into the temple arena. The priest thought of this animal as the embodiment of pollution and immediately attempted to drive the animal out from the temple premise. Jaykali actively intervenes in the scene, ensures the safety by closing the gate and when confronted by the people, stands by her decision. The story ends with a potent twist by Tagore, "This small incident brought great satisfaction to the great god who looks after all creatures of the universe, but the petty village god called the community felt considerably perturbed" (Chaudhuri, 125). It is noteworthy to mention here that, the writer attempts to maintain a status-quo by positioning the animal's survival contingent on Jaykali. Her gendered identity becomes the secondary point of reference to her societal identity as an individual belonging to an upper-caste stratum of the society. When we contextualize this story in respect to the contemporary sociocultural milieu, the radical aspect emerges not from the basis of caste, but due to the particular animal's involvement in the story. It was written at a time, when the fowls and pigs were considered too controversial and polluted to be allowed in an orthodox Hindu household, where the temple space was regarded as the most sacred place. Taking that aspect into consideration, the story performs an act of radicalization by portraying a Hindu window allowing a pig to be sheltered in a temple premise. Seen in this way, the story subverts a narrative of power dynamics and merges the politicization domestic place with the animal rights. The works of the colonial times demonstrate that the trope of temple or the place of worship and the kitchen were the spaces, which were associated, cultivated, and established themselves as the space of the women. It is a significant point that, the animal finds a place of security in a temple of a woman, who is also treated by an outcast in her contemporary time, as colonial India had a long tradition of ostracizing widows. The legitimization of this shared experiences of outcasts, is also a first step towards the radicalization of animal and gender rights against an oppressive, androcentric, speciesist cultural system (Scholtmeijer, 1999). The defiant character of Jaykali is unlike the conventional portrayal of Hindu widows in literature, as they were depicted in an overtly melodramatic ways to elicit sympathy from the populace. But depicting the women in this way, this popular section of the literature also participates in an exercise of power dynamic, which subtly encouraged the women's acceptance and tolerance of this societal coercion, by making it more culturally acceptable (Bandyopadhyay, 1995). When we read this story in light of all these factors, the character of Jaykali stands in defiance of conventionalized mode of presenting the women's plight the narrator hints at her conviction of self esteem and capability in the way she chooses to lead her life. Jaykali's decision of harboring the pig from a brutal death is not an impulsive decision motivated by the sentimental reasons; following the graph of her character development, this crucial decision seems to have borne out of her deeply compassionate yet dignified outlook towards the animals and the world.

CONCLUSION

These texts perform a function of silencing disenfranchised subjects in colonial India. By linking the disenfranchised position of women with the animals, these works document a history of emerging animal rights in literature and create a foray of interconnected discourses on human-animal co-habitation with the history of violence on the excluded section of the society. This chapter attempts to establish the lateral yet equivalent position of the outcasts and the animals. There are numerous ways in which women and animals interact in these narratives. With the inclusion of animal presence in these works, this chapter attempts to establish a trajectory of animal-human relation. In encompassing the perspectives of people with disabilities, with the racially, sexually marginalized, these texts create a space for addressing the comparable movements in India. It is important to contextualize Susan Griffin's argument which points out the legitimization of a dominant, masculinist culture on the feminized status of women, animals, children, disenfranchised other in the mainstream discourse. In exposing the interconnected web of displaced tribal people and the outcasts with the animal consciousness, Tarashankar Bandyopadhyay's stories provide a necessary impetus of Shiva's (1988) critique of domination of western, reductionist technological involvement in deforestation and displacement. In this point, Andree Collard and Joyce Contrucci's (1989) seminal work on the patriarchal domination on women, animals, natural world through the structures of racism, gender discrimination, religion, and mainstream industrial culture may be a point of reference. It sheds light on the structural and systematic violence on the "other" of the male-centered sociocultural canon. On the other hand, the stories of Tagore underscore the marginalization of women in colonial household (Banerjee, 1990) and address this issue with the rising animal rights movement in India. This chapter intends to correlate the laterality of the status of animals in a society, which posits the disabled, the underprivileged in an equivalent position of pronounced disregard by presenting the internalized bonding between these outcasts and the animals.

SELECTED BIBLIOGRAPHY

Adams, C. (1990). *The sexual politics of meat: A feminist-vegetarian critical theory*. Continuum.

Arnold, D. (1980). Industrial violence in colonial India. *Comparative Studies in Society and History, 22*(2), 234–255. http://www.jstor.org/stable/178408

Bandyopadhyay, S. (2008). Caste, widow re-marriage, and the reform of popular culture in colonial Bengal. In S. Sarkar., & T. Sarkar (Eds.), *Women and social reform in modern India: A reader* (pp. 100–117). Indiana University Press.

Bandyopadhyay, T. (1969, March). Nari o nagini, The woman and the serpent (M. Devi, Trans.). *Indian Literature*, 12 (1), 80–85. Sahitya Akademi. www.jstor.org/stable/23329120

Bandyopadhyay, T. (1974). Nagini Kanyar Kahini, The tale of the snake-girl. In *Tarashankar rachanavali* (Vol. 8). Mitra o Ghosh Publishers. (Originally published 1951).

Bandyopadhyay, T. (2014, August). Bedeni, The Gypsy Woman (S. Ghosh, Trans.). (Original work published 1943). https://www.academia.edu/19403171/THE_GYPSY_WOMAN_Translation_of_Bedeni_by_Tarashankar_Bandopadhyay

Banerjee, S. (1999). Marginalization of women's popular culture in nineteenth century Bengal. In K. Sangari., & S. Vaid (Eds.), *Recasting women: Essays in Indian colonial history* (pp.127–179). Rutgers University Press.

Behnke, E. A. (1999). From Merleau-Ponty's concept of nature to an interspecies practice of peace. In H. P. Steeves (Eds.), *Animal others: On ethics, ontology and animal life* (pp. 93–116). State University of New York Press.

Chakraborty, S. P. (2017, Marc). Crossing the threshold: Women in colonial city space. *Sanglap, 3*(2), 127–165. http://sanglap-journal.in/index.php/sanglap/article/view/62/97

Chattopadhyay, S.C. (2004). Bilashi, The snake-charmer's daughter. In *The drought and other stories* (S. Sinha, Trans.). Sahitya Akademi. (First published 1970).

Chattopadhyay, S.C. (2004). The Drought. In *The drought and other stories* (S. Sinha, Trans.). Sahitya Akademi. (First published 1970).

Chaudhuri, S. (2000). Trespass. In *Rabindranath Tagore: Selected short stories.* Oxford University Press.

Cixous, H. (2008). The laugh of the Medusa. In Walder, D (Eds.), *Literature in the Modern World: Critical essays and documents* (pp. 291–301). Oxford University Press.

Collard, A., & Contrucci, J. (1988). *Rape of the wild: Man's violence against animals and the earth.* Women's Press.

Danta, C. (2018). Scapegoats and scapegraces: Becoming sacrificial animal in Kafka and Coetzee. In *Animal fables after Darwin: Literature, speciesism, and metaphor* (1st. ed. pp. 159–185). Cambridge University Press.

D'Stair, S. (2021). "The animals and birds were left in peace": Katharine Burdekin's queer utopian ecology. In A. E. George (Ed.). (2021). *Gender and sexuality in critical animal studies.* Lexington Books.

Forbes, G. H. (2005). Caged tigers: "First wave" feminists in India. In *Women in colonial India: Essays on politics, medicine, and historiography* (11–27). DC Publishers.

Gaarder, E. (2011). Where the boys aren't: The predominance of women in animal rights activism. *Feminist Formations, 23*(2), 54–76. http://www.jstor.org/stable/41301656.

Girard, R. (2013). Sacrifice. In *Violence and the sacred* (P. Gregory, Trans. pp. 1–40). Continuum. (Original work published 1988).

Griffin, S. (1978). *Woman and nature: The roaring inside her.* Harper & Row.

Guin, U. L. (1988). Introduction. In *Buffalo girls and other animal presences* (pp. 9–13). Capra Press.

Kreilkamp, I. (2007). Dying like a dog in *Great Expectations.* In D. D. Morse & M. A. Danahay (Eds.), *Victorian animal dreams: Representations of animals, in Victorian literature and culture* (pp. 81–94). Ashgate.

Kundu, P. (2013–2014). Representing marginality: A case study of Tarashankar Bandyopadhyay. *Journal of the department of English, Vidyasagar University, 11*, 89–99. http://inet.vidyasagar.ac.in:8080/jspui/bitstream/123456789/2048/1/10.pdf

Nocella II, A. J., George, A. E., Lupinacci, J., & Repka, M. (2018). Critical animal studies and the importance of anti-racist and anti-ableist politics. In Nocella II, A. J., George, A. E., & Lupinacci, J. (Eds.), *Animals,* disability, and the end of capitalism. Peter Lang Books.

Palmeri, F. (2020). On cursing with animals. *Journal for Critical Animal Studies, 17*(1), 6–18.

Pearson, S. J., & Weismantel, M. (2010). Does "the animal" exist? Toward a theory of social life with animals. In D. Brantz (Eds.), *Beastly natures: Animals, humans, and the study of history* (pp. 17–37). University of Virginia Press.

Peek, C., Bell, N., & Dunham, C. (1996). Gender, gender ideology, and animal rights advocacy. *Gender and Society, 10*(4), 464–478. http://www.jstor.org/stable/189682.

Sabloff, A. (2001). *Reordering the natural world: humans and animals in the city*. University of Toronto Press.

Scholtmeijer, M. (1995). The power of otherness: Animals in women's fiction. In Adams, C., & Donovan, J. (Eds.), *Animals and women: Feminist theoretical explorations* (pp. 231–262). Duke University Press.

Shapiro, K., & Copeland, M. (2005). Toward a critical theory of animal issues in fiction. *Society & Animals, 13*(4).

Shiva, V. (2016). *Staying alive: Women, ecology, and development*. North Atlantic Books.

Sinha. A. (2016, March 1). Mahesh: Sarat Chandra Chattopadhyay. https://arunavasinha.in/2016/03/01/mahesh-sarat-chandra-chattopadhyay/

Svoboda, K. (2021). Animals and the absent referent in Margaret Atwood's *The Handmaid's Tale*. In A. E. George (Ed.). (2021). *Gender and sexuality in critical animal studies*. Lexington Books.

Tagore, R. (2009). A Wife's Letter. (P. Gupta, Trans.) https://parabaas.com/translation/database/translations/stories/gStreerPatra1.html

Tagore, R. (2010, December 27). Subha. In *Stories from Tagore* [Project Gutenberg]. (Originally published 1918). https://www.gutenberg.org/files/34757/34757-h/34757-h.htm#Page_87

Woloch, A. (2003). Introduction. In *The one vs. the many: Minor characters and the space of the protagonist in the novel* (pp. 1–42). Princeton University Press.

Index

About the Editors and Contributors

Michael Allen is Professor of Social, Political, and Legal Philosophy at East Tennessee State University. He has published extensively on civil disobedience and crimes of dissent in a variety of contexts from undocumented immigration, global poverty, and the unauthorized disclosure of government secrets to illegal hunting and animal liberation. His most recent work concerns the aims, scope, and limits of nonviolent resistance to diverse forms of oppression. Indeed, this work also critically examines the ongoing relevance of Gandhi's philosophy of nonviolence in novel circumstances of interspecies and multicultural conflict.

Will Boisseau completed his doctorate at Loughborough University in 2015. His research focuses on the place of animal rights within the British left, particularly on the relationship between the anarchist/direct action and legislative wings of the movement. His work explores the class and gender issues influencing this relationship, the marginalisation of animal rights in mainstream labour politics and a range of concepts including speciesism, total liberation, critical animal studies, and intersectionality. Will is currently involved in trade union politics in the UK.

Erica Von Essen is an associate professor of Environmental Communication from the Swedish University of Agricultural Sciences, who now works as a researcher for Norwegian Institute for Nature Research in Oslo. Her conceptual and empirical focus is on changing human-animal relations in modernity, with particular emphasis on wild animal welfare, wildlife conflict, and nonhuman animal resistance. Erica has also recently brought together scholars devoted to the ethical implications of animal-based tourism, exploring ideas of animal labor and animals as means to human reconciliation. She is widely published across environmental ethics, rural sociology, and criminology fields, having completed her PhD on illegal killings of wolves in Sweden.

Amber E. George, PhD, is an Assistant Professor of philosophy, cultural studies, and sociology at Galen College. She has co-edited several books including *Education for Total Liberation: Critical Animal Pedagogy and Teaching Against Speciesism* (2019); *The Image of Disability: Essays on Media Representations* (2018); *The Intersectionality of Critical Animal, Disability, and Environmental Studies* (2017); and *Screening the Non/Human: Representations of Animal Others in the Media* (2016). She is the current editor-in-chief of the *Journal for Critical Animal Studies* (*JCAS*).

Jordan Halliday is a long-time activist, former political prisoner, and educator indicted in 2009 for resisting a federal grand jury investigating illegal underground animal rights activities. Halliday was jailed for nearly four months under a civil contempt of court order unsuccessfully trying to compel testimony and was later released on a Grumbles motion only to be indicted with criminal contempt of court to which Halliday pleaded "no contest" and was sentenced to an additional 10 months in prison. Halliday is only the third person in U.S. history to serve time for a criminal contempt charge after already serving time civilly for the same act of recalcitrance.

Jessica Holmes is a doctorate candidate in English Language and Literature at the University of Washington in Seattle, where she teaches in the Interdisciplinary Writing Program. Her research areas include environmental humanities, contemporary poetry, and vegan studies. She is a 2019 Mellon Fellow for New Public Projects in the Humanities. She received a Master of Fine Arts in poetry from the University of Washington and a Bachelor of Fine Arts in English from Lewis & Clark College. Her creative and critical work has been published in *TRANSverse Journal*, *West Trade Review*, and *Auto/Biography Studies*, and is forthcoming in the *Routledge Handbook of Vegan Studies*.

Paislee House graduated from the University of Central Missouri with an undergraduate degree in history, specializing in American labor rights and environmental history. Since this time, Paislee has retained a strong interest in anti-capitalist critique and the environment and dedicates much of her time to total liberation studies. She currently resides in The Driftless Area of Wisconsin working as an electrician's apprentice for a rural solar company.

Tyler Lang is an animal rights activist from Los Angeles, CA. He was convicted under the Animal Enterprise Terrorism Act in 2015 for his role in breaking into a fur farm in Morris, Illinois, releasing 2,000 mink, damaging farm equipment, and spray painting the slogan "liberation is love" on the barn. The liberation resulted in the closure of the farm and $200,000 in damage. Tyler was sentenced to 15 months, most of which was spent at a federal halfway house, ordered to pay restitution, and is now labeled as a domestic terrorist.

Swatilekha Maity has her BA and MA in English from the University of Calcutta, India, and completed her MPhil in English from Jadavpur University, India. Currently, she is a PhD candidate in the Department of English, Jadavpur University, India. Her areas of interest include travel writing, nineteenth century, the practice of ethics in animal rights, and the expressions of human violence toward animals.

Tatjana Marjanović is a full professor of English at the University of Banja Luka, Bosnia and Herzegovina, where she teaches a bulk of linguistic courses to undergraduate and postgraduate English majors. She read for her MPhil at the University of Cambridge's Research Centre for English and Applied Linguistics. Ever since her time in the UK, she has continued to draw inspiration from Hallidayan approaches to language. Different from all her other published work, this essay is an attempt at bringing together linguistics and animal welfare, both of which she feels strongly about.

Anthony J. Nocella II, PhD, is an Assistant Professor in the Department of Criminal Justice and Criminology in the Institute of Public Safety at Salt Lake Community College. He is the Co-Director of JEDI4ST, the research center at Salt Lake Community College. Nocella is the editor of the Peace Studies Journal, Transformative Justice Journal, and co-editor of five book series including Critical Animal Studies and Theory with Lexington Books and Hip Hop Studies and Activism with Peter Lang Publishing. He is the National Director of Save the Kids and Executive Director of the Institute for Critical Animal Studies. He has published over fifty book chapters or articles and forty books. He has been interviewed by *New York Times*, *Washington Post*, *Houston Chronicles*, *Fresno Bee*, Fox, CBS, CNN, C-SPAN, and *Los Angeles Times*.

Samantha Orsulak is a recent postgraduate of University of York, where she specialized in eighteenth- and nineteenth-century Gothic literature and animal symbolism within fiction. She now teaches Humanities at the secondary level with an ecological and social justice lens. Her research interests include animal representations in literature, Gothic monsters, and natural history. She is eager to share the fascinating history of animals—fictional and real—and act as their voice in the fight for nonhuman animal representation. Feel free to contact her at sam.orsulak@gmail.com.

Nathan Poirier is a doctorate student in Sociology at Michigan State University with specializations in Animal Studies and Women's and Gender Studies. He holds an MA in mathematics from Western Michigan University, and an MS in Anthrozoology from Canisius College. His master's thesis for Canisius critically examined the landscape of in vitro meat, focusing on its discourse, comparisons to vegetarianism, and potential cultural implications. Nathan's academic interests focus on critical animal studies, intersectionality, anarchism, in vitro meat, and human domination of the environment. In 2015 he organized a community-focused rewilding event in Grand Rapids, MI.

Amanda R. Williams is an independent scholar and total-liberation activist living in The Driftless area of Wisconsin. Amanda has been engaged in the animal rights movement since 2016, working with organizations such as Saint Louis Animal Right Team, Vegan Outreach, Vegan Austin Community Advocates, and Project Animal Freedom. As a day job, Amanda manages a donor database at the No-Kill, companion-animal rescue nonprofit Austin Pets Alive!.

Ellyse Winter is a doctorate candidate at the University of Toronto, pursuing a collaborative program in Social Justice Education and Environmental Studies. Her research applies the intersecting fields of critical food studies, critical animal studies, and environmental justice to an examination of the changing landscape of food production and the possibilities for alternative foodways. In her work, Ellyse examines strategies for building solidarity or an alliance politics across various community groups and social justice movements. Ellyse also teaches in the Sociology Department at Brock University and the Department of Geography and Planning at the University of Toronto.

CPSIA information can be obtained
at www.ICGtesting.com
Printed in the USA
BVHW030245160222
629155BV00002B/10

9 781793 635228